Observational Filmmaking for Education

Nigel Meager

Observational Filmmaking for Education

Digital Video Practices for Researchers, Teachers and Children

palgrave
macmillan

Nigel Meager
King's College
University of Cambridge
Cambridge, UK

ISBN 978-3-319-90625-6   ISBN 978-3-319-90626-3 (eBook)
https://doi.org/10.1007/978-3-319-90626-3

Library of Congress Control Number: 2018964114

© The Editor(s) (if applicable) and The Author(s), under exclusive license to Springer Nature Switzerland AG 2019
This work is subject to copyright. All rights are solely and exclusively licensed by the Publisher, whether the whole or part of the material is concerned, specifically the rights of translation, reprinting, reuse of illustrations, recitation, broadcasting, reproduction on microfilms or in any other physical way, and transmission or information storage and retrieval, electronic adaptation, computer software, or by similar or dissimilar methodology now known or hereafter developed.
The use of general descriptive names, registered names, trademarks, service marks, etc. in this publication does not imply, even in the absence of a specific statement, that such names are exempt from the relevant protective laws and regulations and therefore free for general use.
The publisher, the authors, and the editors are safe to assume that the advice and information in this book are believed to be true and accurate at the date of publication. Neither the publisher nor the authors or the editors give a warranty, express or implied, with respect to the material contained herein or for any errors or omissions that may have been made. The publisher remains neutral with regard to jurisdictional claims in published maps and institutional affiliations.

Cover image: © Andhika Yauwry/EyeEm

This Palgrave Macmillan imprint is published by the registered company Springer Nature Switzerland AG
The registered company address is: Gewerbestrasse 11, 6330 Cham, Switzerland

Foreword

For several decades, I and my colleagues have been exploring how film and video can be put to better use in anthropology. Anthropological films used to be either what we called didactic 'illustrated lectures', with the images serving largely to support what was said on the soundtrack, or they were simply unedited records of events to be used later for various forms of 'objective' analysis. They made little attempt to engage with the everyday experiences of their subjects.

Observational cinema was a reaction against this static and impersonal view. It attempted to bring anthropological films closer to the actual experiences of people living in other societies. Instead of simply presenting anthropological knowledge previously gained, it was more exploratory, moving closer to its subjects and trying to interpret what was happening to them at the time of filming. This was made possible by the availability of new lightweight cameras that could film almost anywhere.

The anthropology of childhood has had a parallel history. At the beginning, anthropologists hardly acknowledged that children had any role in society, beyond being socialised to become adults. They simply existed on the periphery of society as a general type. Only in recent decades have children's individuality and contributions to society been widely recognised. And only recently have children's own perspectives become important in anthropological research.

Despite these gains, for most people children still remain either idealised or seen as unfinished adults-in-the-making. It was perhaps for those reasons that I started making films about children twenty years ago. I wanted to see what I could learn about the emotional, physical and intellectual fabric of children's lives by filming amongst them. And as I had already been making anthropological films, it was not unlike entering one more society about which I knew very little.

I began by filming at a boarding school, and almost immediately a boy came up to me and said, 'What are you doing?' What could I tell him? I gave him the only answer I could think of at the time. I said I was making a study of life at the school, but instead of writing a book about it, I was writing it with a camera. For some reason, he accepted this as explanation enough. Over the next three years, I spent many months at the school, trying to share the students' world and capture their varied experiences of living at the school. In the end, I edited five films from this material, with the aim of immersing viewers in the school's environment and the students' collective and individual responses to it. The films became essays about the school, the experiences of those I was filming and the situation we were both part of.

Much later, after making more than a dozen observational films about children's lives, mostly in schools in India, I began a new project. I felt I had reached a kind of limit by filming children myself. To learn more about children's own perspectives, I began encouraging them to make films themselves. And in doing so, I introduced them to observational filmmaking.

The project was organised as a series of video workshops in different parts of India. Most of the children had only seen television and Bollywood films, so they were being asked to do something completely outside their normal experience. I asked them to find topics in their own community or family and, after receiving some basic training, to explore them with a video camera. They soon accepted the idea that this was a research project to which they could make a valuable contribution. They often knew their chosen topics more intimately than the adults around them.

I discovered that the children learned the basic skills of camera work much more quickly than adults, and what they didn't know about filmmaking they invented. The results were often surprising. Each film differed from the others in conception and style. Each expressed the personality of the child who made it. It seemed as if, as in the best observational filmmaking, they were using the camera as an instrument to think with. As they learned more about a subject, they explored it more deeply. I met with them each day, and we looked at what they had shot the day before. They learned from their own mistakes and the mistakes of others, and the simple act of viewing their work gave them new ideas.

Today, we can see ever-increasing potential for this approach. Observational filmmaking can bring us new knowledge about the immediate responses of individuals, whether the films are made by children or adults. It can bring a new empirical and qualitative dimension to research that in the past has struggled to express many aspects of human experience in words. It can be employed not only to understand how things are, but how things change—such as how children think and learn.

I welcome this book as a new departure for both observational filmmaking and education. It broadens the scope of observational filmmaking by bringing it into the world of education research, but it also opens up further possibilities for children themselves, as an intrinsically reflective and creative way of engaging with the world around them. The book demonstrates that the core values of observational filmmaking can become both a vital part of learning and a new way of understanding the processes of learning itself.

Canberra, Australia
July 2018

Professor David MacDougall
Research School of Humanities
and the Arts, Australian
National University

Acknowledgements

I wrote this book following the completion of my doctorate at the Faculty of Education, University of Cambridge in May 2017. The Ph.D. followed many years working at various times as an artist, art gallery educator, teacher trainer, arts education consultant and schoolteacher. I am very indebted indeed to my Ph.D. supervisor at Cambridge, Professor Richard Hickman, who looked after me and considered my interests at the University with such care and thoughtfulness from the start. This project would not even have got off the ground without him.

I am enormously grateful to the UK Arts and Humanities Research Council's Doctoral Training Partnership (AHRC DTP) at the University of Cambridge who funded my Ph.D. studies with a scholarship. I found the training and support inspirational at times. I thank Dr. Alistair Swiffen and Professor Chris Young for a programme that extended my horizons across Arts and Humanities disciplines. Established academics and fellow Arts and Humanities Ph.D. candidates whom I met opened my mind to a raft of new ideas and practices. This open-mindedness and cross-disciplinary exploratory freedom fed into this book in many ways.

The Cambridge AHRC DTP and Australian National University (ANU) combined to generate a three-month Visiting Fellowship at ANU in 2015. There, I worked under the guidance of Professor David MacDougall. This was a pivotal time in my doctoral research. Professor MacDougall has been a generous and inspiring mentor. His work as an ethnographic filmmaker, and most recently his work supporting Indian children to be observational filmmakers of aspects of their lives and interests, showed me just how valuable the practice of observational filmmaking might be for education research and children's learning. I have been able to write much in this book because of David MacDougall's pioneering work with children in India.

Dr. Anne Harris of Monash University, Melbourne, convinced me that this topic would be of interest to Palgrave and that potential of observational filmmaking in education should be explored in book form. I found my conversations with Anne very valuable. I would also like to thank Professor Pam Burnard, Professor Fernando Hernadez Hernandez and Professor Susan Wright for their insights and the opportunities they offered and generous encouragement for supporting my work.

Children from Park Street Primary School, Cambridge, contributed a great deal to the first phase of my exploratory research. Their enthusiastic willingness to learn and experiment with observational filmmaking inspired me to stretch much further than I might have. Particular thanks to Alexi Hickman, Ana Zandi, Bella Antunes, Carla Roth, Laurie Pattison, Luke Arnone and those who worked with me from January to July 2016. I also thank those children's class teacher, Laura Smith, their head teacher, Gillian Owen, and their respective parents and carers all of whom were always so supportive of the project.

In 2017, I began been working collaboratively with children and teachers at Escola Dovella, a primary school in central Barcelona. The teachers Mónica Segura Guerrero who taught Grade 6 and her colleague Ita Alabat Ramon helped with the practical side of the project, liaised with parents and carers and facilitated a series of initial workshops with Grade 6 children at the school. Fernando Hernandez Hernandez of the Faculty of Fine Arts at the University of Barcelona (UB) has been a valuable critical friend of the project. He secured Visiting Researcher status at UB for me. This has supported my ongoing research in Catalonia. Two students, Cristina Vianey Casillas and Anne Uijttewaal, studying with the Visual Arts and Education Masters course at UB supported the work throughout. I particularly thank the volunteer children filmmakers from Escola Dovella, Arantxa Saray Aragón Martínez, Rayssa Ramatu Canté Djalo, Eudald Clarella López, Marcel Estany Morató, Jéssica Gimeno Beltrán, Jana Núñez Renau and Ernesto Sassot Puig.

Since 2015, I have supported visual arts practices at King's College, Cambridge. After completing my doctorate, the College offered me Associate membership. This has been very helpful, as King's has become my academic base in the UK. The continued interest and support of fellows and students at the College is very valuable.

Finally, but most importantly, I must thank Dr. Julien Morton of London South Bank University. His sharp reposts are constant foil for my tendency towards emotional, generalising woolliness. I also thank the very same Julien Morton as my best friend. Julien, together with his wife Jo, 4-year-old son Ikey and baby daughter Patti, offers an emotional bedrock that enables almost everything I do.

February 2018   Nigel Meager

Contents

1 Introducing Observational Film — 1

2 Experiential Empiricism and Children's Films — 39

3 Academic Frames — 73

4 Ethics — 117

5 Camera Work and Editing for Children, Teachers and Researchers — 131

6 Epilogue — 197

References — 215

List of Figures

Fig. 1.1	Mayank's Family—still from a film by Mayank Ved (MacDougall, 2014) (https://vimeo.com/139964383)	2
Fig. 1.2	Still from *Kun se tapahtuu* (https://vimeo.com/289441020 and https://vimeo.com/289456020)	17
Fig. 1.3	Still from *SchoolScapes* (MacDougall, 2007) (https://vimeopro.com/roninfilmsaustralia/observational-filmmaking-for-education)	27
Fig. 1.4	Still from *Gandhi's Children* (MacDougall, 2008) (https://vimeopro.com/roninfilmsaustralia/observational-filmmaking-for-education)	32
Fig. 2.1	The Delhi workshop—still from a film by Ravi Shivhare—my lovely general store (MacDougall, 2013) (https://vimeo.com/139964405)	62
Fig. 2.2	Why not a girl—still from a film by Anshu Singh (MacDougall, 2013) (https://vimeo.com/139964414)	64
Fig. 2.3	The food: cooking for tourists in Ladakh—still from a film by Aayan Mateen (MacDougall, 2015) (https://vimeo.com/139964416)	65
Fig. 2.4	My funny film—still from a film by Aniket Kumar Kashyap (MacDougall, 2013) (https://vimeo.com/139964413)	66
Fig. 5.1	Setting up the camera (https://vimeo.com/296849556)	156

Fig. 5.2	Holding the camera (https://vimeo.com/296850103)	159
Fig. 5.3	Framing	163
Fig. 5.4	Interviews	171
Fig. 5.5	Reviewing video clips	178

List of Video Material

Links to view the video extracts are found at the page number shown here. The five films made by Indian children (p 2 and pp 81–84) are from *Childhood and Modernity* project, supported by the Australian Research Council. This material and images and extracts from SchoolScapes and Gandhi's Children are available courtesy of Professor David MacDougall and Fieldwork Films. At the time of writing the following link will take you to Ronin Films who have a collection of children's observational films available on DVD. There is also a link to download a useful study guide: https://www.roninfilms.com.au/feature/15168/childs-eye.html.

Extracts from the Finish television documentaries are provided with permission of the filmmakers, Ulla Turunen and Ilkka Ruuhijärvi from Finland. Extracts from *SchoolScapes* and *Gandhi's Children* are courtesy of Fieldwork Films. If it is needed the password to view video extracts on Vimeo is 951159.

Mayank's Family	2
Kun se tapahtuu (As it happens) and *Tien yli* (Across the road)	17
SchoolScapes	27

List of Video Material

Gandhi's Children	32
My Lovely General Store	62
Why Not a Girl	63
The Food—Cooking for Tourists in Ladakh	65
My Funny Film	66

The remaining illustrative video material was recorded with the support of children and parents who originally worked with me at Park Street Primary School, Cambridge. The password to view on Vimeo is 951159.

Setting up the camera	156
Holding the camera	159

Introduction

Starting with Experience

As I write, I can choose to attend to where these words come from. I am conscious of my physical presence—the pressure of my coccyx on the flat seat of a library chair, the weight on points of both forearms that pivot on the edge a narrow wood table so that my hands can reach and roam the keyboard, and the residue of a cold, which partially blocks one of my nasal passages. There are gentle sounds of others working: books are placed on tables; soft clicks as keyboard keys are tapped; and the shifting shuffling sounds of bodies as they adjust their position on chairs. I am also aware of my thoughts. These are the words I write, which I silently verbalise in my head even as I type (and the words you are now sharing as you read this). But in my thoughts, there is also a conscious recognition of my library membership card face up next to my laptop, a mental note to repair the screen on my phone and a minor anxiety about where to meet a friend later. These thoughts seem to well up and recede, sometimes overwhelming others, sometimes like echoes whilst a foregrounded train continues. They don't stop. Thoughts flow with time. In *my* mind, right now, and at all times, there are no fixed boundaries between ideas. They swirl, come into existence, merge and dissipate—gaseous rather than solid. In short, I am in the midst of a flux of my own corporeal and mental experience. Experience seems to me to be inseparable from my living being and from ideas I have. Indeed, my living being and my ideas are one in my experience.

I begin with these words about myself to illustrate a fundamental stance taken in this book: that all ideas, however cerebral, however abstract, are formed in experience (Dewey, 1934). Therefore, if *I* want to find out more about others and their ideas, then granting their experience, allied with my own, a primary role in research would seem a logical place to begin an investigation.

So, this book will present observational filmmaking as thinking formed in and of experience. Observational filmmaking is a thoughtful experiential practice through which knowledge and understanding of others can be formed and shared in the very medium of experience, and out of which and from which questions may be answered and theories formed. Observational filmmaking starts in experience, is composed of experience and never leaves experience behind. This is the subject of this book, one aim of which is to argue for the potential value of observational filmmaking for children, teachers and education researchers.

Film, Video and Observing with Cameras

Chapter 5 in this book articulates certain techniques of using video cameras and microphones as tools. These tools and techniques strengthen qualities in observation. Processes in editing may enhance recorded outcomes of the way the camera is used. The awareness of a certain craft in camera use and editing is far from arbitrary and unthinking. I will describe camera use as focused and inherently analytic, which is cognitive, perceptual and riven with sensation. This is a form of thought process that allows more ineffable qualities in experience such as the material, aesthetic and affective to be central to generating new knowledge and building understanding. This is experiential thinking for both research and learning. In observational filmmaking cognition is neither 'hidden' in brain function nor dependent of sophisticated forms writing text, it is thinking that is immediately viscerally accessible, a way of thinking that is especially valuable to children. Firstly, indirectly via the outcomes of research, in a heightened beneficial awareness about children's experiences as they live and learn in school; and secondly directly, offering powerful audio-visual process through which children can explore and learn more about themselves, others and the social and material world they inhabit.

Film, television and video are embedded in the lives of children, teachers and researchers, at least those who have ready access to the technologies needed to view and make audio-visual images that move. In considering the 'how' and 'why' of creating and consuming films and videos it is, perhaps, a moot point as to whether it is rapid and continuous technological innovation which is driving cultural change or whether it is a cultural change which catalyses technological innovation. It is certain that market forces drive the ever-changing characteristics of digital cameras, phones and tablet computers with which videos can be made and shared by everyone who might own such devices. It is also clear that understanding film, television and video 'texts' (what is actually shown and seen) is inevitably intertwined in understanding domains of economic, technological, social and cultural practices.

The generality of the previous paragraph should stand as a caveat to everything written from here, because a great deal of contemporary culture is audio-visual and in continuous flux. However, this book is more simply focused on the benefits to education research and children's learning of the almost inevitable fact that when one person points a camera at another person and records what they are saying and doing then they are observing that other. In that act of observing, a camera records not only the experience of the person in front of the lens but also the experience of the person using the camera. Any other person who views the audio-visual material is inevitably drawn into a triangle of experience. This means that as the recorded images are seen and heard, a viewer's experience is formed as they share in the experiences of the camera user and the experiences of those being filmed. Observational film's capacity to catalyse the sharing of experiences in thoughtful ways is at the heart of its value to education research and to children's learning in school.

As I will unfold as the book progresses, I place pedagogy at the centre of observational filmmaking as a research method. The essential nature of observational filmmaking as a shared and collaborative practice between adults and children (and children and children) brings into the foreground omnipresent qualities in teaching and learning. This becomes manifestation of video-based research. Research with video is a vast and still rapidly expanding domain. Anne Harris (2016, 2018) in her book, *Video as Method*, and then in a chapter, *Ethnocinema and Video-Based Research*, in Patricia Leavy's (2018) edited *Handbook of Arts-Based Research*, gives a comprehensive guide to the literature about research which has video at its centre. Highlights include the digital visual and sensory ethnography methodologies of Sarah Pink (2013) and the work of Marcus Banks (2001), which offers an introduction to the practice of visually orientated research. There are many others. Harris (2018, p. 438) writes, 'I make the broader case that video is affecting research innovation in both method and methodology […] and the conceptual, political and aesthetic innovations that this approach and others like it provoke'. Indeed, as Harris (2018, p. 441) later continues, 'As many disciplines are now widely using video in some way due to its easy dissemination and multisensory capabilities, there are equally as many forms of research design as there are uses'. This is a technologically driven, creativity-centred movement, which has stepped away from the domination of different forms of numbers and words in research processes and outcomes. The nature of knowledge and understanding that video-based researchers are creating is challenging deeply held assumptions. Indeed, I take up Harris's challenge that,

> Video is not only a method (a tool, an approach) but also more than that, as it increasingly extends theoretical frames, which means that we not only *do* research differently but also *see* the practice, role and responsibility of research differently. Video-based research can serve different scholarly functions, address different social relations, and suggest new knowledge creation as it goes. (2018, p. 440, italics as in original)

However, taking observational filmmaking *per se* as a subset of video as a research and learning method and methodology, it is not yet, at least, a discrete domain in either the social sciences or the arts and humanities within subjects such as sociology, anthropology or film studies. It is not present as a method in education research. Neither is it a subject or even part of a subject in school curricula. However, anyone who has watched television or been to the cinema will have seen the results of observational methods in camera use and editing. These are found in Hollywood film, world cinema, TV drama series and documentary making of all kinds. They are ubiquitous. Indeed, the observational mode is part of a tradition of documentary making.

In research, observational film has found an identifiable niche within social anthropology influenced by the vast domain of ethnographic filmmaking, which straddles across research, the arts and the entertainment industries. As a social anthropological practice, observational filmmaking is a controversial and still developing research method. This is because the value of the knowledge it generates and shares does not sit so well in academic domains powerfully aligned to forms of social scientificity. So, despite the way observational methods infuse the way video, film and television cameras are used, the place those methods have in research and education is far from being clearly formed, they are at best under development and their relative value is contested.

Finished observational films are centred on fact rather than fiction and as such would usually be considered *documentaries*. But the division between factual and fiction filmmaking is not necessarily clear. For example, in the earliest days of the documentary, the pioneering John Grierson (1898–1972) considered that whereas a documentary would show information about the way people live and work, it would do this by creatively treating the recorded fragments of reality in an aesthetic way as they are fashioned into artefacts (films) which, in their turn, have their own social impact (Izod & Kilborn, 1998). In other words, truth and artistry, reality and artifice, are inevitably intermeshed.

One of the abiding characteristics of the documentary mode in cinema and television is the desire to construct an account. To do this in a way that engages an audience, a convincing narrative is needed. Storytelling takes centre stage. In crafting a good story, filmmakers might consider whether the storyteller should be acknowledged or how entertaining (in the broadest sense of that word) the film should be. Filmmakers select what to film and then edit that selection. Indeed, in that light Izod and Kilborn (1998) draw attention to problematic debates about whether documentaries can claim to be truthful accounts. For example, is it ever valid to re-enact scenes? How is it that 'truth' is so easily blurred by highly selective filming and editing? A film might show something real, but does that automatically mean it reveals truths behind that reality? Immediately a documentary film is considered as authored, the subjectivity, indeed the ideology of the filmmaker, comes into play. At the time of writing this, in late 2017, *fake news* is in the news. It is very easy to construct an entirely fictitious reality.

The *mode* of documentary making employed might be defined by the kind of interaction, either actively or passively, between all who are participating in the filmmaking. For example, in the *expository* mode, a storyteller, seen or unseen, tells viewers not only what they are looking at but also what the viewer should think about it. The effect is that the narrator seems to be standing back, overlooking what is happening, and employing didactic means to explain to viewers what is going on. In the *observational* documentary mode, filmmakers attempt to record people getting on with what they are doing in amongst them, but in an apparently natural way without obviously interfering. There is seldom a voice-over narration telling the viewer what to think. Editing allows shots and scenes run on for longer so that the viewer might become immersed in what is going on, almost as if they were there.

Filming others means the camera user intervenes directly to a greater or lesser degree the circumstances of the filming (unless cameras are hidden and filming secretly). There will always, therefore, be some degree of collaboration between the filmmaker and those being filmed. In many of the examples discussed in this book, there is a very high degree of collaboration between those filming and those being filmed. In this sense, both the camera user and people who are filmed are all *participants*. Indeed, in the *interactive* documentary mode, filmmakers do not attempt to hide the effect of the camera or their presence as they deliberately engage with those being filmed. For example, the camera user might ask questions. The viewer hears the responses and the answers are edited to suggest that all the facts and opinions are coming directly from the subjects of the film rather the filmmaker, who is, nevertheless less actively present. In the *reflexive* mode, it is often the way all the participants, including the filmmaker, interact which is the subject of the film. Such an approach may draw out different points of view, different ideologies and different conceptual frames and show how these are intertwining as a more fluid and less definitive representation is constructed.

Other overarching features of a documentary might be poetic (for example, sometimes music and more abstract visual qualities are used to help poeticise films), artistic (especially as the film might relate to contemporary art practices), blog like (a blog might be like a video diary), and something akin to reality television programming. In the latter kind of filmmaking, participants are part of a particular circumstance chosen for potential dramatic and emotional climaxes and curious mini-narratives. All of those are potentially entertaining, hook viewers into watching and therefore, on TV at least, help sell commercial advertising slots.

If I were to choose a new label for the mode of filmmaking recommended in this book, it might be the *pedagogical* mode. Here, the emphasis is on observational film*making*, rather than observational *cinema*. In other words, the proposition is that the *process* of observing with video cameras is in and of itself valuable for researchers, teachers and children, whether or not finished films are made. The notion of process, in respect of the intended education audience and possible beneficiaries, means pedagogy enters centre stage. The way observational techniques of camera use and editing are understood, taught, learnt and practised deeply affects learning, research, or both learning and research in tandem. The shift towards pedagogy and the processes of filmmaking differentiates this book's discussion of observational filmmaking for education from a notion of observational *cinema*, in which ethnographers, artists and documentary makers often strive to produce a final, polished film.

Nonetheless, especially in the experiential empirical frame this book situates itself theoretically, I suggest it is valuable to engage directly with the nature of observational film at the start. That is to consider the results of an observational style of filmmaking in order to get to know the nature of the domain. Looking at examples of the observational style of filmmaking, as this relates specifically to schools, children, teaching and learning, will help give material and aesthetic form to these abstract ideas. In their useful book entitled *Observational Cinema*, Grimshaw and Ravetz (2009, p. 114) note that there is 'a surprising lack of discussion focused around examples of the work itself'. So, my first suggestion, in seeking a response to such a question, is to turn to the start of Chapter 1 and review the extract of eleven-year-old Mayank's observational portrait of his father. Using examples from films themselves to create a sense of a precinct for activity, rather than starting with a definition of observational filmmaking, plays well with the experiential empiricism inspired, in part, by John Dewey (1859–1952), and developed in this book in Chapter 3. There are links to a number of observational films in the text. All have a focus on the experiences of children, mostly in schools or institutions but also at home. Viewing these film extracts, even before reading the text, will offer an experiential understanding of a practice observational filmmaking, which I am promoting.

There are some overarching theoretical characteristics about the nature of observing with video cameras that are advocated in this book and which overlap into the documentary film modes described above. Firstly, Grimshaw and Ravetz (2009) note tensions between an idea of observation that is, on the one hand, detached and unresponsive, even voyeuristic, and on the other hand an open and engaged way of filming, which allows viewers to partake in a scene because the camera operator was an acknowledged, accepted and intimate part the same scene themselves. This book adopts the latter approach. It is to participatory forms of pedagogy and research in which children and adults—camera operators and those who are participating in the research—all contribute and collaborate in a process of creating new experiences and new knowledge. Grimshaw and Ravetz (2009, p. 115) first sum up the negative connotations of observing with video cameras and then state that observation is a skilled practice:

> Hence we propose to put to one side the familiar discussion that has both conflated and reduced the meaning of observation to a narrowly ocular strategy with a tall order of negative features – voyeurism, objectification, surveillance, looking not seeing, assumed transparency, concealed ideology, lack of reflexivity, quasi-scientific objectivity, the ethnographic present and so on. Our reassessment involves reframing observation as a

particular kind of skilled practice one that has the selective training of the filmmakers' attention at its core.

To draw out a contrast to that position, and echoing the acknowledgement of the expository mode above, in his book, *Representing Reality*, Bill Nichols (1991), notes that the established documentary film mode is most often a form of argument. The camera operator is an anonymous presence recording scenes, which are later edited with an authoritative voice. Such a voice is often presented, literally, as a disembodied voice-over. Another expository device uses constant cuts to a presenter who delivers their argument in a committed and (in what they and the director hope) is a convincing way. David MacDougell (2018) sets out an alternative:

> An observational film differs from this by moving the frame outwards, in a figurative sense, to reveal more of the presence of the filmmaker and his or her engagement with the subject. In doing so it takes the viewer further into its confidence about the process of filmmaking and invites a more active critical response to the contents of the film. In minimising the fragmentation and restructuring of images, the observational film also seeks to give the viewer greater access to continuities of time and space. The film is no longer a set of conclusions about a subject constructed after the fact as a kind of lesson, but a more modest presentation of the filmmaking encounter. Making the film becomes a research process in itself and less the gathering of raw materials to construct a film later.

As Chapter 1 unfolds, and to illustrate MacDougall's statement above, I present examples of films made by adults as variations of a participatory observational style. Each variant takes a further step away from standard didactic documentary forms towards a more inclusive, inquisitive, experimental form or creating opportunities for knowing and understanding more about children's experiences as they live and learn in institutions such as schools.

The first examples are two observational films made by adults for television and the cinema. The first is a French film about a rural French primary school, *Être at Avoir*, made by Nicolas Philibert in 2002.

Following this are extracts from a series by Finish television documentary makers, Ulla Turunen & Ilkka Ruuhijärvi made between 1985 and 1991. These Finish films are followed by extracts from *SchoolScapes* (2007) about a life in an elite Indian boarding school and *Gandhi's Children* (2008), which graphically shares children's experiences in a shelter for homeless boys near New Delhi. Both *SchoolScapes* and *Gandhi's Children* were shot and edited by social anthropologist David MacDougall. In Chapter 2, I introduce examples shot by children in India as part of the innovative *Childhood and Modernity Project*, during which David MacDougall trained children, via a series of workshops in their schools, to be observational filmmakers of their own and others' experiences. The children are empowered to work independently of adults. Coming across these Indian children's films after visiting MacDougall at Australian National University provided a grounding from which I could see how ideas about children's creative thinking, pedagogy and education research intersect in a collaborative practice of observing with video cameras and then organising the results in filmic form. These manifestations of observational camera work and editing show how pedagogy, technology and a craft of inquiry coalesce in children's filmmaking to empower them to share their own and others' experiences. In that process, and in the sharing, new knowledge and understanding about children's experiences as they live and learn in school is born. How that might work in both practical and theoretical frames is the subject of this book.

Summary of What This Book Sets Out to Do

Observational filmmaking is a practice in social anthropology, even if it is controversial. It is part of a broader field of video-based research, which cuts across disciplines in the social sciences, arts and humanities. This book's first aim is to introduce observational filmmaking to teachers and education researchers, where the use of video is commonplace, but where observational filmmaking is not established as a method to support either research or learning.

The book adopts a theoretical stance developed out of a form of experiential empiricism originally advocated by John Dewey. Knowing and understanding more about children's experiences as they live and learn in school, if it is to embrace the fullness and richness of experience, needs to engage with kinds of experiences such as the material, aesthetic and affective, which are difficult or even impossible to express with words alone. Forms of qualitative analysis, which convert children's experience into data to be coded and later analysed, create considerable distance between that experience and the outcomes of research. An aim of this book is to sketch how a Deweyan inspired experiential empiricism might underscore the practice of observational filmmaking as pedagogy and research. This allows children's experiences as they live and learn in school to be in the foreground of research and learning throughout. This is given substance in Chapter 2, through examples of observational films shot by children.

Observing, filming, and recording children in school present significant ethical challenges. Also, ethical issues are prominent when participating in research with children as filmmakers. In addition, observational filmmaking, either as pedagogy or as research, will raise different theoretical critiques. Indeed, there are many caveats to the idea that observational filmmaking might be an education research practice or make a contribution to how children learn, think and express ideas. An aim of this book is to open out the debate about various intellectual domains, which might intersect with observational filmmaking as research and as learning. Therefore, in Chapters 3 and 4, I acknowledge significant theoretical and ethical considerations surrounding a practice of observational filmmaking in education.

How tools are used with materials is evident in the work of artists and designers who wish to craft outcomes of quality. Observational filmmaking uses both technological tools and engages particular techniques. An aim of this book is to explore the interrelation of these technological tools and the way they are used in relation to practices of observational filmmaking relevant to education. This is addressed throughout Chapter 5.

A number of examples of observational films cited are cited in this book. These feature children as observational filmmakers of their own and others' experiences. This book presents, through practical guidance and examples, pedagogy for observational filmmaking (both camera work and editing), which is appropriate for helping children gain knowledge and understanding of tools and techniques so that they can film in an observational style independently of adults. Again, this is addressed in Chapter 5. The text is pitched so as researchers and teachers will be able to support children to practice observational filmmaking through camera use and editing. However, I hope that this opening out of pedagogy is of equal benefit to adults, be they researchers or teachers, who are less familiar with these technologies and processes.

In this book, pedagogy and research coalesce. An aim of this book is to demonstrate a way, via pedagogy and practising a research craft, experience can become an object, medium and outcome of research. In this way research processes and outcomes, which hold ineffable qualities, such as aesthetic, material and affective qualities centre stage, can be readily practised by and shared with teachers and children in schools. A discussion of this as an arts-based rather than social science-based approach to research is found in Chapter 6 and concludes the book.

References

Banks, M. (2001). *Visual methods in social research*. London: Sage Publications.
Dewey, J. (1934). Art as experience. In J. Boydston (Ed.), *John Dewey the later works, 1925–1953* (Vol. 10, 1988). Carbondale: Southern Illinois University Press.
Grimshaw, A., & Ravetz, A. (2009). *Observational cinema: Anthropology, film, and the exploration of social life*. Bloomington: Indiana University Press.
Harris, A. (2016). *Video as method*. Oxford: Oxford University Press.
Harris, A. (2018). Ethnocinema and video-based research. In P. Leavy (Ed.), *Handbook of arts-based research* (pp. 437–452). New York: The Guilford Press.
Izod, J., & Kilborn, R. (1998). The documentary. In J. Hill (Ed.), *Oxford guide to film studies* (pp. 426–433). Oxford: Oxford University Press.
Leavy, P. (Ed.). (2018). *Handbook of arts-based research*. New York: The Guilford Press.

MacDougall, D. (2018). Observational cinema. In H. Callan (Ed.), *The International encyclopedia of anthropology*. New York: Wiley-Blackwell Publishing, Inc.

Nichols, B. (1991). *Representing reality* (pp. 125–133). Bloomington and Indianapolis: Indiana University Press.

Pink, S. (2013). *Doing visual ethnography.* (3rd ed. expanded and revised). London: Sage.

1

Introducing Observational Film

Mayank was eleven years old when he learnt to use a video camera in an observational style. He was part of a small group of children who worked with the ethnographic filmmaker and social anthropologist, David MacDougall, in a series of workshops at his state primary school in Delwara. Mayank asked if could take the high definition video camera home to film his father's working day. An extract from his film, which he shot independently and then co-edited with MacDougall, is available by following the link below. The password for access is 951159. The *Childhood and Modernity* project, of which Mayank's film was a part, is discussed more fully in Chapter 2.

In the centre frame of Fig. 1.1, Mayank is visible, reflected in the mirror of his father's shop. He is wearing a yellow 'T' shirt and leaning against the doorframe to help steady the camera. A careful look at the characteristics and the circumstances of this extract from Mayank's film will help draw out qualities in the observational style of filming.

In his pioneering 1975 essay about observational cinema, Colin Young stressed a camera could be used subjectively and embedded within a setting in a way that allows "a viewer elsewhere to have a sense of experiencing the event" (p. 104). Mayank is sharing with us what he

Fig. 1.1 Mayank's Family—still from a film by Mayank Ved (MacDougall, 2014) (https://vimeo.com/139964383)

experienced as he used the video camera. This is what *he* wanted to film, first at home, as his father prepares for the day, and then later on in his father's barbershop. So, there is nothing objective about what we see. The film sequences are so embedded in Mayank's experience that it is impossible to imagine another person filming in the same places at the same time in the same way. Such overt subjectivity places observational filming in stark contrast to the apparent (and even covert) objectivity of an apparently scientific or fly-on-the-wall use of a video camera. For example, rather than a static camera pre-positioned and left to record whatever passes across the frame, Mayank's camera is within and part of the scenes he films. Therefore Mayank's presence with his camera and his particular relationships and interactions with others in the film are vital to what viewers of the film see. He is a single and identifiable author of the shots he films and a co-author, with his adult guide, of the edited sequences he presents for public viewing.

A characteristic of Mayank's film is that there is no narrative voice-over from a filmmaker who is telling us what to notice or who wants to expand on the implications of what is shown to develop an argument or make a point. Nor is there an attempt to construct performances or present us with scenes for entertainment. Mayank mostly follows what interests him as it happens. He cares about his father and so what his father does interests him. What happens has not been pre-planned or set-up. Mayank is able to patiently show us ordinary kinds of events as they spontaneously unfold around him. There is a naturalistic narrative element in how the film is structured as it follows, sequentially, how events unfold through time. But Mayank is not attempting to present a didactic narrative; he is simply looking thoughtfully. He is observing from his position, which is clearly visible and at the centre of his film. Others share something of his experience when they view the film.

There are conversations in Mayank's film, including conversations between him with those around him as he films. These are spontaneous interactions and cement our understanding that Mayank is at the core of the setting he is recording. This is quite different from filmmakers and researchers who conduct interviews or record what people say with discreetly placed microphones to listen in on afterwards. The hugely influential ethnographic filmmaker, John Rouch (1917–2004) described collaborations between the filmmaker and those filmed as a shared anthropology. It is in the spirit of collaboration that Mayank's mother and father at home and the customers in the barbershop are happy for the boy to be there and seem to get on with what is at hand, accepting he has a video camera and is recording what is going on. Clearly they are sharing the circumstances they are all part of and collaborating with Mayank as he films.

What can be learnt from the extract of Mayank's film? There is no attempt to explain what we see. Mayank has no special thesis he is trying to convince us of by presenting his film as evidence; neither did he construct his film as a form of argument. We are, however, able to appreciate qualities he is experiencing in ways that other kinds of accounts, especially accounts reliant on words and analyses of data, would simply fail to render. For example, we have a material and aesthetic sense of the sounds together with the size, positioning, colours and forms of the home shrine, as his father completes his morning religious ritual. Also, we have a strong consciousness of the combination of sensuality and forcefulness as soap is lathered onto the customers face preparing for the razor blade that scrapes the beard before a powerful face massage completes the shave. Therefore, even in such a short extract we are learning there are material and aesthetic qualities that are an essential part of Mayank's experience of himself, his home and his parents. We learn these through his filmmaking encounters whose process is visible to us in the raw film material, which, however it is edited, cannot be rewritten. The decisions Mayank makes in the way he films and what he chooses to film offer us his contingent, subjective and experiential analysis of the circumstances he filmed, which is able to convey, as his teacher David MacDougall puts it, "the multiple features of social events, not through dissociating them from one another or in the abstract, but in the simultaneity and their material and sensory dimensions" (2018).

It may be tempting to argue that Mayank's film comes close to an unmediated record of his experience whist filming—purer somehow. But he is still the author of what we see, as he makes so many decisions about what and how to film. He may only be eleven but he is still very much in control. Mayank is therefore consciously mediating what we see through his use of the camera. After filming, and together with MacDougall, an anthropologist, he took part in negotiating how what he shot was edited into a finished film. Thus, the final filmic sequences have a refined anthropological quality in their editing, which Mayank alone would not have contemplated.

The whole process may leave viewers with an uncomfortable sensation of voyeurism, even manipulation, as we look in on the boy's life (and his family's life) from afar. Even more so as we know what this involved. This necessarily puts both Mayank's observation with camera and our observation of his film under some reflective scrutiny. There is a tension couched in such a voyeuristic implication, especially when adult researchers and children are working together. For example, there is an aesthetic tenor in play, which has been valorised by adults. This becomes part of what the boy senses he should be doing. This aesthetic is part of the nature of the specific craft skills of video camera work that Mayank learnt and practiced during the observational filmmaking workshops at his school. It appears adults may not have told Mayank what to film but by they have suggested how he should film. However, that same particular approach to filming and the associated practical skills Mayank needed, empowered him to film and share with us parts of his experience he values highly. The boy was tutored by adults and learnt what to do, but he clearly has benefitted from their knowledge and is able to share his experiences in a coherent and useful way because of that pedagogical relationship.

In terms of research, Mayank collaborated with social anthropologists, and learnt from them a way of filming. As he instigated his own inquiry through his independent filmmaking at home and at his father's shop, Mayank become integral to the academically orientated adults' research process. This was designed to open pathways to knowing and understanding more about the individual children's lives and how their lives are lived in contemporary India by placing children's own knowledge and experience centre stage. There are procedural, methodological and ethical challenges in considering this kind of observational filmmaking as research, especially if children are camera operators and editors. This book, which is centred on observational filmmaking for education, will take up those challenges because the benefits to children both directly as participants and indirectly through the outcomes of such research are substantial.

The Observational Style in Film

Doing ethnography is naturally and ubiquitously associated with observing others. During the twentieth century, the continual technological changes in audio and visual recording technologies meant that using cameras to record became increasingly available to all ethnographic researchers as a way and a means to observe and hold onto the raw material of observations. At one end of a wide spectrum of possible methods, a passive camera can be left running in a fixed (or even from a hidden) position, on predetermined settings, to observe and record whatever humans are doing or saying as they pass across the frame. The resulting material usually becomes data for subsequent analysis. Somewhere in the middle of this spectrum a camera can be deliberately used to document the customs and conventions of people (including children) as they get on with what is at hand. In this situation the camera is active, specifically targeted by the filmmaker, who responds as events unfold, in order to record elements that help address whatever questions are being asked in the research or demanded by the objectives of the intended film. Although data can be extracted from such material for qualitative analysis using any number of possible conceptual frameworks, often the filmmaker produces an explanatory or expressive documentary film, which presents, or contributes to, a particular viewpoint or argument.

However, as Mayank's film shows, the observational filmmaking style, which is the focus of this book, is further along the spectrum of ways of using a camera to observe. This is also a highly active and engaged technique, which takes the camera into the centre of a situation but without the overtly didactic or explanatory aims of documentary filmmaking. The camera documents with the material, aesthetic and affective subjectivity of the camera user in the foreground, rather than a didactic or explicatory intention. These qualities are amplified because the user observes by responding intuitively and naturally to what is going on. Thus, the camera becomes an extension of the filmmaker's sensations, perceptions and thoughts. The filmmaker seems more physically present in the resulting filmic material.

Academic writers, notably Roger Sandall (1972), Colin Young (1975), David MacDougall (1998, 1999, 2006, together with Anna Grimshaw and Amanda Ravetz (2009) have each critically documented elements of the history of observational cinema, where the term 'cinema' refers to the production of films. This book focuses on the theory and practice of observational *filmmaking* as an educative process, be that for research or for classroom pedagogy, rather than on observational *cinema*, which suggests an imperative to produce finished films as an end product. This is an important distinction, as I will argue this places the accent on using cameras and editing software as a form of thinking, before it becomes a form of representation. This process is valuable to education in and of itself whether or not filmic material is highly crafted and released as a film. Therefore, the focus in this book is different than that of the anthropologists cited above. However, from the very first cinematic experiments, it is contextually useful to render something of the emergence of an observational style through a social anthropologic filter.

The Lumière brothers shot some of the earliest examples of film using their invention, the *Cinématographe*, in 1895. They quickly amassed a collection of short films, which they presented at public screenings. These cinematic illusions of real life were a triumph of a science and showmanship (North, 2001). To early audiences films were an entertaining and beguiling magical technological trick. They demonstrated how a deliberately placed camera, which continuously records what is happening in its field of view, could simply reveal humans getting on with what they are doing without obvious comment or manipulation. Although, the Lumières quickly discovered that a humorous set up, *L' Arroseur arrose* made in 1895, and technological manipulation, *Démolition d'un mur*, made a year later in 1896, bought entertaining drama to scenes a camera might observe. Many of these early Lumière films can be viewed on YouTube.

In 1898, Alfred Hadden, who led the Cambridge Anthropological Expedition to the Torres Straights, demonstrated that a camera might be a useful, if cumbersome and troublesome, tool to help capture more information about society in its context (Quiggin, 1942). For many anthropologists, however, as the twentieth century progressed, the temptation to create a kind of visual catalogue of how societies looked missed more conceptual and revealing aspects of social life, such as kinship, friendship and beliefs. Nevertheless, certain qualities of social interaction simply could not be recorded or represented fully by writing. A film camera could be a tool to help an anthropologist capture, for later analysis and reflection, different kinds of information that written notes could not hope to capture alone. As an example of this, in the 1930s, anthropologist Margaret Mead decided a camera would help research. However the ways film cameras might be used had changed significantly since the Lumière brothers' early experiments. This resulted in theoretical and practical tensions in filmmaking as a research method.

Mead had a view that the ideal camera should be a neutral tool and simply be left running in a situation (Mead & Bateson, 1977). Life would be recorded running before it. She saw the personality and technique of a camera operator as a danger to the objectivity and neutrality demanded by science. In contrast, Gregory Bateson, her husband when he worked with her on their Bali expedition from 1936, was a skilled camera operator and argued that a camera was nothing without the person behind it. The person with the camera established relationships with those being filmed and made constant decisions about where a camera was and where a camera would point as well as technical decisions about aperture, lenses etcetera. This, he argued, was in contrast to a futile attempt at a neutral kind of scientificity. There was valuable authenticity as the researcher reflexively acknowledged the camera was *not* objective in how it is used. The camera demonstrated a point of view. For Mead, the kind of reflexive, edited ethnographic film that might result was art and not science; this artistry would not support the *science* of anthropology. There are transcripts of a lively argument between Mead and Bateson that illuminate fundamental dilemmas in reconciling conflicting qualities of subjectivity and objectivity in using video cameras as a research tool in the social sciences (Mead & Bateson, 1977).

In contrast to Mead, during the 1950s and 1960s, the filmmaker and anthropologist, Jean Rouch, orginator of *Cinéma Vérité*, explored how a cinematic truth was created through improvisation, collaboration and performance as, for example, people could re-enact their own lives and memories, stimulated and provoked by the presence of a film camera. The camera and the researcher become instruments of an exploration of the reality of others as they openly probe and prompt their subjects whose ideas and viewpoints become very much part of how a film unfolds.

Steven Feld (2003) unpacks key theoretical themes from Rouch's films and writings. He draws out the way Rouch brought into play conversations about anthropologic film techniques, elements he found exemplified in previous attempts by filmmakers such as Robert Flaherty (1884–1951) and Dziga Vertov (1896–1954). Informed by this history, in his essay *The Camera and Man* (1974), Rouch illuminates the tensions between the film as a conscious attempt to stage, construct and present a *version* of real life and the possibility that film can observe, record and present life as it unfolds.

Rouch practised pioneering approaches to filming social realities. He developed processes of *ciné-vérité* as ethnography. In this practice, participants were integral to the process of their observation, as they often became collaborators with Rouch in how and what was filmed. Rouch improvised camera techniques and took advantage of developing technology to record improvised life in an improvised way. He frequently put the camera and camera user in the midst of the situation. He openly revealed the process of filmmaking and acknowledged the necessary subjectivity of authorship. Rouch did not simply subscribe to stances on this kind of inter-subjectivity. He catalysed the role of the filmmaker as authoring film, not only about others' experience, but also about the filmmaker's experience in the filmed settings.

To illustrate this, in the first three minutes thirty seconds of a film made for Dutch television, Philo Bregstein (1986) shows Rouch at work in 1977 in a rural village in Nigeria. He has a portable film camera, sound recording equipment and the willing collaboration of different people, some of whom are being filmed; others are helping him or just watching what is going on. Immediately as Rouch starts filming, the nature of the technology he is using is apparent. A helper carries the sound equipment. The microphone, about a metre in length, appears to be a large diaphragm condenser type covered in what is known as a 'dead cat' muff to lessen the effect of wind noise. Much of the camera casing seems to comprise a film canister. A battery that Rouch has slung on his waist powers the camera. Rouch rests the camera on his right shoulder so that he can both see through the eyepiece and change the focus manually using the focus ring. The film is announced to all as "The Two Hunters", as the sound recorder taps the microphone on camera to help with synchronising his recorded sound with image during editing.

Rouch first films a tall constructed wall rendered in mud before slowly turning the camera towards the scene he will focus on. He then moves, walking carefully, towards a small pick-up truck. This is surrounded by a number of young men and boys. They are watching as

Rouch approaches. As he arrives, they begin talking. Rouch is filming the open back of the pick-up where, as the truck is organised, viewers hear metal objects of various kinds moved around.

Rouch stops and says, "Let's go again". There is now a second 'take' with the sound recorder repeating the tap on the microphone. The truck needs water and one of the boys stoops to collect water from a well just by the truck. Rouch follows the movement of the boy as he dips a container in the well. But Rouch is unhappy; he cries out forcibly, "You're an idiot! You should ask Lam if he wants a lot of water or not. Dja Dafo!" There is loud laughter and same process is repeated and filmed again, but this time the boy asks Lam how much water is needed. There are comments about how little water there is in the well. With the water in the truck, a group of six push the vehicle away. Rouch follows, walking with his camera.

The villagers and Rouch seem to be working together to shoot what appears to be a very ordinary scene. But, many are watching Rouch and the goings on and it is clear that filming is not an everyday situation. The eventual film remained unfinished. It was going to be an allegory about two men who claimed to be great hunters, whereas in fact they were charlatans who loved telling exaggerated stories (Henley, 2010).

The film extract described above shows how Rouch worked within communities and filmed with participants rather than merely filming participants. But it also graphically reveals the tensions between constructing a *narrative* and recording what it is that is going on, regardless of whether that fits the intended narrative. Most of all, the extract immediately reveals the effect of the available technology on what and how Rouch filmed. The 1970s saw the emergence of really mobile film recording technologies, but these were still cumbersome compared with what is readily available in digital audio-video technologies to recreational consumers at the time of writing. It is already clear that throughout the historical development of film and video, from the Lumière brothers to the present day, how technology is both understood and worked, profoundly influences what is recorded and so its value in terms of research. This is a theme that becomes prominent as this book progresses.

There are many critiques of Rouch, who suggest that he is an ethnographic entertainer by presenting, even revelling in, the strange, primitive and unusual. His self-critical, self-aware pronouncements are poor camouflage for an underlying preoccupation with colonising the lives and experiences of others (Gabriel, 1982; Harrow, 1999; Hennebelle, 1972; Ukadike & Gabriel, 2002). However, the example from Rouch I wish to highlight, and that taken up by MacDougall and others, leaves to one side overarching, predetermined conceptual frameworks for the categorisation and organisation of filmic material as data. It also leaves behind overly constructed and pre-planned filmic narratives and documentary techniques designed to narrate *only* the producer's and director's view. Instead, these pioneers employed the film camera as integral to the experience of both those who are filmed *and* the filmmaker. Rouch suggested that filming could be "a way of moving through the world [...] at the heart of the inquiry was a mobile, embodied camera—a camera that became an extension of the senses of the filmmaker" (Grimshaw & Ravetz, 2015, p. 262). Looking at such filmic material, viewers share in and share through experience rather than being told about that experience. The *Cinéma Vérité* of Rouch, and those who developed their own filmmaking styles inspired by his example, suggested the filmmaker was able to actively participate in scenes, make artistic choices in how film material was shot and assembled and therefore create artifice to reveal something of what lies beneath the surface of appearances.

Taylor (1998) implies that filmmakers such as Rouch, and later MacDougall, create knowledge as they film and edit, rather than illustrating knowledge with audio-visual material, or collecting data from which knowledge is later extracted. In social anthropology, Rouch helped set observational filmmaking as a counterpoint to the dominant tradition of filmmaking as a *servant* to knowledge (Taylor, 1998). The style of observational filmmaking can generate knowledge directly. David MacDougall is a filmmaker and anthropologist who has taken these key aspects from Rouch's methods and extended the participatory nature of observational filmmaking practice. As an example, which became a model from which I developed my own research method, I will go on to demonstrate in Chapter 2 that in MacDougall's *Childhood and Modernity* project—still running at the time of writing in 2017—it is the children themselves who use video cameras and shoot audio-visual material without the researcher on hand.

In parallel with *Cinéma Vérité*, but in many ways in contrast to it, *Direct Cinema* (which emerged as a form of documentary filming in North America in the 1960s) the filmmaker stays apart from the scene and lets it unfold without any overt intention to change what happens through the presence of the camera. It is as though the intention is to suggest that the camera made no difference to what the viewer sees and hears and was, as the expression runs, a fly on the wall. For example, in a film such as *Salesman* directed by Albert Maysles, David Maysles, and Charlotte Zwerin (1969), it appears that participants agreed, either openly or implicitly, to just continue with what they were doing and saying as though the camera was not present. *Salesman* is edited for characterisation and narrative punch. The subject was chosen because of the drama in the ethics of selling lavishly illustrated bibles to strangers in their homes. The filmmaker is actively engaging an observational style to present a viewpoint about moral behaviour when selling bibles. This kind of observational documentary, which takes a stance on social issues, grew out of frustrations of the Italian Neo-realist filmmakers after the Second World War. They rejected a bourgeois cinema of wealth, intellect and privilege in favour of the gritty realism of life as it is lived by the poorer working class. At the time of writing *Salesman* is available to view on YouTube.

The style of observational documentary, which is still a powerful force in television documentary making today, first became known as (and then developed out of) both *Direct Cinema* and *Cinéma Vérité*. It is apparent from the brief sketches above that a predilection for using a camera to observe and then using editing techniques to construct films with an observational feel have influenced factual films as documents of social life, the gritty realism of many fiction films, as well as films for anthropology and ethnographic research. Those elements of cinematic processes have an intertwined history. They also resonate through the accounts and examples of observational filmmaking for education in this book.

Examples of Observational Films

To further illustrate observational filmmaking in more specific relation to children's experiences whist living and learning, I will now describe extracts from three different filmmakers, which were shot and edited by adults. Each demonstrates elements of the observational style. The first of these is a review of a series of observational films focused on the lives of the same children in Finland over a number of years at school as the and at home. These films were made for television in the 1980s by Ulla Turunen and Ilkka Ruuhijärvi. The second example is *Être et Avoir* (Philibert, 2002) a French documentary shot in a rural primary school. This is followed by a discussion of two films *Schoolscapes* (2007) and *Gandhi's Children* (2008). Both are ethnographic observational film made by David MacDougall. In Chapter 2 there is an account of David MacDougall's subsequent *Childhood and Modernity* project, which ran from 2012 to 2018. During that project, MacDougall handed video cameras to children and taught them observational technique of filming, so that that they might observe, record and share their experiences with others.

Films by Ulla Turunen and Ilkka Ruuhijärvi

Between 1985 and 1991, Ulla Turunen and Ilkka Ruuhijärvi (1987a, 1987b, 1989, 1990, 1992) collaborated to make five observational films. These were broadcast by the Finish television channel, YLE TV1. In 1985, TV1 commissioned the first documentary from the Aalto University of Art and Design in Helsinki. In 1985 both Ulla and Ilkka were film students at Aalto. They had already discovered the work of Richard Leacock (1921–2011) and other filmmakers who adopted the *Direct Cinema* and *Cinéma Vérité* styles. Turunen and Ruuhijärvi were asked to take part in the project. The resulting films ended up by following the same group of children as they grew and progressed from Class 1 to Class 6. In Class 1 children are 6 or 7, by Class 6 they are 11 or 12 years old.

TV1 invited Turunen and Ruuhijärvi to make the first film focusing on children's experiences in school. The television channel left the students free to find the school and negotiate how and when to film. Their instinct was to avoid the wealthiest areas, sleepy suburbs, and very big schools. Eventually, they found a promising, small school building in the middle a concreted urban landscape, dominated by blocks of flats. This was in a working class area of Kallio called Merihaka, which Helsinki had started to build in 1970s. It is close to the sea. At that time the area was one of the most polluted in the country. One of the largest coal fired power stations in Finland was located very near the school, and some of the children lived in flats on the same level of chimney tops. There was dust and dirt everywhere and the environment was not designed for children in any way, but this didn't stop their outdoor activities, which became a feature in the films as children made the most of being outside, despite the nature of their 'concrete jungle'.

Having found a possible school, Turunen and Ruuhijärvi were offered a chance to film in Class 1 by the class teacher, who was also a student at the time. The filmmakers then sought and got permission for the filming from The Education Department of City of Helsinki. But, because schools were public places in Finland, there was no objection in principle to filming in school. So, on the first day of the school year, Turunen and Ruuhijärvi were already filming and it was then they met parents for the first time. Later in the autumn 1985 the filmmakers attended a parents' evening and explained their idea for the documentary project more fully. The parents asked them not to interview the children or allow filming to interrupt their play or studies, but were otherwise happy for children to be involved in such a project. As the film series followed the same group of children over the succeeding years, the filmmakers got to know parents well and checked with them at each new stage of the project.

The filming style remained remarkably consistent throughout the project. Turunen and Ruuhijärvi worked as a team of two. The used a Super 16 mm film camera and a separate sound recorder. This meant sound had to be synchronised later whilst editing. All material was filmed using the same focal length, which meant, for example, there was no zooming into or out of detail. Observing the children and what was happening as they were learning and living their lives both at school and at home was approached in the spirit of *Direct Cinema* and *Cinéma Vérité*. The filmmakers have noted that they were doing more than merely recording the events. They were far from passive observers and responded to what they were seeing and hearing. They found that how they spontaneously used the camera created a structure to what was captured during the filming sessions. In effect, the component scenes of each film already had some sense of a form before editing started. The flow of the film was important. So, there was no script or pre-planned storyboard—indeed, the television station did not ask for it. The final film only began to take shape during editing: Turunen and Ruuhijärvi choose the best scenes and put them together in a way that made sense to them as they recalled what was happening as they filmed the various scenes and settings over time. They wrote (Personal Communication, 2017):

> The conflicting situations in the characters' life as well as the narrative conflicts in the story bind the viewers into a common framework of the experience of childhood and youth: the viewer's sympathy and emotions spring from their own childhood experiences, memories and friends who make up a part of every human's own story.

Turunen and Ruuhijärvi (Personal Communication, 2017) also wrote to me about the children's first response to filming in their classroom:

> In the very beginning some pupils wanted to disrupt the filming. They screamed loudly into a microphone, or they put their heads straight to the camera's matte box [a device used on the end of a lens to block the sun or other light source in order to prevent glare and lens flare]. In that case we allowed the pupils to do so for a while. One boy was interested to try the camera, an Aaton. It is surprisingly heavy. Ilkka let him shoot some footage. Ulla gave pupils headphones so they could listen to the recorded sound. The children were satisfied, and they didn't disturb the filming any longer. The children were aware of the camera, they always knew when

it was on, because the small internal motor it made noise. Despite the camera and the microphone, the children were more absorbed by their schoolwork, plays, or conflicts. They soon ignored the filmmaking. One parent recognized from our documentaries, that we have not filmed secretly. It is true.

The filmmakers comment on the relationship with the children. They did not try to become the children's friend: "The children had their own friends, families and relatives. We filmmakers were only visitors during their schooldays". That might serve to argue that Turunen and Ruuhijärvi distanced themselves from the children's experiences. But they argue this was far from the case, by remaining more neutral in respect of interpersonal relationships with the children, they found that they and their equipment was accepted, but with the minimum of interference in what children were doing and saying.

Adults often film children from a standing position, so that the camera is angled down to a child from the level of the filmmaker. In those films a child seems to be an object, not a subject. That point of view is one that chimes with the power of an adult over a child. It is notable how Turunen and Ruuhijärvi always filmed on the same level with the children's eyes. In 1985 the children were around 100–120 centimetres tall, so that if the adult camera operator was standing, the handheld camera was always at armpit height or lower. The filmmakers (Personal Communication, 2017) wrote more about their approach:

> In our films the camera movement and the angle are always very controlled. The controlling of the camera movement is filmmaker's way to tell a story. He decides when to film, what to film, how to move, how to edit during the filming. He observes a child, but at the same time he respects the inner life of the child. He doesn't want to open or reveal the child's secret world. In the class some pupils had behaviour problems, learning problems, health problems etc. They had weekly contacts with therapists, doctors, curators etc. Some had quite stressful lives. We think, that the children were calm and easy in front of the camera just because they didn't need to do anything special. We were the only outsiders who didn't ask or beg anything of them. Our role was to be quiet and listen. In the classroom and in the schoolyard we moved like stalkers, but very close.

1 Introducing Observational Film

Fig. 1.2 Still from *Kun se tapahtuu* (https://vimeo.com/289441020 and https://vimeo.com/289456020)

The films were difficult to locate, but thanks to Ulla Turunen and Ilkka Ruuhijärvi some Betamax cassettes were found and the contents have been digitised as MP4s. It is now appropriate to let the filmmaking speak for itself. I have selected some extracts, which with the kind permission of the filmmakers, are available to readers on Vimeo. Please follow the link above and use the password 951159 to view. The first extract is from the first film *Kun se tapahtuu* (As it happens) (1987a), the second from the third film *Tien yli* (Across the road) (1989) (Fig. 1.2).

Être et Avoir

Être et Avoir (2002) offers a portrait of children and their teacher in a single class rural primary school in the Auvergne region of France. Nicolas Philibert, the director, shot the film over a period of six months in 2001. He used a crew of four people, a cameraman, a sound engineer, an assistant cameraman and himself. *Être et Avoir* was premiered at

Cannes, won considerable critical acclaim and a raft of awards, including the prestigious best film of the year from the French Syndicate of Cinema Critics. I include a critical account of this documentary here, because it demonstrates the dissonant relationship between the observational style of camera work, editing, and the demands of a publically released film, which is offered to cinemas and television for commercial reasons. The making and distribution of this film draws attention to both technical and ethical issues about the intentions, practices, and outcomes of close-up factual filming of children's experiences. Parallel issues also pertain when the audio-visual processes and outcomes, which are a record of children's experiences, are in education research domains or part of teaching and learning in schools and universities. For example, if researchers, teachers, parents or, indeed, children themselves wish to know and understand more about children's experiences in school, then attending carefully to those experiences is likely to play a central part. But, the nature and processes of observation will affect both what is observed and how outcomes of that are shared with others. Not only that, how is it that being observed is in the best interests of children?

Filming *Être et Avoir* began in the midst of an icy winter of 2001 and ended six months later in high summer as children are leaving for the summer holidays. The crew were in the school for ten weeks spread out over this period. When in school, they limited filming in the classroom to around 40 minutes per day, so as to minimise disruption to children's learning. Philibert also filmed children traveling to and from school, children at home doing homework with parents and one pupil working on farm chores. He also filmed the surrounding landscape in various weather conditions in an evocative and poetic way. There is no commentary, although there is a short and impromptu interview with the teacher, Georges Lopez towards the end of the documentary. Whist editing, Phililbert inserted a few brief playful music sequences to accompany transitional movement such as a child cycling to school.

The style is reminiscent of *Direct Cinema* more than Rouch's form of *Cinéma Vérité* and, indeed, a number of critics label this as a fly-on-the-wall film (Rotton Tomatoes, 2017). Philibert (2003, p. 2) admits he "broke the style" so that he could film teacher Lopez talking with him on camera. That interview is towards the end of the film. The clip helps cement the viewers' understanding of the teacher as the main 'character' in the documentary.

Philibert has assembled the clips into a film with an identifiable formal structure (2017). During the production process a huge amount of what was filmed was rejected. He writes, "A film's final cut is not a 'best of', but a construction which complies as much with the director's desires as the laws peculiar to film". Therefore, he decided that the final film should show nothing of children's interaction with a crew of four adults and their equipment. In *Être et Avoir* children seem to be getting on in their single classroom school oblivious to the filming. This is the powerful effect of selective editing, but it is also an indication that children became thoroughly used the crew being in the school. They simply got on with what was significant to them as children, rather than paying too much attention to matters (the filming), which neither overly interested them or had any obvious bearing on what they were doing at the time. The issue was not that the camera and crew of four were ever forgotten; it was that they were fully accepted, so children and their teacher appear to ignore the camera and crew, at least in the shots presented in the final edited film. Nevertheless, Philibert (2017) did not wish to extend that acceptance of the filmmaking process to viewers. So the camera operators were "permanently on the alert for our reflections in the window and on the blackboard". The illusion that the camera and crew were *not* in the classroom with the children was intended.

Philibert filmed and edited to draw out characters from the 'cast' of twelve children who interacted with each other and with Lopez, the teacher. Jojo is a relentlessly busy, communicative four-year-old who struggles with the disciplines of learning. Julien, who is 11, has a taciturn acceptance of difficulty both as he works with the cattle on his parents' farm, deals with conflict, and struggles with homework. Olivier, also 11, is more emotional, but is coping with his father's serious illness. Nathalie is so shy that she hardly speaks, a worrying trait for her mother and teacher that has nothing to do with the presence of the camera. Not all the children in the class feature as strongly. Philibert (2017) explains that the filming "bothered" some children. These children were filmed less and some barely appear in the film. So it is the depictions of those who do feature that are important to how the film is constructed. The director uses these developing individual characterisations, as they build through the film, to help construct dramatic narratives and episodes woven within the structure of the film. Those mini-dramas work better within the story of the film because viewers have got to know some of the children and their teacher.

This was a film made for public distribution. It is a documentary, but was also made to engage and entertain. Its profitability depended on sales. But the close observation of children's lives in the sanctuary of their school classroom does not necessarily sit easily with the director's aim to make an acclaimed film for public release in cinemas. The efficacy of small individual dramas and narratives, together with the poetry of cinematography with children at its heart, make for a product that viewers may enjoy, but a product that becomes more about the filmic form than what that form portrays. Philibert (2017) acknowledges some of the tensions:

> It was necessary to find "the right distance", a distance that varies according to the context and nature of the relationships that you have with the persons that you film. Each film is a singular story and this question of limits is posed over and over again [...] A film imprisons the people that you film in a certain image, at a precise moment in their lives and you have to remember that this image will stick to them, that they won't always be able to rid themselves of it. That's the whole difference between documentary and fiction.

Philibert's intentions dominate what is produced. To set up the project, the director visited at least a 100 schools, after contacting more than 300. He was looking for a small enough class so that children could become identifiable characters. A wide age-range would bring variety, different dramatic scenarios and therefore interest for viewers. The classroom had to be large enough for a crew of four to film without disrupting classroom life and light enough so that the crew would not need additional lighting. Philibert chose to work with traditional film stock rather than digital video because of the cinematic richness that he argued such medium brings to screenings. This way of filming meant that the available light limited depth of field. Therefore, focusing a film camera accurately in unpredictable circumstances of the classroom needed the considerable skill of a highly experienced camera operator (Andrew, 2003; Falcon, 2003)

The collaborative character of the experienced male teacher, Georges Lopez, in the setting of an old-fashioned stone schoolhouse in a small, poor, rural community offered Philibert (2003, p. 2) the chance to make, as he says, "*cinema* [sic] with something from the everyday". This project was carefully designed. The setting and the participants would have to be in tune with the filmmaker's aims, although Philibert did not know what the film would contain when he began, that would emerge in the process of filming and reflective reviewing of takes. But, nevertheless, he controlled, quite tightly, the choice of the environment he chose to work within so that the circumstance of the little school in the village of Sainte-Étienne sur Usson enabled *Être et Avoir* to resonate with big themes.

There is the harshness of a physical and emotional outside world in comparison with the physical and emotional sanctuary of the classroom. This major thematic thread is introduced at the very start as, following shots of farmers struggling to herd cattle in a windswept and bitter winter landscape, the camera shows two pet turtles walking across the floor of a quiet, clean, warm classroom. The classroom appears as a controlled sanctuary for vulnerable independent living beings cared for and sheltered from the torments of what lies outside. But not all is what it seems and the gentleness of a mythically idyllic small rural school is inhabited with day-to-day personal challenges that are inevitably part of real, not mythical, children's lives. The film reveals that an attractive stone built schoolhouse with its light airy classroom, small family-like atmosphere and spaces to play outside is also the backdrop for the intense emotions of childhood. Philibert shows how these emotional traumas of childhood sit in relation to the all powerful but seemingly unlimited benevolence of a supporting adult—the teacher.

Young children's faltering communication about the simplest of concepts, such as seven follows six, is set alongside the teacher's patient explanations and demonstrations. It seems that it is in *how* Lopez and children communicate about what they are learning that the very fabric of coming to know and understand more is revealed. Julien, a child who has autonomy, trust and important roles on a family farm, is less adequate, even diminished, by maths and literacy work in school. Four-year-old JoJo, although insistent that counting comes to an end, is led by Lopez towards the idea of infinity. Young and old find ways to collaborate and peacefully co-exist within the reliable society of the class despite their obvious different and intensely subjective experiences.

To achieve the sense of intimate connection with children and Lopez there are long, unbroken shots of unfolding scenes, where the camera is frequently at children's rather than an adult's eye level. Careful framing helps to focus on a particular event. Surprisingly, there is only one shot that attempts to survey the whole class. The points of view taken up by the camera, and the often apparent closeness of the lens to the children, gives the impression that viewers are sitting alongside children at the classroom tables rather than looking down on them from a distance. However natural frames appear, Philibert was active in physically changing elements in the setting that might clash with the ethos of the film. There were computers in the class, but they are left out of the film. When a television was on in Julien's home as he did his homework Philibert asked if could turn it off (Falcon, 2003).

In the contextual shots of the village, landscape and children travelling to and from school, the camera is often less close-up and personal. It takes in scenes from a distance. The differences between interior and exterior viewpoints have a metaphorical as well as a formal function. They help show the passage of time, the changing of the seasons and the sense of an ever-moving physical landscape within which the classroom sits. But, children, as well as the world in which they inhabit, are also in constant flux.

There is an epilogue to the *Être et Avoir* story. The film was a surprising home and international success. Tourists began to visit Sainte-Étienne sur Usson and ask for photographs with the children, the 'stars' of the film. The teacher Lopez, now retired, filed a lawsuit against the film's producers. His legal team argued he should be cited as a co-author and that he was, in effect, an actor who should receive payment. Lopez wanted financial compensation for the use of his voice and his image. His legal claim for €250,000 failed. His comments afterwards are revealing. He related that he and the children had been exploited. As Amelia Gentleman (2004) reports in her *Guardian* newspaper article, he said:

> We were misled. The production company told me and the children's families that they were making a small documentary about the phenomenon of the one-teacher village school and the film would be used primarily for educational purposes [...] They said it would have a restricted screening and never discussed marketing the film to make it such a commercial venture.

The French press and public turned against him. The filmic illusion of the altruistic, value fuelled schoolteacher who only cares for his pupils appeared shattered. The French tribunal ruled that he had enjoyed his personal and the film's success, attended Cannes and had spoken in public about his role without ever once asking for financial reward. French media critics discussed what might happen to the idea of a documentary if protagonists were paid to take part. But Lopez insisted they had all been deceived. Was the film really an honest form of observation of school life or had the filmmakers manipulated the 'cast' of characters to create an entertainment, which reputedly made a €2 million profit (Gentleman, 2004)? It was also reported that out of 12 children who appeared in the film, 9 families made a claim for payments of €20,000 each.

Two Films by David MacDougall: *SchoolScapes*: Scenes from a School in South India (2007) and *Gandhi's Children* (2008)

David MacDougall has an extensive catalogue of ethnographic films, which can be traced back to influential work filming with semi-nomadic pastoral people in Northeastern Uganda in the early '70s. That work resulted in the critically acclaimed *To Live with Herds* (MacDougall, 1974). During the 1990s, after filming with aboriginal communities in Australia, MacDougall's research relocated to India, where he developed observational filmmaking methods in response to ethnographic challenges when observing children. The two films in this section were made in vastly contrasting institutions for the education and welfare of children. Firstly, *SchoolScapes* (2007) is set in the Rishi Valley School, a fee-paying co-educational boarding school founded by the philosopher Krishnamurti. Secondly, *Gandhi's Children* (2008) shows the daily lives of children in the Prayas Children's Home for neglected, destitute and working boys at Jahangirpuri, Dehli. So, whereas both *SchoolScapes* and *Gandhi's Children* investigate children's lives in institutions, the privilege of the former stands in marked contrast to the implied poverty of the latter. Both films are characteristic of MacDougall's style of observational camera work and editing. Each presents a set of scenes joined together in a sequence. However the structure of the final films has less to do with narrative (although narrative elements inevitably become part of how events unfold) than an intention to create heightened awareness of where MacDougall was and what he and the children were experiencing in the circumstances they all were part of.

At the time, MacDougall presented films such as *SchoolScapes* as part of a broader initiative, which he termed an 'Observation Project'. Grimshaw and Hockings (2011) explain how MacDougall's concern with observation is not focused on dictating to others what he saw was important and explaining to them how that should be understood, but rather on catalysing a heightened form of awareness so that viewers can see and hear what the camera records with their own eyes and ears. Understanding other's experiences is difficult, especially from their point of view. This is especially so with children. MacDougall's methodology is a catalyst for the possibility of heightened awareness of people in the circumstances of their lives. This is a necessary precursor to more definitional models of understanding. In simple terms, if researchers and educators can be with children and share something of their experience they will get to know them better. It is hard to imagine, in the context of day-to-day family and friendship relationships, that understanding someone in depth is possible without getting to know them. Getting to know people requires spending time with them. MacDougall's use of observational filmmaking as research prioritises that simple aim.

1 Introducing Observational Film

SchoolScapes is one hour and seventeen minutes long. The film is comprised of 40 single takes of no more than five minutes and often of a minute or so in length. In almost all the 'scenes' the camera does not move. When it does it is a gentle purposeful movement, which connects two elements of the scene together. The following paragraphs, each and in turn, briefly describe the content from a part of the film from the opening credits.

First we hear sounds from a landscape. Mostly birds. The initial frames are black. Starting at 42 seconds, and after minimal titles, there is a still shot of a rocky hillside at dawn animated by birdcalls and songs. This lasts one minute.

A close up full frame of twigs, branches and leaves moving in the wind follows for a further minute. The movement intermingles within a complex layered space receding to distance. Sound is again prominent. Both opening shots suggest aesthetic force is important to MacDougall in how the film will be shot and structured.

The camera is in a dormitory. One boy is still in bed. There are a number of other beds. These are untidy, just left. A mechanical sound (air-conditioning or a fan) dominates. Just on the left edge of the frame a red curtain is moving in a draft of air. A man enters to wake the boy who is about 14 years old. The camera is at about waist level of a standing man. It is possible to imagine MacDougall kneeling or sitting for this shot, or, perhaps, standing holding the camera at waist height. The boy slowly rouses and gets up and dressed before sleepily laying his head back on the pillow. The process takes almost 5 minutes.

Three teenage girls are lying flat on thin cotton rugs. The girl closest to the camera is visible from mid torso to head. The camera is at floor level and appears close to the nearest girl. The girls are meditating and a man is leading a breathing exercise. Eyes are closed. The meditation class continues with stretching stomach exercises. There are faint mural paintings of large birds on the far wall. The man counts the length of each stomach crunch hold.

Thirty seconds of an empty classroom of single wooden school desks follows. The room is white, high ceilinged with large bright windows. The sounds of birds from the first clip recall the landscape outside.

Large grey patterned thin-cottoned floor mats are drying on clotheslines outside. There are adults and children's voices off camera.

The camera is at floor level. Many sandals, slip-ons and flip-flops are left on a polished concrete floor at the transition of a large internal space to outside. There are six square receding concrete columns and bright external daylight. Gradually, the noise of pupils leaving an assembly of some kind builds. Legs appear as a busy throng; feet are slipped into the sandals. The framing only shows feet and trousered ankles of those closest to the camera. Whole figures are visible further away. The frame is held for three minutes. In that time the pupils leave the assembly, slip on their shoes, gather and talk briefly before heading outside into the bright light. An apparent dustiness of colour in denim, concrete, landscape, painted walls and cotton fabrics, is an emergent aesthetic theme.

There is a loud mechanical chattering of printers and the human talk of voices in an active administration office. MacDougall, with the camera, seems to be seated, a little apart and away from the desk of a man who appears in charge of busy comings and goings. The frame is held for almost two minutes.

The camera is at floor level, lower than two men who are seated cross-legged on the reed-matted floor of a large hall space open to the outside. There is a sound of a bagpipe like drone and one man is singing and attempting to find rhythm by repeatedly hitting his knee and clapping. The second man holds a drum in his lap. He joins in. They appear to be practicing. The frame lasts for almost two minutes.

For over one minute, the camera seems to be on a metal counter in a kitchen. On one side, a number of men wearing beige and cream shirts are preparing chapattis. They are placing these on the counter in shiny stainless steel plates where a woman in a blue sari collects them from the other side.

The paragraphs that follow describe the next sequence of four clips. David MacDougall and his Australian distributers, Ronin Films, have kindly made this sequence of shots available to view on Vimeo. Please follow the link below. At the time of writing, *SchoolScapes* is available to purchase in Australia from Ronin Flims, in the USA from Berkeley Media LLC, and in the UK from the Royal Anthropological Institute, London (RAI) (Fig. 1.3).

The camera seems a few inches from a boy's slightly bowed head. He has clasped his hands over his eyes. His fingers grasp jet-black short hair. This

1 Introducing Observational Film 27

Fig. 1.3 Still from *SchoolScapes* (MacDougall, 2007) (https://vimeopro.com/roninfilmsaustralia/observational-filmmaking-for-education)

is first shot where the camera moves slightly. It follows the boy's hands as he moves his head. There are sounds of boys' voices and a man's. This is a teacher. But he is only present through his voice. The camera moves down to show two closed books on the table in front of the boy. He handles them absent-mindedly.

There are two animated boys sitting at a table in class. They are both reading a thick textbook or encyclopaedia. They could be twins. They are collaborating on a project. MacDougall holds the camera at their head height. It seems to be actually at the table with them. The boys argue about what to do and can't work together.

The next shot shows a reflected scene close up in a mirror. A girl is dancing and a man sits apparently playing a drum. He is singing to a rhythmical percussion accompaniment. It appears the girl is dancing almost in conversation with the musician. In contrast to the highly structured dancing and music, the walls and posters in the background appear scrappy and scruffy.

There is a cassette tape recorder loudly playing Indian heavy metal style music on a workbench. Two boys appear to be doing homework close to the radio. There are loud boy's voices both on and off camera. MacDougall seems to be on the bench close to the seated boys for almost four minutes. The camera is below their eye level. The music is switched on and off as pupils interact and talk loudly. The film has now been running 26 minutes from the first black frame before the titles.

What did MacDougall's strategy for filmmaking make me aware of as I watched *SchoolScapes*? Initially, it was not what I saw but what I heard which began to inhabit my consciousness of the Rishi Valley School. It is easy to forget the significance of sound and that sound and images are recorded together and that what is noticed is often dependent on what is heard and vice versa. The soundscapes in *SchoolScapes* are a powerful part of each scene. I realised I could determine natural sounds, the human voice, mechanical sounds, and sounds that people were making especially music. Secondly, I gradually noted more about the physical contexts. Prominent were landscape and then the inside and outside of buildings (often characterised by materials such as concrete and stone or the colour of paint used). I became aware of clothing, furniture, the objects used by children and adults in the school, plus what was hung, pinned or stuck on the walls. Thirdly, I realised that people, especially but not exclusively children, were working, relaxing, learning, teaching, concentrating, playing, listening, talking, reading, writing and engaged aesthetically with music or dance for example.

The film presents Rishi Valley School as a place occupied by people. That may seem an unimportant and obvious comment, but the interrelationship of the physical environment with what people are doing, saying and experiencing is vital to building an understanding of how an institution such as a school works. Within the school there are different kinds of places—settings for activities and living. These included dormitories, kitchens, offices, assembly halls, practice rooms, classrooms, and pupils' studies. There are outside spaces for sport, domestic chores and just hanging out. In the film, each of these places (settings) became scenes animated by the sounds and movements of people. It should be reemphasised that in *SchoolScapes* there is no commentary or voice over explaining what is going on or telling the viewer what to notice. There is no overt defining narrative to hold the film together as a story, although, in the first part of the film, there is a natural progression of scenes through a day. Narrative structure has been absorbed by

MacDougall's intention to prioritise awareness of what is seen, heard, sensed and felt.

SchoolScapes invites viewers to be with, as though alongside, the filmmaker (MacDougall) and experience a heightened awareness of a selection of circumstances of the school, the pupils and the adults who people the scenes. The ordinary, everyday and overlooked in daily life are in the foreground. MacDougall's filmmaking offers consumers of his research, if they attend to what he shows, a perceptual, felt and almost physically aesthetic sense of what it might be like to be a pupil at Rishi Valley School. He is able to do this because he allows his own highly tuned subjectivity to lead how he uses the camera and its attached microphone. Viewers are with *MacDougall* (the emphasis is deliberate) as they experience what he recorded with the cameras. There are usually long unbroken takes of self-aware attention during which it is possible to become acutely aware of the filmmaker's presence holding the camera, despite the inevitable fact that he is hidden behind the lens and that his voice is almost never heard.

MacDougall selects the shots he wishes to share during editing and assembles a film. His film thus becomes a gentle and persuasive guide to pupils' experiences. He writes no explanatory text about the school or pupil, nor separately analyses his film material into a social anthropologic text. He openly, carefully and respectfully frames the scenes he records to present to viewers the school, the pupils and the objects that surround their lives. Notably, in *SchoolScapes*, MacDougall avoids building a film from a series of mini-dramas. He creates no overarching literary style narrative, nor does he create a biographical narrative structure by following one or more pupils. Grimshaw and Hockings (2011), in their review of the film, point out how this echoes earliest cinematic aesthetic of the Lumière brothers and reflects qualities in simply looking with attention promoted by Krishnamurti, the school's founder. This suggests that viewing MacDougall's film is less like being a spectator, necessarily outside of a scene created to entertain or inform (as in much Hollywod cinema and television production including reality TV), and more like being the filmmaker's and pupils' invitee to share with them what they and the school are like.

It would be a mistake to compare *SchoolScape's* structure and aesthetic directly with that of a narrative driven documentary. It is a different kind of a film. Rather than having a story to tell MacDougall has first-hand perceptions to share. In his theoretical writing about observational filmmaking MacDougall (2006, p. 7) has attempted to articulate his position. He writes that this "sensory state" is one of "heightened awareness", which precedes judgement and categorisation and "prepares us for a different kind of knowledge". It is not that the researcher "projects oneself onto things in themselves" but frees minds to first of all perceive them. In the case of pupils, their lives and experiences in schools, the implication is that this looking, this state of observing, this heightened awareness, is a vital prerequisite to a deeper and fuller understanding of their circumstances. Surely this is something of enormous benefit to education research about schools, teaching, learning and how adults might improve children's lives.

In **Gandhi's Children** David MacDougall shares his and children's experience in a very different Indian institution from the elite Rishi Valley School. The Prayas Children's Home for Boys (also the Prayas Institute of Juvenile Justice) is located in Shahjahanpuri on the northern edge of Dehli. There are *courtwallas*, boys who are living in the home because of a court order and *homewallas*, who are there because it is their only home. Perhaps there is no adult prepared to look after them, perhaps they have run away, or perhaps they have been found living on the streets. In the case of *courtwallas* the boys may be petty criminals such as pickpockets and thieves. The film includes sequences tracking the arrival for a large number of children rescued by the authorities from illegal forced labour in an embroidery factory. In one scene boys speak of being raped in another penal institution in another part of Dehli. Clearly, many of the boys have had harrowing past experiences. Many, nevertheless, seem not just resilient, but practical and pragmatic, determined to get on and make the best of the situation by looking forward not back.

As in *SchoolScapes*, MacDougall's technique draws out an awareness of pervasive qualities in the material and aesthetic circumstances of the physical surroundings. However, in *Ghandi's Children* the camera is often more active. It follows and listens as the personal dramas of individual children form a tapestry of scenes, which have more of an overtly narrative intent. This filmmaking is not only observation but story telling as well. Human processes and emotions are followed. Despite what might be thought of as the disturbing circumstances of these children's lives, MacDougall does not take a position on this by explaining to viewers or leading their thoughts with a commentary. The film is not structured to form political or socially conscious arguments (although it may well be used as evidence for those). Rather, it is constructed in a way that allows others to share the children's day-to-day experiences and listen to their thoughts, hopes and fears.

This is a long film, running to just over three hours. A screening is preferable to watching on a small monitor or television as the sound and visual sensations are part of the fabric of what MacDougall shares and deserve to be delivered well. The phenomena in *Gandhi's Children* are immersive. It is not easy to watch. This is not a documentary film designed to capture an audience, to entertain, to convince or to teach.

Materiality as colour, light, and sound is not a mere backdrop, it is integral to children's experiences to such an extent that one can feel MacDougall's thoughts—not just alongside him, but also almost as if inside him, as he watches and listens along side these boys. It is because of that immediacy, that intimacy, that after three hours of attentiveness watching *Gandhi's Children* I had a powerful sense of receiving memories, as though I had been at the Prayas Children's Home with MacDougall. I had a visceral pathway towards understanding of those children's experiences as they lived their lives. What I might do with the discovery of that pathway is another matter. However, what I am convinced of is that this is a form of knowledge is essential to building a well-rounded understanding of children's experiences in institutions, including schools. Whatever might be written about those Delhi children and their Prayas home, words could never convey all there is to be known.

Thanks to the generosity of David MacDougall and Ronin Films, readers of this book can view two extracts from *Gandhi's Children* on Vimeo. Please follow the link below. At the time of writing *Gandhi's Children* is available to purchase in Australia from Ronin Flims, in the USA from Berkeley

Fig. 1.4 Still from *Gandhi's Children* (MacDougall, 2008) (https://vimeopro.com/roninfilmsaustralia/observational-filmmaking-for-education)

Media LLC and in the UK from the Royal Athropological Institute, London (RAI) (Fig. 1.4).

Conclusion

This chapter presents four examples of observational films, which centre on children's experiences. They range from the French documentary *Être et Avoir,* which had a successful release in cinemas, examples from a Finish TV documentary series following children in a Helsinki school, followed by two films made in contrasting children's institutions in India—an elite boarding school and a home for destitute children. To begin the chapter I commented on extracts from a film shot in the observational style by 11 year-old Myank, who shared with us his view of his father during a working day. Myank had learnt about using a video camera in this way from MacDougall, but had gone on to film independently of adult direction.

The intention of this chapter has been to draw out characteristics of observational filmmaking. The book goes on to weave two threads that intertwine in how observational filmmaking may contribute to education, in particular to the education of children in schools. Firstly there is the value of observational filmmaking as a form of education research and secondly the value of observational filmmaking as pedagogy. A stance taken and developed as the book progresses is that as children become observational filmmakers, research and pedagogy become inseparable—a melding of practice that is to the benefit of both. There are theoretical, ethical and practical issues, which accompany observational filmmaking as a practice in education. These are discussed as the book unfolds.

To conclude, here is a list of sentences that gather together a summary view of what might be said about the observational style of filmmaking as a result of reading this chapter and viewing the referenced film extracts on Vimeo.

- Observational filmmaking heightens attentiveness and fosters an awareness of children and their experiences in the circumstances they are in.
- The camera is integral to those circumstances and not separate from them.
- The camera quickly becomes a natural and usually unremarkable part of those circumstances.
- Observational filmmaking is a collaborative practice as the camera operators (be that a film crew, a single adult or a child) and those being filmed are necessarily aware of each other. They allow each other to get on with what is at hand.
- Observational camera work is subjective and the camera is an extension of the subjective experience of its user.
- Viewers come to know more about people in the films, and what they are doing and feeling in the circumstances they are in, because observational camera work forms knowledge directly in those circumstances.
- Observational camera work is contingent to the specific situation. That is the experience of the person using the camera, in a particular time, in a particular place, surrounded by what it was that was going, and the individual and collective experiences of others who were there at the time.

- Scenes are generally not planned in advance or set up. A person with a camera follows what is happening without necessarily being able to predict what the outcomes may be.
- There is a focus on sensory experience in real time and details often emerge within the slow unfolding of often un-dramatic moments.
- The camera as a tool connects filmmaker and viewer, whether researcher, teacher or child, with aesthetic and material phenomena integral to children's experience.
- Observational filmmakers often do not hide the presence of the camera. Sometimes an interaction between the camera operator and those being filmed is obvious. However, selective editing may create an illusion of a hidden or magical camera, which does not intrude in any way on what was going on in the scene.
- Observational films may be aimed at different audiences and be made for different purposes. The intentions behind filming will affect the outcomes.
- The nature of camera and editing technology affects the outcomes.
- How the camera and editing technology are used affects outcomes.
- Specific techniques of camera use and editing for observational filmmaking help adults and children to share experiences with others.
- Children, as well as adults, can learn to use a video camera as an observational tool. This aids them in looking at their circumstances and then sharing what they experience with others.
- How researchers, teachers and children come to understand and practice using the camera as an observational tool will significantly affect the nature of the outcomes. This places pedagogy centre stage in research as well as learning.
- The observational camera offers researchers access to the aesthetic, material and corporeal experience of others.
- Spontaneous, intuitive and aesthetic decisions are made as the camera user is filming. Results of these decisions are visible in the film material regardless of any subsequent editing.
- Aesthetic decisions have a vital role in how a sequence of shots is edited together as a final film.

- The observational camera is not primarily an instrument to record data for later analysis, or to create an explanatory or didactic document.
- The observational style permits viewers to watch and learn as much as possible on their own terms, rather than according to those directed by the filmmaker. There are no voiceovers or explanatory texts.
- The continuous development of film recording technology and the way that it is used continuously and significantly affect the outcomes.
- Observational filmmaking generates open-ended thinking before fixed representations.
- Observational filmmaking generates knowledge and opens possibilities of understanding in forms quite different from writing.
- Observational filmmaking is a way of thinking.
- Practical considerations in camera use, such as the height of the camera, the angle of the camera and its distance from a subject, all contribute to the observational style. How a camera is moved, how the camera user moves with the camera, the focal length, aperture, focus control and other elements of the craft of camera use all have an effect on the process of looking.

The thesis, which underpins this book, is that observational filmmaking can make a powerful contribution in the education of children, be that as an eminently sharable research method and methodology extending knowledge of children's experiences in schools or as pedagogy which promotes attentiveness, awareness and thoughtful processes of looking in forms that can be shared with others. The following chapter considers observational filmmaking from a theoretical standpoint as a deep form of experiential empiricism and, in that light, considers more carefully further examples of observational films made by children.

References

Andrew, G. (2003, June 11–18). Massive hit. *Time Out*, p. 2.
Bregstein, P. (1986). (TV Film). *Jean Rouch and his camera in the heart of Africa*. Documentary Educational Resources.

Falcon, R. (2003, July). Back to basics. *Sight & Sound*, p. 38.
Feld, S. (2003). Editor's introduction. In S. Feld (Ed.), *Cine-ethnography—Jean Rouch* (pp. 1–28). Minneapolis: University of Minnesota Press.
Gabriel, T. (1982). *Third cinema in the third world: The aesthetics of liberation*. Ann Arbor: University of Michigan Research Press.
Gentleman, A. (2004, October 3). Film's fallen hero fights on for his class. *The Guardian*.
Grimshaw, A., & Hockings, P. (2011). Two recent films from David MacDougall. *Visual Anthropology, 24*(4), 391–399.
Grimshaw, A., & Ravetz, A. (2009). *Observational cinema: Anthropology, film, and the exploration of social life*. Bloomington: Indiana University Press.
Grimshaw, A., & Ravetz, A. (2015). Drawing with a camera? *Ethnographic Film and Transformative Anthropology, 21*(1), 255–275.
Harrow, K. (1999). *African cinema: Post-colonial and feminist readings*. Trenton: Africa World Press.
Henley, P. (2010). *The adventure of the real: Jean Rouch and the craft of ethnographic cinema*. Chicago: University of Chicago press.
Hennebelle, G. (1972). *Les cinémas Africains en 1972*. Dakar and Paris: Société Africaine d'edition.
MacDougall, D. (Director). (1974). *To live with herds* [Motion Picture]. USA: University of California, Los Angeles.
MacDougall, D. (1998). *Transcultural cinema*. Princeton, NJ: Princeton University Press.
MacDougall, D. (1999). Social aesthetics and The Doon School. *Visual Anthropology Review, 15*, 3–20.
MacDougall, D. (2006). *The corporeal image: Film, ethnography, and the senses*. Princeton, NJ: Princeton University Press.
MacDougall, D. (Director). (2007). *SchoolScapes* [Motion Picture]. Australia: Centre for Cross-Cultural Research, Australian National University.
MacDougall, D. (Director). (2008). *Gandhi's children* [Motion Picture]. Australia: Centre for Cross-Cultural Research, Australian National University.
MacDougall, D. (Producer). (2014). *Eleven in Delwara* [Motion Picture]. Australia: Childhood and Modernity Project, Fieldwork Films and Research School for Humanities & the Arts, Australian National University.
MacDougall, D. (2018). Observational cinema. In H. Callan (Ed.), *The International encyclopedia of anthropology*. New York: Wiley-Blackwell Publishing, Inc.

Maysles, A., Maysles, D., & Zwerin, C. (Directors). (1969). *Salesman* [Motion Picture]. USA: Maysles Films.

Mead, M., & Bateson, G. (1977). On the use of the camera. *Anthropology*, *4*(2), 78–80. Retrieved from https://repository.upenn.edu/svc/vol4/iss2/3.

North, D. (2001). Magic and illusion in early cinema. *Studies in French Cinema*, *1*(2), 70–79.

Philibert, N. (Director). (2002). *Être et Avoir* [Motion Picture]. Paris, France: Maïa Films, Arte France Cinéma, Les Films d'Ici, Centre National de Documentation Pédagogique.

Philibert, N. (2003, June 11–18). Massive hit. In G. Andrew, *Time out*, p. 2.

Philibert, N. (2017). *A camera gives you incredible power over others*. Retrieved November 10, 2017 from http://nicolasphilibert.fr.

Quiggin, A. H. (1942). *Haddon, the head hunter: A short sketch of the life of A. C. Haddon*. Cambridge: The University Press.

Rotton Tomatoes. (2017). *Critic Reviews Être et Avoir*. Retrieved December 19, 2017 from https://www.rottentomatoes.com/m/to_be_and_to_have/.

Rouch, J. (1974). The camera and man. In P. Hockings (Ed.), *Principles of visual anthropology* (pp. 79–98). Berlin: Mouton de Gruyter.

Sandall, R. (1972). Observation and identity. *Sight and Sound*, *41*(4), 192–196.

Taylor, L. (1998). Introduction. In D. MacDougall (Ed.), *Transcultural cinema* (pp. 3–24). Princeton, NJ: Princeton University Press.

Turunen, U., & Ruuhijärvi, I. (1987a). *Kun se tapahtuu* [Television Documentary]. Finland: YLE TV1.

Turunen, U., & Ruuhijärvi, I. (1987b). *Koko ajan jossakin* [Television Documentary]. Finland: YLE TV1.

Turunen, U., & Ruuhijärvi, I. (1989). *Tien yli* [Television Documentary]. Finland: YLE TV1.

Turunen, U., & Ruuhijärvi, I. (1990). *Aina eikä milloinkaan* [Television Documentary]. Finland: YLE TV1.

Turunen, U., & Ruuhijärvi, I. (1992). *Elämä* [Television Documentary]. Finland: YLE TV1.

Ukadike, N., & Gabriel, T. (2002). *Questioning African cinema: Conversations with filmmakers*. Minneapolis: University of Minnesota Press.

Young, C. (1975). Observational cinema. In P. Hockings (Ed.), *Principles of visual anthropology* (pp. 99–114). The Hague: Mouton Publishers.

2

Experiential Empiricism and Children's Films

Introduction

So far, I have suggested that observational filmmaking is a usable and productive method, which generates potential for deeper forms of knowledge and understanding about children's experiences. As this is a book focused on education, the experiences most in play are those that children have in school. In the Introduction and Chapter 1, I allude to an inevitable and unavoidable subjectivity when a researcher, teacher or child takes a video camera into a setting. The subjective view is an essential component of what is recorded and, perhaps, later shared. How the camera was held, where the camera was held and to what the camera user pointed the lens is evident through the examples cited in Chapter 1. These are often intuitive choices made by the observer within a situation, as they follow a process or a person. Such subjectivity is a challenge for education research. It is as if an allegiance to an overt social scientificity diminishes forms of knowledge and understanding formed in and through aesthetic, material and affective experience—kinds of experiences that are part and parcel of observational filming and the kinds of experiences through which one human comes to know more about another.

© The Author(s) 2019
N. Meager, *Observational Filmmaking for Education*,
https://doi.org/10.1007/978-3-319-90626-3_2

Chapter 3 will bring into play some of the issues and concerns that researchers and teachers will have after viewing some of the examples of observational filming presented in Chapter 1. These are always and necessarily present and will constantly help form the fabric of discourse around observational filmmaking with children and in schools. First of all, this chapter unfolds a possible abstract framework of ideas which might support how knowledge and understanding is formed in and through experience.

As in all forms of education research or pedagogical methodology, in this account of observational filmmaking there is an underlying conceptual landscape which contextualises practice in a framework of ideas. As I first expressed on the first page of the introduction, I am suggesting that a deeply empiricist and experiential conceptual basis for inquiry is needed to research children's experiences if the fullness of those experiences, especially aesthetic, material and affective qualities, are to be present in research. This chapter sets out the theoretical origins of such experiential empiricism described in this book. I then summarise the argument for a possible conceptual landscape in which and from which observational filmmaking might be acknowledged as a useful route to forming knowledge and understanding about children and their experiences in schools.

Firstly, I discuss John Dewey's philosophy of experience in *Art as Experience* (Dewey, 1934). The appeal to attend to experience as a first route to knowledge (an attention at the core of observational filmmaking) is confirmed by Dewey's deep distrust of "transcendental standards that hide from inspection even as they pretend to guarantee the validity of judgements" (Fesmire, 2015, p. 4). I make no new claims about Dewey's philosophy. I do not challenge the conceptual roots of pragmatism or empiricism. However, Dewey's argument, in which aesthetic experience is a pervasive quality, melds distinctions between ideas and experience. I do, therefore, suggest that the theory and practice of observational filmmaking as education research, and as pedagogy, is illuminated by Dewey's experiential empiricism.

The chapter, therefore, first introduces Dewey and describes the interconnectedness between his view of art as experience and experience as art. I introduce the consummatory force of aesthetic experience, which

Dewey argues is a pervasive quality in all experience. I draw out the way in which Dewey conceptualises meaning in experience as a precursor to his establishing a qualitative and ethical logic for a situated and deeply empirical methodology. This is generative rather than definitional research, appropriate for observational filmmaking as research and as pedagogy. I return to a wider take on experiential empiricism in the final chapter of this book via outlining how the late philosophy of Gilles Deleuze (1925–1995) offers a parallel route to theorising for generative empirical routes to knowledge built within experience. This chapter concludes by returning to examples of observational films shot by children. I have placed these alongside the following discussion of Dewey's take on experience as they demonstrate so much of what he argues.

Introducing Dewey

John Dewey (1859–1952) is a towering figure who, earlier in the twentieth century, was at the summit of American philosophy (Westbrook, 1991). Yet, by the 1960s the Anglo-American tradition of analytic philosophy had condemned Dewey's discursive, nuanced and generative form of intellectual thought as soft, woolly, and lacking rigour (Sleeper, 1986). Although Dewey disliked the term *pragmatism* (Alexander, 2013) he was, nevertheless, seen as a classical American pragmatist alongside others such as Charles Pierce (1839–1914), William James (1842–1910) and Herbert Mead (1863–1931).

Dewey, like William James before him, argued that intellectual thought grows best out of perceiving, thinking and acting in situations (Westbrook, 1991). It is worth noting here, that James' ideas also found traction in the second half of the twentieth century, as sociologists and psychologists grappled with the complexity in interpreting people's experiences. For example, Erving Goffman (1974) cited James, as he articulated his own argument about paying close attention to the specifics in experience in order to understand human interaction. When investigating social circumstances, Goffman saw that applying the abstractions and representations in philosophical thought, so admired by Anglophone analytic philosophers, hindered rather than helped illuminate complex interactions between humans and their situations. Goffman's (1974) work on framing experience echoed Dewey and he was also, as Dewey was, critiqued for abandoning systematic and replicable analytic structures (Chriss, 1995).

As a philosopher for education, Dewey is often regarded for his theories on experimental inquiry, which places direct experience at the heart of learning and in a form that aids education's responsibility for ensuring democratic values for citizens. However, his work on aesthetic experience seems to have had less attention from educators. This is despite the place of aesthetic understanding at the core of Dewey's philosophy—perhaps it is because aesthetic experience resists definition. There is also an implication of a collapsing of dualities, which may seem counter-intuitive in education frames dominated by the separations between thinking and feeling, knowledge and experience, instrumental and definitional teaching and learning, and between what is known and what is not yet known.

However, I now turn to Dewey to illuminate how observational filmmaking might be conceptualised both as education research and as pedagogy. As Fesmire (2015), Baldacchino (2014) and others confirm, Dewey advocates generative and open philosophical thinking based in process and experiment. This points to a creative underpinning for research, which generates rather than defines knowledge. Furthermore, Dewey's work to conflate qualities in experience with qualities in art is, I suggest, a valuable starting point for education research endeavour that seeks to make a significant contribution to how research might learn more about the value of children's experiences in schools.

I will use Dewey's *Art as Experience* (1934), together with interpretive accounts by Westbrooke (1991), Alexander (1987, 1998), Fesmire (2003, 2015) and Baldacchino (2014), amongst others, to draw out the relevant functional concepts, which illuminate the understanding of art as aesthetic experience. These include: meaning within experience, imagination and aesthetic experience, collapsing duality in qualitative thought, methodological ethics of experience, and freedom to create ideas before domination by ideas. I will then draw out a methodological underpinning of approaches to observational filmmaking, which suggests the practice of observational filmmaking, illustrated with examples of the children's films, is supported by a Deweyan inspired philosophy of experience. This deeply experiential empirical stance will underpin the way in which the book describes observational filmmaking as a practice for education research and classroom pedagogy.

Dewey on Aesthetic Experience

Westbrook (1991) recognises in Dewey a reciprocal elucidation of art and experience through the usefulness of expanding on their mutual interrelationship in aesthetic experience.

> It was to aesthetic experience, he [Dewey] argued, that "the philosopher must go to understand what experience is" [...] As Edman noted, "the whole of Dewey's philosophy of art is not so much what is commonly called 'esthetics' as it is a work on experience *in excelsis*". (Westbrook, 1991, p. 393)

Dewey's preoccupation with experience as a foundation for thought grew out of developments in the natural sciences in the second half of the nineteenth century (Joas, 1996). His emphasis on attending to experience to build understanding of how humans feel, know and act originated in his fascination with Darwin's evolutionary theories about how living organisms interact with their environment (Perricone, 2006). In his essay *The Reflexive Arc in Psychology*, Dewey argued forcefully that psychology must take into account the situatedness of the organism (Dewey, 1896). These ideas were a precursor for Dewey's later writings in *Art as Experience* (1934), where he argues that humans, like all organisms, are constantly seeking to adapt to the ever-changing conditions in which they find themselves. If the organism is out of kilter with its environment (its situation), there is a drive to rebalance. If an animal is hungry it seeks food, if a human is lonely it seeks company. Because of these needs, argues Dewey, living organisms are constantly seeking fulfillment—to fill what is lacking. However, fulfillment is transitory as both environment and organisms are constantly changing; this process is forever and necessarily in flux.

Therefore, in *Art as Experience*, Dewey (1934) explains that the 'environing' conditions and the live creature interact in the process of living: "Experience occurs continuously, because of the interaction of the live creature and the environing conditions [...] in the very process of living" (p. 42). Experience is dynamic, in relentless inevitable movement through transactions between humans and their environment (including transactions with other humans). For humans, crucially, and in a way that differentiates human experience from that of animals, the conditions of the organism and its environment embrace thought, language and culture. This makes the drive for balance and equilibrium a hugely complex phenomenon. The 'process of living' is the source of new ideas and, as such, creativity is at the heart of experience. This stands in contrast to determining experience according to fixed theories, formal logic, systems and ideals. For Dewey, understanding thinking (and everything else humans do) must start and be located in experience.

Dewey (1934) argues that consummatory aesthetic is a force which binds multifaceted, many-layered and multidimensional experiences—the flux of the continuum of our present experience—into simpler packages with which the mind can work. This works because aesthetic experience occurs constantly in everyday life as we unify past experiences into *an* experience (Dewey's italics). Aesthetic experience is thus part of the fabric of everyday experience, not just artistic experience. This phenomenon is easily recognised: it seems simple enough to say, "I enjoyed that dinner party", but inviting the guests, planning the menu, shopping for and cooking the meal, eating the meal, and having conversations throughout the evening are all, potentially, hugely complex events in themselves, as they are laden with perceptions, sensations, emotions and ideas. The dinner party, and each of its many inextricably interlaced components becomes a unified single whole, as expressed as all those experiences are melded into *that* dinner party. This melding of complexity into a simple unity is aesthetic. I might imagine a friend saying, "That walk with you along the beach was an unforgettable experience". The unity embraced by the singular experience encapsulated by the two words 'that walk' resonates with meaning, emotional power and beauty. This is an example of how *'an* experience' is a concept at the core of Dewey's notion of the aesthetic, which is a unifying force that synthesises experiences into wholes which humans can think about, react to and act upon (Joas, 1996).

To augment this argument further, Dewey (1934) explains that in forming an awareness of *an* experience, there is a "continuous merging" of all the potentially disparate elements (if taken out of the flux and examined separately)—these "melt and fuse into unity" (p. 43). *An* experience "takes on a single *quality* [Dewey's italics]" (p. 43). If we decide to interpret the experience, as we create a discourse about it, we might make use of adjectives to describe it (emotional, intellectual, practical). The danger of the interpretive discourse is that it can appear that these descriptive, representative components form an understanding of experience as though it is the product of a sum of its different characteristics. However, in the living of the experience and in the unifying force, which forms a synthesis into *an* experience, these descriptive interpretive components "were lost in it as distinctive traits" (p. 44).

> Thinking goes on in trains of ideas, but the ideas form a train only because they are much more than what an analytic psychology calls ideas. They are phases, emotionally and practically distinguished, of a developing underlying quality; they are its moving variations, not separate and independent like Locke's and Hume's so-called ideas and impressions, but are subtle shadings of a pervading and developing hue [...]. (p. 44)

If the aesthetic is pervasive, it is not usually notable in terms of how we get on with things in the day-to-day. However, *distinctive* aesthetic experience is visible in a heightened form as we have powerful indissoluble experiences looking at and making art, listening to music, in places of natural beauty, watching sport, and making love. So, "the factors that determine anything which can be called *an* experience are lifted high above the threshold of perception and are made manifest for their own sake" (p. 57).

In art, the aesthetic as an expressive synthesis is tied to a medium of expression and so integral in the overt outcome such that: "the roundedness and meaningfulness of experience become immediate goals" (Joas, 1996, p. 141). It is *process* in making art that transforms experiences into new experiences with new forms. The working of artistic media forms these new experiences for the artist and for their audiences. The art object is a coalescence of experiences into a cohesive unified form:

> The creative process [...] explores new avenues of experience which then gel to a new totality of meaning [...] the striving for *an* experience, for the wholeness of action pervaded with meaning, leads to works which bring into the world new modes of sensory experience. (Joas, 1996, p. 142)

In terms of the narrative of argument unfolding through this book, almost all research in education is social science based and demands analysis. However, if a Deweyan style of ontology and epistemology, as expressed in *Art as Experience* (1934), inform an arching conceptual frame, then analysis may seem at face value to be an inappropriate way to research aesthetic experiences, which meld rather than separate, categorise, label and define. By separating and dividing experience (for example children's experiences in school) into component parts, then analyses, pure and simple, may miss the very qualities that pervade meaningful action (as children experience learning for example) and reflection upon it (research about how children learn).

Meaning and Aesthetic Experience

To help explain a distinction between meaning taken to be external to experience and meaning within experience, Dewey (1934) comes up with a dictum: "Science states meanings, art expresses them" (p. 90). Whereas a scientific statement of water as H_2O represents with precision what constitutes water in a supremely useful way, it does not necessarily help understand our experience of water. The aesthetic expression of water in poetry, music, or art does something different from pointing to or stating what water is; it constitutes an experience inspired by water. These artistic expressions draw closer to the experience of water. In this way, Dewey argues, "the poem, or painting, does not operate in the dimension of correct descriptive statement but in that of experience itself" (p. 91).

However, there is an opposing danger where meaning is thought of as an esoteric aesthetic experience unique to each work or as internal within the mind of the artist or viewer and therefore disconnected to all other external references. Attacking the separation of an internal self from an external object: "If an art product is taken to be one of *self*-expression and the self is regarded as something complete and self-contained in isolation, then of course substance and form fall apart" (p. 112). The material of the art object is a material of the physical world. The maker assimilates that material in a distinctive way to re-form it as a new object. The material cannot be essentially private, it is physically present, but the manner of thinking and acting with it is individual and unique. Thought, material and making are indissoluble, one from another, in a form of art. Form and thought are unified both in the making and in the viewing of art:

> The work itself *is* matter formed into aesthetic substance [...] The undefined pervasive quality of an experience is that which binds together the defined elements [...] making them whole [...] A work of art elicits and accentuates this quality of being whole [...] in the act there is no distinction, but perfect integration of manner and content, form and substance. (pp. 111–113)

Although distinctions in experiences making art may be reflected upon and signifying meanings drawn out, if these defining components are too separate and fractured from the experience, then full meaning is lost. In *Art as Experience* Dewey (1934) had already shown how this separating tendency leads to an intellectual dislocation of art objects from their nature as experience. In contrast to understanding due to intellectual categorisation and definition, if there is an aesthetic understanding in experience, the intrinsic meaning is *experienced* in the materiality of the art. The viewer experiences the art object as meaningful in that unique circumstance of being present with it.

As art is made (and experiences experienced), there is an intimate interweaving of doing and perceiving: "The artist embodies in himself the attitude of the perceiver while he works" (p. 55). There is constant interaction between artist and material. He explains:

> In short, art, in its form, unites the very same relation of doing and undergoing, outgoing and incoming energy, that makes an experience to be an experience [...] Every art does something with some physical material, the body or something outside the body, or with or without the use of intervening tools, and with a view to production of something visible, audible or tangible. (p. 54)

Dewey waxes lyrical about the "exquisite intelligibility and clarity" the "esthetic intensity" that somehow a work of art operates "to raise to great clarity that sense of an enveloping undefined whole that accompanies every normal experience" (p. 119). Making art and experiencing art accentuates the fundamental conditions of being in the world that constitute experience: "we are carried out beyond ourselves to find ourselves" (p. 119). Meaning and, therefore, understanding is a unified quality of substance, expression and form. If this is fractured, full meaning and deeper understanding of aesthetic experience is not possible. Here lies the challenge for art education research.

In terms of the intention of this book, academically orientated text in the field of education can only go so far in building knowledge and understanding of what is happening as children experience school, because, argues Dewey, referring to the arts, "meanings are actually embodied in material which thereby becomes the medium for their expression" (p. 277). It must be necessary to attempt to maintain the integrity of experience, if it is to be better understood. To put another way, to understand more completely what is happening as children have experiences in school, the essential embodiment of meaning in the materiality of those experiences must be sensed.

This becomes the basis for an argument to build an experiential research method where analytic methods alone will fail. To put this in Deweyan terms: in this way research is freed "from factors that subordinate experience as it is directly had to something beyond itself" (p. 278). I also suggest that for children, if adults support their practice as observational filmmakers, that pedagogy connects them directly with experience, both their own and that of those they observe in ways which deepen awareness, promote reflexion and feed learning. An intriguing thought exercise is to reread this section replacing the word 'art' with the phrase 'observational filmmaking'. Although this tactic will not work in every case, it will draw out how an experiential empiricism might illuminate how and why observational filmmaking embraces material, aesthetic and affective knowledge.

Methodological Ethics and Qualitative Aesthetics

In a modernist tradition of splitting science from the arts, knowing is separated from feeling, and processes of reasoned logic and a priori are set in opposition to the processes of art and aesthetic experience. Science is reasoned and the arts are imaginatively expressive, may run the cliché. The dispassionate and rule-driven thinking, which governs scientific inquiry, must then be essentially different from artistic and aesthetic experiences, which form artistic inquiry and outcomes. Baldacchino (2014) argues that the thrust of much of *Art as Experience* is to deny those constraints to knowing imposed by reason versus imagination and thinking versus feeling. Indeed, before *Art as Experience* (1934), Dewey (1931) argued that the qualitative basis of scientific and artistic thought is indistinguishable within experience.

It has been established that Dewey constantly railed against the supremacy of cognitive knowledge as superior to non-cognitive experience (Fesmire, 2015). As Baldacchino (2014) argues, dualisms such as subject and object, interiority and exteriority, contingency and universality are collapsed in Dewey. Indeed, Dewey rejects all kinds of duality, which he considered artificial. Such dualities may be useful facets of explanations but are limiting constructions external to the deepest knowledge of life as it is lived. By insisting on the primacy of experience, Dewey obverts the resulting "ossification of human thinking" that artificial dualisms can produce (Baldacchino, 2014, p. 5). If scientific and artistic thinking are equally sprung from the deepest forms of knowing in experience, then it is to that experience that research about teaching and learning (which surely should embrace all forms of thought) should go.

This view is confirmed by a reading of Dewey's essay, *Qualitative Thought* (1931). Indeed, it is here that experience is described as a pervasive qualitative medium from which both science and art grow. As Fesmire (2015, p. 207) states, Dewey: "de-subjectivised the aesthetic and de-objectivised understanding" so that qualities in experience are dominant and pervasive. Qualities in experience can be simultaneously objective and subjective, reasoned and aesthetic. Qualities are "the background, the point of departure and the regulative principle of all thinking" (Dewey, 1931, p. 248).

In *Qualitative Thought* (1931), all experience is qualitative; all thought is a form of experience; all thought is qualitative; as all experience is aesthetic in its process, all thought is also aesthetic in its process. Aesthetic experience is a qualitative force in all thought. Thus, Dewey's (1931) essay argues qualitative thought is internal to logic and reason in the same way as it is internal to artistic expression. It is drawn from the same experiential *field* as artistic thinking; although, as scientific outcomes, qualitative thought manifests in different ways from artistic outcomes. Therefore, in Dewey, artistic thinking is not in a different realm from scientific reasoning. They inhabit the same realm. In other words, a qualitative experiential field drives, situates, mediates and forms all thought as experience. This is melded in a continuous flux, as a qualitative experiential field, in which dualistic thinking is appended, not core.

A problem arising for the journey this book charts, is that children's experience often appears ineffable, aesthetic, material and affective. Language and scientific method, especially the academic language of the social sciences in which almost all education research is located, appears to fall short of embracing such a complex and rich matrix of qualities as is found in children's experience as they learn and live their lives in school. Taking arguments formed by Baldacchino (2014) and Fesmire (2015), which are drawn out of Dewey (1931, 1934), the absence of direct contact with aesthetic and material experience from the realms of inquiry diminishes and limits inquiry.

Moreover, consummatory aesthetic qualities are as internal in logic and reason as they are bound into artistic and everyday experience. Thus, it can be argued, attending to aesthetic qualities in experience is not a lesser source of knowledge than scientifically framed analysis.

An aesthetic materiality in research and pedagogy draws into the foreground qualities, which are supremely difficult to codify as data and subsequently analyse yet, which are pervasive throughout human experience. Meaningful expression of experience "is the culminating event of nature as well as the climax of experience" (p. 8). So, for Dewey an inquiry is "at its best an art that has the enrichment of immediate experience as its principle charge" (Fesmire, 2015, p. 214). This is a dictum that drives this unfolding methodology.

Given the preceding arguments, it is not surprising that commentators show that for Dewey ethical problems are situated in experience (Putman, 2011). Confirming this reading, Fesmire (2003) implies that Deweyan inspired methodological ethics should emanate in experience before being dominated by predetermined ethical criteria. Indeed, echoing the ontology of a flux and fabric of experiences, Dewey (1931) argued that with such moral questions it is impossible to reduce all the elements to principles. If this is recognised, it highlights the ethical demand to attend more fully to the concrete elements in each situation where ethical questions are present. The alternative is the assumption that humans should put experience to one side and address ethical dilemmas with rational order and with laws derived from founding principles. Dewey suggested that this entirely misses vital qualities in experience. This is because an idealised form of ethics can veil the materiality of the situation and, therefore, become disconnected with how to act in situations. Ethics based ideas that are artificially separated from experience may be unethical because it is harder to know how to act. So, as Fesmire (2015) describes, Dewey's ethics imply a necessary pluralistic approach, which rejects potentially dualistic, limiting and prescribing dogmas in favour of careful intelligent situated debate about how to proceed. An intelligent reconciliation between conflicting factors is needed. It is "a relational moral philosophy of the twentieth century" (Fesmire, 2015, p. 119).

What Dewey demands is that when difficult questions are asked, including difficult ethical questions, different connections and possibilities in those questions are drawn out. The challenge, writes Fesmire (2003), "is to respect the uniqueness of imagination, artistry, the aesthetic, and the moral, whilst also disclosing their relations to one another" (p. 5). This both develops the questions and aids the process towards acting effectively. In this way, Deweyan experientialism suggests an ethical route to understanding based in experience. Rules and principles *supplement* a research ethic, they do not constitute it.

If observational filmmakers follow a Deweyan inspired methodology for education research, they should not base an approach to research on bedrock principles based in a Kantian style of rational logic, pre-imposed onto research according to predefined theoretical frameworks. If the rules and principles are the "tethering centre of either ethical theory or practice", then this can become dogma, which obstructs understanding experience (Fesmire, 2003, p. 3). The implication of this argument is that observational filmmakers will miss much if they apply pre-ordained systemised rules to programme a method for their research, or impose a delineating overarching theoretical framework onto the hugely complex tangle of circumstances and phenomena that make up what is happening as children experience learning and living in schools. Stating this in terms of practice: knowledge about what happens when children are learning and living is more likely to be found by entering into and paying attention in those circumstances. Equally, a Deweyan inspired methodological ethic will be situated in and built out of each particular research circumstance.

Freedom to Create Ideas Rather Than Domination by Ideas

Richard Rorty (1980) describes Dewey as the "great edifying peripheral thinker [someone who mocks] the classic picture of man, the picture which contains systematic philosophy, the search for universal commensuration in a final vocabulary" (p. 38). Unlike systematic philosophers, "edifying philosophers want to keep space open for the sense of wonder which poets can sometimes cause—wonder that there is something new under the sun, something which is not an accurate representation of what was normally there, something (at least for the moment) that cannot be explained and can be barely described" (Rorty, 1980, p. 38).

Dewey has the courage not to pin anything down—not to constrain, control and limit. He allows and sustains paradox which "seeks no ultimate resolution, but which keeps the conditions and possibilities of creativity alive" (Baldacchino, 2014, p. 5). There is, of course, no rest, as we live in the continuum of presents; no resolution into certainty. Dewey did not believe there could be such a state of rest or any absolute form of realisation (Baldacchino, 2014). This means that we are always continuously in a state of flux, of permanent experiment and discovery. New ideas are always being born. Baldacchino argues that a "reading of Dewey which fails to understand the Deweyan rejection of fixed thinking would result in a philosophy that is at best a method, and at worst a pedagogical creed" (2014, p. 6).

This means for me that using Dewey to underpin a conceptual framework for observational filmmaking for education must mean that this underpinning and framing is less overtly structural (like a building) and is more like unfolding a process of exploring undiscovered realms. There is no pre-drawn map. What is initially planned must be continuously adapted according to what is being discovered. Which, of course, does not mean exploration is arbitrary, on the contrary, knowledge and understanding of uncharted experiences emerges out of simultaneously being immersed in and paying close attention to their circumstances. How might one find out about the strange land one is shipwrecked on? By acting and thinking. Staying put because a travel guide might turn up is unlikely to get one very far. Baldacchino (2014) puts it like this:

> I want to insist that Dewey needs to be carefully followed in his logical travels between thought and action where thought becomes action and where action becomes thought […] Dewey presents us with a horizon of creativity where artificial distinctions that are often made between doing and thinking, reflecting and acting, knowing and being, become obsolete. (p. 8)

Dewey's approach remains critical and ever-changing. Because there are no foregone conclusions, no absolutes, there is continuous experimentation inherent within experience. So, "students and teachers work from the premise that everything changes" (Baldacchino, 2014, p. 11).

In terms of research, the outcomes of method must be positioned within a space where there is freedom to "engage, contest, dispute and indeed take ownership of knowledge" (p. 11).

Researching Children's Experience

It is now productive to examine concrete ways of researching children's experience. This becomes a process of *making* new knowledge. It requires attentiveness and imagination from me as researcher, from participants and from consumers of the research, as we are able to explore and create knowledge about children's experiences as they live and learn in school because of our shared disposition towards experience freed from domination by pre-structured ideas (Baldacchino, 2014).

Observational filmmaking is a method, which deals directly with the experience of others. It provides a practiced, if controversial, approach that brings qualities in experience such as the aesthetic and the material into the foreground throughout the research process. But it is not merely a research process. For some anthropologists, the filmic material forms outcomes of their research and sits independently from academic text as a form of anthropological knowledge. A tenet of this book is that this form of knowledge is particularly valuable when researching children's experiences, especially because it offers a way that children can collaborate with teachers and researchers as they share experiences and share in experiences in a thoughtful way. This is particularly valuable for children because observational filmmaking is not dominated by a reliance on words and text.

Practitioners and theorists of observational filmmaking have not overtly articulated a relationship with Dewey's philosophy of experience. However, I will show that if the methodological underpinning of observational filmmaking is set alongside Deweyan thought about experience, a more powerful argument for its value as a research method can be better put. This deep experiential empiricism offers a creative and ethical pathway to generating knowledge with and about experiences of others. This knowledge is embedded in experiences of participants and researchers alike. In terms of knowing and understanding more about children's experience living and learning in school, this is able to embrace aesthetic, sensory and material manifestations of experience, not just explanatory and interpretive ideas. This means that a more complete understanding of essential qualities in that experience is possible. Better teaching and learning will result from improved understanding. But, more crucially, adults who help children grow and develop may be persuaded to acknowledge just how vital a thoughtful awareness of a child's view of those experiences can be. I suggest the *Childhood and Modernity* project, which is given form through the resulting children's films, is a powerful example of a research project within and experientially empirical frame. I will now explore that project and examples from those films in more detail.

Introducing the Childhood and Modernity Project

As the examples from Chapter 1 demonstrated, the form of observational filmmaking I wish to draw on in this book is dependent on a set of interrelated practices which allow the video camera and whoever is using it to be knowingly and openly in the heart of the circumstances being filmed. The qualities implicit in the processes of *observation* result from *collaboration* between the filmmaker and others, including those who are being filmed and those who are responsible in institutions such as schools, communities and families. There is *participation* as those who are being filmed take an active part in making the film. Everyone accepts the presence of the filmmaker with the camera. This is reflected in the possibility of dialogue between the filmmaker and those being filmed. The filmmaker's presence in the film is tangible. There are a set of basic techniques, a *craft*, which underscore an observational style of camera work and editing. How the camera and editing *technology* are used as a tool is pivotal to the filming process and its outcomes. I suggest qualities addressed through observation, collaboration, participation, craft and technology will apply whether it is an education researcher, a teacher or children who are filming and editing. As will be articulated later in this book, it may be that different forms of partnership between researchers, teachers and children are formed, as the act of filming becomes a shared activity. The nature of the process will both depend on and become a product of the intention of the activity—for example: teaching children observational skills, answering a research question about children's experiences in classrooms, observing how children are learning to help train teachers.

This chapter opened with a discussion of and extract from eleven-year-old Mayank's film about his father at home and work. The film was made during a five-year research project, began in 2012, called *Childhood and Modernity Indian Children's Perspectives*. Funded by the Australian Research Council and supported by the Australian National University, this ethnographic and social anthropologic investigative and experimental inquiry, explored how children might be supported, via a workshop program, to use video cameras in an observational style. As they developed camera skills, the project offered children a direct role as researchers to film circumstances from their own, their friends and their family's lives. Crucially, before they embarked on filming, each participating child came up with a considered topic, theme and approach to what it was they wanted to observe. This was not a random or arbitrary use of a camera, recording what ever just happened to be going on. Children deliberately set out to explore circumstances about a setting, process or person with an aim of finding out more about that. In that way it was hoped that children are able to be actively part of the generation of new knowledge about matters that they have a special access to and an understanding of.

David MacDougall instigated and led the project. Rowena Potts (2015), who at the time was a Ph.D. candidate in sociocultural anthropology at New York University and who took an active part in facilitating at least one set of children's films, interviewed MacDougall about the project. Readers will find detailed information about *Childhood and Modernity*, together with both theoretical and practical discussions about children as filmmakers in Potts' (2015) paper. Nevertheless, relying both on Potts' account and my own conversations with David MacDougall, I will now briefly outline how he arrived at a point where he believed that children could be observational filmmakers and collaborate with him as researchers.

From 1997 and up to the time of writing in 2017, MacDougall's filmmaking focused on ethnographic studies of children's lives in schools and institutions in India. Apart from *SchoolScapes* (2007) and *Gandhi's Children* (2008), which were introduced in Chapter 1, the most significant body of work, where MacDougall himself was the filmmaker, was a series of five films made at Doon School, an independent boys boarding school in Dehradun, Uttarakhand, India. Other films followed until MacDougall's interest in how film might reveal nuanced and pervasive emotional, material and aesthetic qualities in children's experience within the social and cultural milieu of institutions, naturally led him to explore how children themselves might be better placed than any adult to share such ephemeral qualities in their lives, if only they had a means to do so.

Together with his theoretical writing about the observational style of filmmaking for social anthropology (MacDougall, 1999, 2006), MacDougall's growing portfolio of acclaimed ethnographic films meant that he was much in demand as a workshop leader supporting graduate students use filming techniques in their research. MacDougall often led workshops in partnership with the filmmaker Judith MacDougall, his wife. Inevitably they began to develop a pedagogical approach, which used an analysis of how and why observational filmmaking worked as a research method to create a pedagogical structure for the workshops. When MacDougall started filming in schools, he realised he was also able to offer children similar kinds of video workshops. His experience helping children use video cameras in an observational style, and the lessons learnt, led to the proposal to the Australian Research Council to fund the *Childhood and Modernity* project.

For *Childhood and Modernity*, MacDougall wanted to see what happened when he offered children of a particular age (between 10 and 13) an opportunity to use cameras to help them think about themselves, others around them, where they live and how they live. MacDougall thought that paying attention to how children used video cameras, together with where they chose to and what they chose to film, would enlighten viewers about how children were part of the social and cultural worlds they inhabit and what children were thinking about those worlds. As children learnt and practiced the craft of the observational style, they would be able to share ideas in away that would impossible for them to do using words. There was never any intention that children were going to be expected to continue as filmmakers. Rather, the workshops and the opportunity to film was designed so that children, who were all volunteers, would enjoy the experience and that it would benefit them.

Over a period of five years during from 2012 to 2017, during component projects and associated workshops, in various locations in India, it was clear that children would create a great deal of audio-visual material. MacDougall worked alongside children to edit short films from a wealth of original footage for public viewing. However, it was also hoped that children's film clips and takes would become an archive of their perceptions of contemporary India, focused through the specificity of the experiences they chose to share, at that particular time and place. In short, different kinds of people (for example: psychologists, teachers, parents, friends, researchers), who look at the children's films, will learn different kinds of things depending partly on what they are looking for. The crucial feature of *Childhood and Modernity* was that MacDougall had found a reliable way to help children generate the original film material about their experiences from their perspective, an emic perspective, rather from an adult perspective, as is the case in the films I used as examples earlier in Chapter 1.

By applying a consistent workshop pedagogy, across place and time, a certain consistency emerged which enabled judgements to be made as adults compared one child's film with another—a potentially valuable cross-cultural and cross-generational research method. This is a lesson I wish to place at the centre of my intention in this book. A consistent pedagogy for observational camera work and editing enables children, researchers, teachers, parents—indeed anyone who might have an interest in children's experiences and what happens in schools—to film from their individual point of view. Each of those viewpoints may have a comparable weight in any future comparative critical commentary. I will set out in Chapters 4 and 5 in a practical way how observational filmmaking can provide a structure for expanding how education researchers learn about children's experiences and what happens in schools. It adds to the possibilities for the kinds of knowledge that research may encompass.

To explore how his method worked in practice MacDougall and colleagues set up series of workshops, each lasting between 8 and 10 weeks, with small groups of volunteer children (aged ten to thirteen) from different backgrounds in different parts of India. Locations included a government school in New Delhi, a school in Delwara, in Rajasthan, and school in Ladakh. In the different locations MacDougall explored different ways for engaging children in what they might film, this ranged from deciding on a shared theme, which all the children would explore, to the children carefully selecting their own topics for research. MacDougall taught children a set of basic camera techniques. The pedagogy was designed to facilitate the observation style of camera work. Children were asked to take the project seriously as co-researchers with MacDougall. This was not a game. Because of the emphasis in the workshops, the observational style predominated, but, naturally and often, children playfully crossed over to imitate styles of fiction filming, such as Bollywood, and the kinds of factual filming they saw on television in news reports for example.

As well as practicing exercises in the workshops, children took the cameras home to shoot aspects of their lives that they had specifically chosen to explore and explained carefully in advance to MacDougall and their teachers. They would then share this filmic material with each other and with MacDougall for an hour or so each day during the project. Immediately, the researcher (and the other participating children) saw things they would not normally ever see about an individual child's experience. Knowledge is being constructed in the very act of the filming and the sharing of the raw audio-visual material with others. The viewing together, the talking and sharing of ideas, the critical awareness of what and how they were filming, all that enabled children and adults to collaboratively get to know a great deal about the circumstances in which children had filmed.

Towards the end of the stay in each location, MacDougall reviewed each child's filming. The child began to decide what is the most important part of the filming and how that might be ordered in the final film. They then decided together what is to be rejected (often because technically it was not so useful for a finished film or because it didn't fit with the child's idea about what they want to show). MacDougall then made a rough edit for the child. MacDougall reviewed the rough films together with the children and any changes they want were made. The material was then fine tuned by MacDougall before he and the children agreed to release it as a finished film out into the world for public viewing.

MacDougall relates how relationships with the institution hosting the workshops such as a school can be complex. There are conflicting interests between the demands of a school and that of research. Other children, who have not been selected to take part in the filming (however that selection was undertaken), may be resentful. Children need to be trained to take care of the equipment. There may be tensions at home as siblings, friends and adults want to use the cameras themselves in inappropriate ways. Adults may try to censor or filter what the children film and how they go about filming, sometimes for very understandable reasons, at other times because they don't trust the child or don't take the child's agency as a filmmaker seriously (Potts, 2015).

There are stringent formal ethical procedures and protocols for any university based research project involving children, but especially when photography or video are involved. *Childhood and Modernity*, as a project supported by Australian National University was no different. Providing written information, clear communication and obtaining considered permissions from adults who are responsible for the children was essential. Making sure that children were fully informed and understood their role in the project they were taking part in, is also a vital part of the pedagogy. However, any fixed rules, regulations and approved procedures are often less than helpful in the specific circumstances of each project and in relation to the uniqueness of each individual participant child. A sensitive, caring and self-aware approach to a situated ethics by the researcher that protects children and always puts their interests first is MacDougall's practice. It is important that children as well as the researcher benefit from taking part. I will set out the ethical issues, debate ethical principles and illustrate some examples of practice in Chapters 4 and 5.

Examples of the Indian Children's Films

As well as the extract from Mayank's film, which began Chapter 1, readers can view further extracts from examples of children's films from the *Childhood and Modernity* projects. The collections of films, which reflect the locations of the projects, include: *Delhi at Eleven* (MacDougall, 2013), *Eleven in Delwara* (MacDougall, 2014a), *Eleven in Kolkata* (MacDougall, 2014b) and *Ten and Eleven in Ladakh* (MacDougall, 2015). Extracts from a selection of the films shot in New Dehli and Ladakh are presented here. To view directly online, readers should follow the link embedded in and underneath the illustration from the relevant film, using the password *951159* to view.

A great deal of the fascination in what these children show with the camera comes from the inevitable fact that, for many viewers, these films depict a different cultural world. There is a danger that these films are interesting only because of their novelty. However, subtracting the effect of a fascination with an intimate view of cultural worlds that viewers may have little knowledge of still leaves a great deal of detailed information about what and how these child camera users choose to film. For example, viewing and analysing the filmed material might answer the following questions: What do children choose to include in the frame? How do adults respond to the child-with-camera? What activities of day-to-day life do children decide to show? Why? Ginsburg (2014) notes that using a camera provided children with a licence to explore their everyday lives. This becomes a means to a "clear-eyed curiosity in ways they might not have thought to do without the passport provide by a camera and the charge to go out and record their world for others to see" (Ginsburg, 2014, p. 456).

I have included a brief critical commentary about each film. I suggest that MacDougall's research outcomes are evidence of the way that his research method might contribute to answering research questions about places, people and the processes of living in a way that puts in the foreground affective, material and aesthetic experience. It is possible to experience the kinds of knowledge produced through the corporeal and thoughtful nature of the observational filmmaking method. These are immediately apparent as accessible and shareable research outcomes for all participants, beneficiaries and users of the research. Teachers will notice that children have developed considerable skill in using the camera to observe and record in the various circumstances they choose to film. Not only are the films evidence of learning in and of themselves, what they show might be a rich source of material to support learning across curriculum domains. In my view, they are powerful examples of how valuable observational filmmaking might be to education research concerning children's experiences and, indeed, to children themselves. The following extracts were included in a paper, Children make observational films exploring a participatory visual method for art education, for the *International Journal of Education Through Art* (Meager, 2017). Katy Marriner (2018) has written study guide for children and teachers about the *Childhood and Modernity* films.

Ravi Shivhare's Film

The combination of the effect of MacDougall's methods, the privileged access a child has to a certain circumstance, and the capacity of children to use a digital video camera for observation is particularly evident in Ravi's filming of his favourite streetside general store. Ravi begins by being crystal clear about what he wants as he explains to the camera before his film is seen. He says, "When I finish my film, I will know how a shop functions" (Fig. 2.1).

Fig. 2.1 The Delhi workshop—still from a film by Ravi Shivhare—my lovely general store (MacDougall, 2013) (https://vimeo.com/139964405)

Ravi appears to have honed ethnographic instincts as he becomes fascinated by the details of the objects and actions of retail processes, such as stocking shelves and engaging with customers. All this goes on in the tiny space of the shop. He is able to slip into cramped spaces with an ease and fluency that an adult would find difficult to emulate. Grimshaw (2014) suggests that this is a kind of choreography. Ravi does not conduct interviews with the owners, employees and customers, as he might have done, nor does he impose a pre-thought-out plan on his filming, which is not to say he was unclear about his objective. Rather than preparing a storyboard to plan the filming, which might have resulted in a drier more distanced film, Ravi is simply there, in and around the shop, and follows what happens. This child's ability to gain access to both the social and physical spaces of the streetside shop creates opportunities for constructing new kinds of knowledge about the shop and those we see in the film. This comes out of the visible and auditory social interactions with the physical environment and with other children and adults. This is achieved, as Grimshaw (2014, p. 468) notes, because it is as though the camera and Ravi's body, senses and perceptions have merged together; the camera is "an extension of his eyes, ears and body – eager, inquisitive, flexible". In his theoretical writing about observational filmmaking, this is an example of what David MacDougall (2006) has termed the corporeal image. As a confirmation of the value of this film to anthropological research, Assa Doran (2014) gives a more detailed account of how Ravi's film offers unusual insight into social relations and the practical economies of the Delhi streets.

Anshu Singh's Film

As Grimshaw (2014) reminds us, the camera that draws out social issues by revealing an individual's experience can be effective in political argument. In her film, Anshu is passionate about her view that girls are treated unfairly in the family home. Boys are allowed to play, while girls have to do domestic work (Fig. 2.2).

Anshu shows how the camera can become an extension of herself, as a friend delivers a stream of consciousness complaints about

Fig. 2.2 Why not a girl—still from a film by Anshu Singh (MacDougall, 2013) (https://vimeo.com/139964414)

the domestic work she has to do. It is doubtful that her friend would have spoken so freely and unaffectedly to an adult, let alone an adult researcher from outside her circle of family and friends. Anshu shows just how much she has learnt about an observational camera's strength, which is to empower others to speak, rather than recording the often stiff and unproductive form that a series of questions and responses in an interview can take. At the end of her film, Anshu retreats to the roof of her house at dusk to whisper a soliloquy to the camera. The camera has become a catalyst to the fluent expression of deeply felt and sophisticated ideas she would have found much more difficult, if not impossible, to verbalise or write about in a school context.

Aayan Mateen's Film

Some of the ways adults might interact with a child filmmaker are evidenced in Aayan's portrait of pizza making for tourists in Ladakh. The camera has given Aayan licence to get almost into the pizzas he so obviously adores. This allows us, as viewers, to build a quite comprehensive

Fig. 2.3 The food: cooking for tourists in Ladakh—still from a film by Aayan Mateen (MacDougall, 2015) (https://vimeo.com/139964416)

and almost physical understanding of the pizzas, the pizza makers and how pizzas are made in this restaurant (Fig. 2.3).

Petheram (2014) notices that adults react in various ways to being filmed by a child. Some ignore the camera and the child; others see it as an unconcerning game or, in some cases, as a school project probably worth tolerating. A few adults seem a little disconcerted by the confident child-with-camera. Some adults cannot resist a comment. Aayan's film suggests that the camera gives the child some additional authority to be close to a scene where usually their presence would be seen as interfering and a nuisance.

Aniket Kumar Kashyap's Film

In a way that would have been impossible for him to couch in words, Aniket becomes fascinated by the teenage bride, his new aunt, who is a newcomer in the family home (Fig. 2.4).

In response to Aniket's new young aunt, and his emergent feelings, the camera becomes a self-reflective extension of the boy's mind as he

Fig. 2.4 My funny film—still from a film by Aniket Kumar Kashyap (MacDougall, 2013) (https://vimeo.com/139964413)

lies back and sings a love song in his own languorous, expectant but not entirely serious way. Through the quality of his engagement, 11-year-old Aniket also shows us not just his intense subjectivity but also the new bride's loneliness and passivity. He frames her, using the LCD screen of the digital video camera, with a visual artist's sensitivity to a range of compositions and their potential expressivity. Ragazzi (2014, p. 461) suggests that Aniket's view of his new aunt "registers her corporeality: she appears both self-consciously posing and spontaneous in her languor". The filmmaker prompts many questions about the young woman and her circumstance through his film. For example, is it an expectation for the new bride to stay inside the house dressed in luxurious-looking garments and wearing so much jewellery? What is evident is that Aniket has given tangible form to his aunt and his feelings for her "without a narrative or plot, without interview or staging […] because the filmmaker seems to understand the power of heightened perception the camera induces, he can allow his way of filmmaking to fill our senses" (Ragazzi, 2014, p. 461). This is an example of how film-making is able to explore and represent ineffable experience within a research method.

There is a study guide to accompany a collection of twelve Indian children's films. The study guide is free and can be downloaded from https://www.roninfilms.com.au/feature/15168/childs-eye.html. The films are also available via following that link in a collection on DVD called *The Child's Eye*.

Conclusion

If observational filmmaking outcomes can be presented in the most straightforward of terms as a form of "presentation of objects and the re-enactment of experiences in the world" (MacDougall, 2006, p. 272), then the status of observational filmmaking as an education research method is less straightforward. For example, participant observational ethnographic films are not a series of propositional statements or replicable generalisations. However, in beneficial contrast, the method MacDougall uses brings into our view a material embodiment of the children he works with, and the presence of those they film.

This is because observational films in an education context, whether authored by researchers or co-authored with children who shoot the filmic material, tactile qualities—such as light, colour, sounds, and movement—evoke the materiality of people and their circumstances. These qualities can be sensed through filmic sequences. In the examples presented in this chapter, the way video cameras are used demonstrates that observational films have the power to present information and draw viewers into the circumstances that are filmed in a sensory way, which is quite different from written text. Generalisations, which are easy to make in writing, can be set aside. Instead, viewers see "the very instant in which the general is transformed into the particular. [This] has not only widened our vision of life it has deepened it" (Balázs, 1970, p. 54). Objects, including the object of the person, are given unique physical presence that de-objectifies and de-commercialises the participant in the filmic image. In this way, the resulting knowledge generated by filming such situations is very far from being objective. As BBC documentary editor Dai Vaughan (1999) reminds us, such objectivity is, in any case, a chimera. Can a filmmaker or viewer, even if present, see simultaneously from each corner of the room? Can all the whispered side remarks in a busy classroom be heard? Could, in any imaginable world, this objective viewer have no preconceptions or possible criteria for taking an interest in what is going on?

So, seeing the looking, gesturing, and touching, in sequence with talk and actions, helps a viewer understand the depicted circumstance through emotions, sensations, aesthetic and ineffable experience. This highly visual and social activity seems to defy both categorisation as data and representation in words, even poetic words. It gives form and substance to the ineffable. I take 'ineffable' in this context to stand for manifestations of different kinds of ephemeral, indefinable, transient, emotional, sensory, perceptual, aesthetic and embodied experiences that are either impossible or hugely difficult to encompass with words. Viewers can see these qualities along with others shown in film and feel these qualities themselves; viewers also sense the environment of those circumstances, the material things, the aesthetic and natural qualities in which, and with which, participants act. I suggest that examples of the observational style in filming offers education researchers, teachers and children potential practical solutions for the investigation of aesthetic and material experiences in the emotional, sensual, sensory, and material nature of living in the complex social context of both schools and homes. It is this potential that is explored as a practical method later in this book.

In terms of research, the apparent conflict inherent in the particularity of the sensual when considered with the abstract generality of scientifically-orientated outcomes is reflected by MacDougall (2006) when he writes: "many anthropologists still feel caught between the possibility of conceptual advances from visual anthropology and the more constructive paradigms of a positivistic scientific tradition" (p. 224). This implicates analysis and description of visual-auditory-tactile experience by written means as potentially contradictory. The danger is that when written forms dominate ethnographic description, this tends to reduce all knowledge to information. The valuable knowledge gained from direct perception is lost. As MacDougall (2006) argues there is much richness when what is heard, touched and seen interplay.

One route to debating how observational filmic images can form new knowledge in an academic context is to draw out the tension generated with academic writing. MacDougall (2006) states that:

> The encounter with visual images demands more of us than the mental facility that language has given us […] in considering the use of images, it is no good simply insisting that we must do a better job of adapting them to scholarly writing. This will only lead to bad compromises. If we are to gain new knowledge from using images, it will come in other forms and by different means. (p. 2)

In *Writing Culture* (Clifford & Marcus, 1986) showed from an anthropological perspective the wedge driven between what happened during ethnographic fieldwork and what was written as published anthropological texts. This suggests the nature of what the reader can come to know only through academic writing about the subjects and circumstances of ethnography is highly prescribed within a narrow band of an accepted textuality. So, within anthropology, observational filmmaking methodology challenged and challenges the dominance of such text-based discourse, however reflexive and dialogic, by a commitment to ensuring that the researcher shares a direct penetrating engagement in the circumstances of the research. Reflexivity is inherent in the research method and dialogism is deferred as a reflection on, rather than a veiling component injected onto, the unfolding experiences embedded within the filmic material. As anthropologist MacDougall himself argued (2006, p. 268), his kind of filmmaking is "a different kind of anthropology, not a substitute for anthropological writing".

Feld (2003, p. 20) writes that Rouch's work "forcefully dissolves and obliterates parochial distinctions between fact and story, documentary and fiction, knowledge and feeling, improvisation and composition, observation and participation". In this view, filmmaking transits the real and the imaginary and conceptual domains of filmmaker, viewers and participants are merged. MacDougall (2006) expands on this by exploring relationships between images, consciousness awareness, vision and feeling. He argues that we assume "the things we see have the properties of being, but our grasp of this depends upon extending our own feeling of being into our seeing" (p. 1). To take an opposing view, the observational film exposes the contingency and provisional nature of the way researchers might acquire knowledge of others in the field. However, the material recorded at the moment of contact with the subject is the fabric of the work and will always carry the indelible stamp of the original encounter. Ethnographic film material is very different from academic writing because, although it can be selected from, combined, and edited in various ways, it cannot be rewritten.

Finally, I suggest that teachers and education researchers will recognise that using video cameras in an observational style is valuable for children. Because observational filmmaking is a form of thought, children are able to explore what is happening around them in a careful and considered way. There is a record of their experiences as a camera user together with a record of others' experiences in the circumstances they share. These audio-visual recordings are available immediately (or after some editing) for review, analysis and interpretation. All that is based in a material, aesthetic and affective form which is not dominated by text so that it is readily accessible and sharable by children, teachers and researchers. This process of considered observation and reflection supports children's learning.

References

Alexander, T. (1987). *John Dewey's theory of art, experience, and nature: The horizon of feeling.* Albany: SUNY Press.

Alexander, T. (1998). The art of life: Dewey's aesthetics. In L. Hickman (Ed.), *Reading Dewey* (pp. 1–22). Bloomington: Indiana University Press.

Alexander, T. (2013). John Dewey's uncommon faith: Understanding 'religious experience'. *American Catholic Philosophical Quarterly, 87*(2), 347–362.

Balázs, B. (1970). *Theory of the film: Character and growth of a new art.* New York: Dover Publications.

Baldacchino, J. (2014). *John Dewey: Liberty and the pedagogy of disposition.* Dordrecht, The Netherlands: Springer.

Chriss, J. (1995). Some thoughts on recent efforts to further systematize Goffman. *Sociological Forum, 10*(1), 177–186.

Clifford, J., & Marcus, G. (Eds.). (1986). *Writing culture: The poetics and politics of ethnography*. Los Angeles: University of California Press.

Dewey, J. (1896). The reflex arc concept in psychology. *Psychological Review, 3*(4), 357–370.

Dewey, J. (1931). Qualitative thought. In J. Boydston (Ed.), *John Dewey the later works, 1925–1953* (Vol. 5, 1988). Carbondale: Southern Illinois University Press.

Dewey, J. (1934). Art as experience. In J. Boydston (Ed.), *John Dewey the later works, 1925–1953* (Vol. 10, 1988). Carbondale: Southern Illinois University Press.

Doran, A. (2014). Deciphered by children: The city's view from below. *The Asia Pacific Journal of Anthropology, 15*(5), 470–473.

Feld, S. (2003). Editor's introduction. In S. Feld (Ed.), *Cine-ethnography—Jean Rouch* (pp. 1–28). Minneapolis: University of Minnesota Press.

Fesmire, S. (2003). *John Dewey and moral imagination*. Bloomington: Indiana University Press.

Fesmire, S. (2015). *Dewey*. New York: Routledge.

Ginsburg, F. (2014). Chronicles of the ephemeral: Some thoughts on Delhi at eleven. *The Asia Pacific Journal of Anthropology, 15*(5), 455–457.

Goffman, E. (1974). *Frame analysis: An essay on the organization of experience*. London: Harper & Row.

Grimshaw, A. (2014). Delhi at eleven: Reflections on filmmaking as a tool for social exploration and personal expression. *The Asia Pacific Journal of Anthropology, 15*(5), 467–470.

Joas, H. (1996). *The creativity of action*. Chicago: University of Chicago Press.

MacDougall, D. (1999). Social aesthetics and the Doon School. *Visual Anthropology Review, 15*, 3–20.

MacDougall, D. (2006). *The corporeal image: Film, ethnography, and the senses*. Princeton, NJ: Princeton University Press.

MacDougall, D. (Director). (2007). *SchoolScapes* (Motion Picture). Australia: Centre for Cross-Cultural Research, Australian National University.

MacDougall, D. (Director). (2008). *Gandhi's children* (Motion Picture). Australia: Centre for Cross-Cultural Research, Australian National University.

MacDougall, D. (Producer). (2013). *Delhi at eleven* (Motion Picture). Australia: Childhood and Modernity Project, Fieldwork Films and Research School for Humanities & the Arts, Australian National University.

MacDougall, D. (Producer). (2014a). *Eleven in Delwara* (Motion Picture). Australia: Childhood and Modernity Project, Fieldwork Films and Research School for Humanities & the Arts, Australian National University.

MacDougall, D. (Producer). (2014b). *Eleven in Kolkata* (Motion Picture). Australia: Childhood and Modernity Project, Fieldwork Films and Research School for Humanities & the Arts, Australian National University.

MacDougall, D. (2015). *Observational cinema*. Manuscript Submitted for Publication.

Marriner, K. (2018). *The child's eye: 12 films from India by child researchers*. Melbourne: Australian Teachers of Media (ATOM).

Meager, N. (2017). Children make observational films exploring a participatory visual method for art education. *International Journal of Education Through Art, 13*(1), 7–22.

Perricone, C. (2006). The influence of Darwinism on John Dewey's philosophy of art. *Journal of Speculative Philosophy, 20*, 20–41.

Petheram, L. (2014). Insights into Indian children, their spaces and lives through four films. *The Asia Pacific Journal of Anthropology, 15*(5), 478–479.

Potts, R. (2015). A conversation with David MacDougall: Reflections on the childhood and modernity workshop films. *Visual Anthropology Review, 31*, 190–200.

Putman, H. (2011). Reflections on pragmatism. In J. Shook & P. Kurtz (Eds.), *Dewey's enduring impact: Essays on America's philosopher* (p. 52). Amherst: Prometheus Books.

Ragazzi, R. (2014). Challenging our view of temporality. *The Asia Pacific Journal of Anthropology, 15*(5), 457–461.

Rorty, R. (1980). *Philosophy and the mirror of nature*. Princetown: Princetown University Press.

Sleeper, R. (1986). *The necessity of pragmatism*. New Haven: Yale University Press.

Vaughan, D. (1999). *For documentary*. Berkeley: University of California Press.

Westbrook, R. (1991). *John Dewey and American democracy*. Ithaca and London: Cornell University Press.

3

Academic Frames

Introduction

At the heart of this book is the question of an empirical practice, observational filmmaking, which places children's experience in the foreground throughout all phases of an inquiry into such experiences. I have already suggested that pedagogy catalyses observational filmmaking in research and learning. For example, children find ways of using video cameras and editing software to share their own and others' experiences. Children can film in an observational style independently of adults. Observational camera techniques help them pay close attention to what they can see and hear as they look at what is going on around them. This is a valuable tool for learning. Observational filmmaking gives children control and offers adults a child-centred view of children's experiences as they live and learn in school.

In Chapter 2, I argued that Dewey's deeply empirical articulation of experience, in *Art as Experience* (1934) and his essay *Qualitative Thought* (1931), supports a theoretical methodological underpinning for observational filmmaking as an education research method. Using functional concepts such as: inquiry, experiment, situation, imagination, and aesthetic experience, with the consummating notion of *an* experience, Dewey argues that starting in experience, with experience, is fundamental in both artistic and scientific practice. From that qualitative logic, which Dewey unpicked in his subsequent book, *Logic, the Theory of Inquiry* (1938), knowledge in the arts and the sciences is built. In a common sense kind of way, saying that humans have experiences and that ideas are experienced, along with everything else, is not saying very much. But if experience is a given, its significance can easily be lost as researchers seek theories and explanations in only abstract terms. There are qualities in human experience that the thoughtful practice of observational filmmaking allows others to share. These are not usually present in theoretical, explanatory discourse.

Drawing on Dewey as an inspiration, my position is that an education research project exploring children's experiences as they live and learn in school should stay as close to *all* qualities in that experience as is possible. This is because, if essential qualities are lost, such as the aesthetic, material and affective, then potential understanding of that experience, and therefore an appreciation of its value, is significantly diminished. However, that position, and my claim that observational filmmaking implies a challenge to education research methods which fail to deal well with experience, draws out theoretical and methodological critiques. This chapter introduces some of these relevant dilemmas, issues and questions. I acknowledge the unsatisfactory brevity of each sub-section in this chapter in relation to the vastness of each of these domains of interest. However, each sheds a valuable and differentiated critical light onto observational filmmaking for education. Each sub-section introduces themes, which readers may explore further if they wish to delve more deeply into observational filmmaking as either an education research practice or as pedagogy.

Phenomenology

To begin their introduction to an edited volume about the phenomenology of thinking, Thiemo Breyer and Chrisopher Gutland (2015) write:

Do we experience our thoughts and thinking, or are they subpersonal factors that functionally determine our experience without themselves being experienced? And if we do experience them, do they have a certain qualitative feel to them like pain or color sensations? (p. 1)

This debate is about how humans experience thinking and how experience is manifest in thought. This draws into focus the fluid and hazy boundaries when dealing in terms such as *thought* and *experience*. But such questions also lie at the heart of the value of observational filmmaking as research—for example, consider the experience of the filmed experience of children's experience in school. Is this thoughtful and already a form of useful knowledge, or is it an experiential undercurrent only of value if more overt forms of cognition, such as interpretive meaning-making, come into play? Although the philosophy of phenomenology is a vast domain, and so a thorough investigation of observational filmmaking for education as a form of phenomenology is beyond the scope of this book, there are significant methodological critiques implicit when applying a phenomenological frame to this research about experience, which must at least be flagged here.

Phenomena that seem to make up human consciousness and direct experience are at the heart of phenomenological philosophical discourses. How is it that all that makes up the world, including others, and ourselves, becomes manifest to us? *The Oxford Dictionary of Film Studies* (Kuhn & Westwell, 2012) draws on two trends in phenomenology that are particularly relevant to considering experience as it relates to film. The first, originating in ideas expressed by Edmund Husserl (1859–1938) focuses on a reductive description, analysis and critical reflection about phenomena of which humans are conscious. The second originates in the writing of Maurice Merleau-Ponty (1908–1961). This emphasises the corporeality of perception which embraces the world as it is lived, the body as it lives, and the qualities of sensations and perceptions. Encompassing both traditions in an attempted definition, Galen Strawson (2011) writes: "Phenomenology is the general study, theology, of appearances, of the experiential character of experiences – the experiential or qualitative what-it's-likeness character that experiences have for those who have them as they have them" (p. 286).

One relevant issue at the heart of phenomenological discourse are the dissonances that come about when saying that two people in the same circumstance may have quite different sensations, let alone thoughts, of 'what-it's-likeness' is like. Right away, a tension implicit within ideas about the mind and the body, thinking and feeling, synthesis in experience and analysis through ideas, are manifest in those simple headline characterisations of phenomenological debate. These debates are complex, evolved and evolving phases of detailed philosophy, which are best located in what Glock (2008) describes as families of resemblances, rather than as part of any homogenous, clearly defined traditions.

To draw on just one thread in phenomenology, Vivian Sobchack (1992) cites the approach of Merleau-Ponty to draw out forms of filmic experience that cannot be analysed in structuralist, semiotic, or cultural terms. The experience of film is at least three-way. It is in the film, embodied in the human-with-camera just as it is in those whose experiences are recorded by film. Experience is also located within the viewer of those experiences as they are recorded in audio-visual forms. In this way, there is a vital and inevitable exchange of experience when any film material is viewed because it is in the melding of the thoughts and feelings of viewers with those before and behind the camera that film is experienced. In this sense, both making and viewing film is corporeal and sensual. I suggest that this is of particular value when researching such embodied, material, affective and aesthetic phenomena, which are so much part of children's experiences. Without such an approach, those qualities may not even sensed, let alone explored and understood.

However, thinking about phenomenology might promote dualistic thinking about feeling. The very existence of phenomenology as domain of thought, even though it riles against its own nature, suggests a possible separation of mind and body, thoughts and feelings. It is, therefore, easy to miss the unified phenomena of experience—the phenomena of thought and experience as one. Phenomenology raises questions around the filmic experience and how film shows or infers experience in terms of the qualities of knowing which observational filmmaking as methodology engenders, but it is not, in itself, sufficient as a conceptual frame for this unfolding methodology.

Empathy

In this book about observational filmmaking, the camera operators, participating children, users of the editing software and the viewers of the filmic outcomes (teachers and researchers, for example) may each have a sense of others' experiences. So, it may be argued that if a person has *empathy* with another, then in one sense they have an idea of what it might be like, as it were, in their shoes—perhaps to predict and explain what they are thinking, feeling and doing (Coplan & Goldie, 2014). This might be a useful quality if research seeks to embrace the full sense of experience that Dewey (1934) intended.

However, the concept of empathy is a hazy one. To illustrate how easily confused—and even glib—discussions of empathy can become, Coplan and Goldie (2014) usefully draw out some of the common uses of the term. These include: feeling what someone else feels; caring about someone else; being emotionally affected by others' emotions and experiences; imaginatively being in someone else's situation; inferring the mental state of another; and any one of all or several of those combined. Discourses that engage with unravelling dilemmas within a concept of empathy find a home within philosophy, medicine, evolutionary science, neuroscience, psychology, psychoanalysis, anthropology and education (Hollan & Throop, 2011). Empathy is also a component in critical engagement and production within the arts (de Bolla, 2001). Here, I simply wish to draw attention to the concept as a methodological component, which must be acknowledged as present in how observational filmmaking may be taken to function.

Jodi Halpern (2001) describes empathy as an experiential understanding of others situated in and acknowledging first-personality. The experience of someone else resonates and provokes an imaginative conception of another's point of view. It is, suggests Halpern (2001), difficult to disentangle combinations of cognition, sensation, and emotion. This is not, "a third-person observer's detached insight or pure theoretical knowing or predictions and forecasts, however accurate […] Nor is empathy solely an affective merging, identification, or attunement with another" (Hollan & Throop, 2011, p. 3). Empathy then, is neither a detached calculation nor a submersed emotional union. A better model, and one which builds the quality of empathetic understanding, is to regard empathy as an essentially communicative and generative process, which helps create a first-person style perspective on the thoughts, feelings and actions of others (Margulies, 1989).

In a scientific frame, relatively recent discoveries about the brain have established that motor neurons fire in a passive way (not causing movement or intended action) just on seeing another's actions (Iacoboni, 2008). The potential of a biological, brain based, automatic root of empathetic feeling and thinking is questioning a positioning of empathy as a disembodied, language bound, calculative, rational or cultural abstraction (Hollan & Throop, 2011). In social anthropology and education research, where face-to-face participant observation, interaction and collaboration is a feature in research, the possibility of empathy and its relative value colours what is seen, recorded and interpreted. If empathy is rooted in our biology, it may be as much a corporeal as a cognitive component of critical and self-critical reflection on the experience of others.

A dilemma rooted in the methodology of observational filmmaking is the appropriateness of bringing into focus different routes to knowledge. These epistemic pathways might be characterised as belonging to traditions of *verstehen* (understanding) and *erklaren* (explanation). Those nuances in *understanding* others as separate from *explanations* about others dog disagreements in the social sciences about how to access and interpret the experience of others (Kogler & Stueber, 2000). Stueber (2006) avoids such distinctions in an acknowledgement that empathetic knowledge and understanding is complex and re-enactive, in which basic empathetic brain functions are part of a qualitative flux in which the cognitive, emotional and imaginative work as one. This qualitative unity is an engagement that needs *all* that is experienced, including thought itself. This is not a conceptual and explanatory framework that has been adopted from a detached perspective (Stueber, 2006). Neither is this simply a projection of a researcher's experiences in the form of self-centred thoughts and feelings onto observed others—a process of centring observation through the self that overwhelms rather than draws out the experience of others.

I posit that the notion of empathy as an engaged and enactive synthesis of brain function, affect, cognition, explanation and so on could be set in a Deweyan notion of experience. This supports arguments that the qualitative engagement with the experience of others through observational filmmaking is a potential pathway towards embracing the possibility of empathetic forms of knowing more and understanding more about children's experience as they learn and live in school. Offering possibilities of empathetic understanding is part of how observational filmmaking creates knowledge about others' experiences. The children's film extracts presented in Chapters 1 and 2, can be viewed in this light. They show that empathetic understanding may be qualitatively part of the kinds of knowledge observational filmmaking creates. This particular train of ideas is not part of the thrust of book, but might be part of future debate about the value of observational filmmaking to both research and learning in school.

Aesthetic and Aesthetics

I discussed Dewey's particular notion of aesthetic experience in Chapter 2. More generally, aesthetic experience and experience of aesthetic qualities are inextricably part and parcel of both the filming process and part of watching examples of the observational films referenced in Chapters 1 and 2. The prominent nature of aesthetic qualities in film means that in a research context knowledge gained through observational filmmaking is quite different from that in academic texts. Such knowledge is, in part, more likely to be corporeal, affective, perceptual and material. As an example, a filmmaker such as David MacDougall (2006) addresses the way social aesthetics underpin children's experiences in the institutions in which he films. His films deliberately conjure the sensory feel of everyday and institutional life. In a boarding school, such as the Rishi Valley School featured in *SchoolScapes* (2007) a broad spectrum of social and natural features come together to express an aesthetic character of a community. These include its physical setting, buildings, formal and informal rituals, styles of speech and gesture, types of clothing, dominant objects and colours, and other more elusive features, all of which might be considered to have prominent aesthetic qualities. These deeply affect the way children—and of course adults—live lives, learn and teach in institutions such as schools. But, the essential physicality of such phenomena is often ignored in research, which constantly seeks forms of abstract knowledge.

In a wider frame of reference, the term and word *aesthetic* is not fixed or easily definable. It is used in a variety of ways. It cuts across disciplines with different force depending on context. For example, it may simply be equated with taste. My aesthetic is different from yours and that is why we will decorate a room in different ways. However, *good taste* may be intended as something more general, a supposed fine cultural aesthetic perhaps. What is considered aesthetically beautiful will certainly vary from society to society in different historical and geographical contexts. An artist's aesthetic is bound into the cognitive, affective and material processes making art. That argument can be paralleled in observational filmmaking, where experiencing aesthetic qualities and making aesthetic decisions are indissoluble from the filmmaking process and evidenced in the filmic outcomes. It is worth noting, that in contemporary art an appropriate aesthetic may engage with the materiality of political and collaborative conceptual forms as in the concept of a *relational aesthetics* (Bourriaud, 2002). In the philosophy of ideas and in technical philosophy there is a history of considering *aesthetics* as a domain of theorising around what art is, what art does and how art and artistic and aesthetic experiences work. A theory of aesthetics such as the transcendental idealist aesthetics, as expressed in the work of Immanuel Kant (1724–1804), broadens debates about the aesthetic into core arguments about epistemology.

It is common to set aesthetic experience apart from ordinary experience in a way Dewey (1934) rejected. For example, Peter de Bola (2001) characterises aesthetic experiences in relation to the arts as wonder—a "state of 'in-between-ness', as it were, part physical and part mental, in the orbit of the emotive yet also clearly articulated or potentially articulable within higher orders of mental acuity" (p. 3). With an ambiguity that haunts attempts to define 'higher order' aesthetic experiences, de Bola's accounts of wonder in aesthetic experience still engage with the aesthetic quality of coming-togetherness of thoughts and feelings in experience (2001). This resonates with the qualitative unifying of thinking and feeling that Dewey argued placed aesthetic experience at very core of understanding all experience. Peter de Bola, who is a professor in English literature, draws out an understanding of intense aesthetic experience—that is "to be moved profoundly" (p. 3). Although that clashes with a Deweyan conception of the everydayness of the aesthetic, helpfully for my project, de Bola approaches aesthetic experience from a context of understanding experience in the arts, not primarily from the context of philosophy, psychology or social sciences.

Putting the work of art centre stage (I will substitute *observational film* for art in this context), de Bola (2001) rejects the argument that affective experiences are somehow disconnected from cognitive experiences. He argues for the converse. But he does this by considering very carefully qualities in aesthetic experience of *specific* art works ranging across painting, music and architecture. Peter de Bola is suggesting meaningful and useful knowledge about experiencing works of art are possible, if very careful attention is paid to those experiences in their particular manifestations. Those qualities of experience must be at the centre of that process, not sidestepped or overwhelmed by theory or scientificity. Dewy would agree. This is a position that is at the very core of this book, and, as de Bola's work illustrates, it finds a natural home in the arts and humanities, rather than in the social sciences. The point to take away, is that in both the process and outcomes of observational filmmaking the particular nature of experiences in the particular circumstances within which filming is taking place are at the centre. They demand attention in the material, aesthetic and affective ways they are manifested, they cannot be overwhelmed by theorising to be best understood or else their very qualities are likely to be missed. Observational filmmaking is a way of thinking in which experiencing is indivisible from ideas.

These threads of argument can help draw out one aspect of observational filmmaking, which sets it apart from most other education research paradigms. It deals in, functions through and presents aesthetic experience centre stage. There is no choice in that as the craft of how a filmmaker handles the tool of a camera within the unfolding, unpredictable settings depends on aesthetic judgements. Moreover, as the raw shots are edited in the software environment powerful aesthetic forces are in play about how the final sequence of shots hangs together—how they will look and feel. Viewers will inevitably respond to extracts of observational film material in an aesthetic way, sensing the plays of light, the craft of a camera angle, the feeling way one shot is juxtaposed with another. Viewers will also see and sense children's aesthetic responses as they are learning, playing and living out their lives. No other research methodology, especially ones that try to treat experience as data to be coded and then analysed under some predetermined intellectual frame can hope to be as useful or effective in creating knowledge and understanding of the nature and value of children's aesthetic experiences in school.

There is widespread belief that individuals' aesthetic responses are locked within the containment of their own experiences and feelings deeply located within a psychology of representation (Gombrich, 1961). For example, in school, an art teacher's job is to open pupils to their unique and essentially private individuality (Hickman, 2010). In this view, how art is meaningful and representative is therefore located in those internal states as well as in cultural norms and psychologically resonant symbols and motifs. Indeed, virtually all of twentieth century aesthetics taught that each human, whether as creator or perceiver, brings his or her own feelings to the expressive object (Depew, 2005). The danger here is that this dualistic view of inner mental states as separate from the external world suggests that aesthetic meaning is private, somehow unreachable and bound into individual consciousness. Observational filmmaking as a away of thinking, which is so evidently sharable, bucks against this view as filmic thinking is manifest through a materiality of colour, light, space, texture, movement and sound.

This book presents aesthetic experience, as it applies in observational filmmaking for education, more in that loosely expressed "part physical and part mental" sense with which de Bola (2001, p. 3) asks his readers to engage. But, rather than a separate and special quality in human thought and experience, a Deweyan conception of aesthetic experience would each reject such implicit dualities and hierarchies of inner and outer worlds. Dewey's concept of aesthetic experience is in process rather than definition. It is open, generative and creative of new knowledge. It is a qualitative unified flux of all that is material, affective and cognitive. This has to be one of the first ports of call to build understanding of human experiences, especially, I suggest, if these are aesthetic experiences.

Observation and Questioning Looking

Dalston and Lunbeck (2011) relate examples of scientific observation across the centuries, which seek methods and the associated tools to focus on components of a larger whole by separating this or that part out from its wider circumstance. The reduction and distilling of these parts from the potential confusion of their environments renders them more rather than less visible. This methodology is fine if the aim is to, say, isolate and make visible particles in atoms or to observe black holes within galaxies. However, particularisation and the discrimination to select one phenomenon over another will not help make visible the 'process field' of the unity of lived experience implied in a Deweyan sense. Yet, in the history of both the sciences and the arts, observation is a core practice. Indeed, in the introduction to the edited volume, *Histories of Observation*, Daston and Lunbeck (2011) address many issues equally applicable to artistic as to scientific observation. For example, is it preferable to use the naked eye or rely on instruments to help observe? Different people may look carefully at the same phenomena and yet end up observing different things.

When Grimshaw and Ravetz (2009, p. xiii) write in the context of filmmaking that, "observation has come to be conceptualised in terms of sites, technologies, skills and performances", they are also implicitly questioning how it is possible to observe from the situation of the observer in terms of the situation of the subject. They also imply that observation is a skilled practice and one can learn to observe. This is not only about learning to construct research tools and how to use technologies effectively, although these are vital. There is also a process of heightening observation through the *practice* of using tools. The technologies at hand can become conduits for sharing an attentiveness and sensitivity to aesthetic and sensory knowledge as well as a mechanism for collecting data of all kinds. Such debates draw out the many-layered frames that overlay any observational research practice, particularly a practice of observing the experience of others.

To generate and share knowledge through observational filmmaking techniques, MacDougall (2006) suggests that *looking* comes first:

> [Observational] filmmakers compose images into a form for others to see and are then frequently asked, "What were you trying to say"? They have tried to say or mean certain things, but that is perhaps the least of their intentions. Most of their effort has gone into putting the viewer into a particular relation to a subject and creating progression of images and scenes for understanding it [...] But before filmmakers can compose images in this way, they have to film them, and this has required looking. Thus, before films are a form of representing or communicating, they are a form of looking. Before they express ideas, they are a form of looking. Before they describe anything, they are a form of looking". (pp. 6–7)

Filming can register, argues MacDougall (2006), the process of looking, which captures the interest and will behind the camera. There is a dissonance between trying deliberately to make something visible (simply seeing) and deliberately *looking* with a camera to follow a person or a process as it unfolds in a setting. However, looking is aided by seeing better. Improved lenses on optical devices allow humans to see more so that they can look more carefully. In using digital video camera as a research tool an observer can be bought closer to the object-in-the-world rather than the-object-as-an-idea. One possible metaphor is that observational filmmaking functions a little like the process of drawing with one interesting advantage. Drawing unfolds through time and can show the process of looking as a visible trace in the final object, but only very rarely can this process be witnessed. What we are left with is the object at the end, in which everything that went on (all those lines and marks that were individually drawn) has been bought together into one—the drawing. Filming, however, is a temporal process, within which the camera is recording every moment of how the camera operator was looking and the way that person was part of the setting. Such thoughtful looking is as integral to the way the resulting filmic material appears as what those in front of the lens were doing and saying.

Such filmic *looking* embraces a state of being attentive. This requires a certain consciousness. However it is seldom a state without any abstractions and concepts. Many conventions and pre-conditions are inevitably bought to bear, either unconsciously or, if considered self-reflection is exercised, consciously. These may include: conventions in camera use; already knowing participants as people; the nature of the technology; awareness of participatory research ethics, and much else. The looking an observational filmmaker undertakes with a camera is imbued with those abstractions. Indeed, when discussing learning how to look towards the close of *The Corporeal Image* (2006), MacDougall implicitly acknowledges that "*looking* implies a more selective, intentional activity, a search for an investment of meaning" (p. 242).

If to look with a camera is to look with purpose then that is thinking. Abstractions in psychological and sociological conventions and pre-conditions, whether consciously acknowledged or not, are present and the intentional activity of using a camera to observe is a form of thought. The process *and* the outcomes embrace qualities in thought, and thoughtfulness is present as much as colour, light, movement and the passage of time are recorded by the filming.

As consumers of the filmed research material, we can pay attention to how the camera was used and so how the camera user was looking. The evidence is apparant. This helps merge the experience of the camera user (the observer in situ) with our experience as observers (viewers in our own place and time). As we attend to what the film shows and listen to what the microphones recorded, we bring together ourselves as viewers, the camera user, the participants (getting on with what was at hand in their specific circumstances in time and place) into one experience.

Dewey might argue that those moments of looking (which embody the observer in that situation) flow as one experience. This flux is not divisible, if the nature of the experience is honoured. A process, which separates experience into parts to analyse those parts more effectively, may deny the unity of experience and distances us from it. The challenge for an academic, who is arguing that observational filmmaking can make a significant contribution to research, or a teacher, who argues observational filmmaking can contribute to learning, is to show that this tangible form of visible thinking (which is embodied within the succession of 25 frames that make each second of film) opens access to kinds of knowledge about experiences that abstract thinking, thinking in words, cannot approach on its own.

Ethnography

Ethnography has been drawn from its roots in anthropology into a wide range of research domains such as medicine, education, geography, and sociology (Wolcott, 2008). This ubiquitous tendency contributes to the way in which the concept of ethnographic research has become almost interchangeable with the concept of qualitative research, where researchers attempt forms of in-depth interpretive descriptions of others in social and cultural situations (Hoey, 2014).

There is an underlying assumption in ethnography that it is possible to see how humans construct meaning within social and cultural interaction and how they act with purpose towards specific outcomes (Iphofen, 2013). By entering the circumstances of the research, researchers can feel closer to what is going on and, indeed, become part of the processes of meaning-making. If that happens, a problem is that manipulating and controlling subjects will deny a sense of naturalism and authenticity (Iphofen, 2013). To set meaning-making in a social and cultural context, ethnographers often present something of the whole setting. Awareness of places, times, objects and other non-human qualities form part of interpretive understanding of what is going on in the circumstances under investigation. By engaging with participants, ethnographers open research to the assumption that there are always multiple perspectives in play concerning what is going on, as advocating one viewpoint over another may deny knowledge of other views that are powerful influences on the social and cultural circumstances (Iphofen, 2013). Broad principles such as these apply to an ethnographic *process* in which researchers engage, more or sometimes less so, with others in situations. They deeply affect the nature of ethnographic outcomes, which become ethnographies of the people, circumstances and settings of the research.

When ethnographers go to a research setting and become part of that setting, this can be termed participant observation. The researcher is both participating in the setting and observing. This creates a conflict between immersion in the lives of others (what they feel, think and do) and a necessary detachment in order to offer insight and interpretation of what it is that is going on in cultural and social terms. Ethnographic techniques can be instrumental in identifying with others in order to speak for them or to offer a way that their voices can be heard. A socially conscious, politically motivated form of ethnographic research is common. However, the need to construct a narrative, the purpose of which is predetermined, colours both research processes and outcomes (Wolcott, 2008).

In introducing ethnography for art education research, Richard Hickman (2008) emphasises its value as a naturalistic, interpretive methodology for social and cultural phenomena in educational contexts. He confirms the centrality of observation, especially reflexive participant observation where the "researcher is immersed in the phenomena observed" (p. 18). Hickman stresses how emic knowledge underpins forms of intuitive and empathetic understanding that ethnographic research may draw out. Whereas phenomenology tends to focus on individual experience, ethnography draws on cultural and social interaction. However, the interconnectedness of the experience of the individual, the experience of researchers, the experiences of the consumers of research outcomes and the experiences of any and all of these in the social and cultural context mean that that a phenomenological interest is part of an ethnographic approach, and vice versa.

The nature of observational filmmaking as an ethnographic practice is complicated when the participants observe themselves, as in a number of examples of the children's films presented in Chapters 1 and 2. The dissonance between extreme intimacy, as witnessed in Ravi's film discussed in Chapter 2, and a demand for a more detached frame for interpretation is acute. This must be acknowledged and discussed. However, to draw the argument back to the holistic threads found in Dewey, observational filmmaking techniques are a "repudiation of methods that fragmented ethnographic realities as a preliminary to reassembling them with a conceptual framework imposed from elsewhere"

(Grimshaw & Raveez, 2009, p. 4). They describe how Sandall (1972) and others laid foundations for a conceptual scaffold for an observational epistemology that is built from within the ethnographic situation as observational filmmakers interact and collaborate with subjects. All become participants contributing to the outcome—a film. At the very least, researchers, participants and consumers of research will share in knowledge about those situations through watching the filmic material. This knowledge is experiential and it is the immediate ground on which an interpretative understanding is drawn from whichever point of view.

Some relevant principles in ethnography, which I have outlined briefly here, find focus through observing cultural and social interaction, from which the meaning of cultural and social interaction may be drawn out. I suggest observational filmmaking brings to this practice, and embeds within it, qualities in experience that often defy the textual processes of meaning-making so prevalent in social science research. If this is ethnography, it is one in which the material and aesthetic are inextricable from the way in which knowledge and understanding result.

Filmmaking as a Research Practice and Process

In practice, as Pink (2007) argues, most visual anthropologists and visual sociologists create and present images to form part of a dialectic with writing for knowledge creation, rather than seeing images as a uniquely discrete realm of knowing. However, Grimshaw and Ravetz (2015) suggest that the theory about how academic writing and image making work together in research has yet to catch up with this practice. The way that academic writing and social science analytical practices might usefully intersect with observational filmmaking is a question arising from observational filmmaking as a research method. As the camera captures the sounds and sights of children's experiences living and learning, it seems experiential. Yet, academic research in education will often ignore qualities such as the material and aesthetic to focus on abstract meaning found in social and cultural contexts. Because of this, as I will describe in the following section of this chapter, video material in social science orientated research about children is more often than not counted as data. From this data what children say and the mechanics of what they do might be coded and analysed, in order to pin down elements of what is going on so as to understand those children better. As I have argued earlier in this book, experiential qualities such as aesthetic experience—which are central to children's experience as they live and learn in school—are, on the whole, ignored. These cannot either be adequately explored through a dualistic approach to analysis or adequately expressed in text. They are, therefore, largely absent in impactful education research.

In contrast to education research, which uses video material as data for analysis so that interpretive definitions might be subsequently drawn in academic text, the discussion of observational filmmaking in Chapter 1 suggested that it is an experiential practice. This is a generative route to knowledge. The researcher uses the camera actively as a tool to generate new knowledge with participants. In a parallel line of argument, Ingold (2007, 2011, 2013) and also Taussig (2009, 2011) have suggested that drawing is a practice, which creates a kind of knowledge. They intersect with debates in contemporary anthropology about knowledge pursued and expressed in media other than text (Grimshaw & Ravetz, 2015). I will draw out this argument here, as it offers an insight into how I suggest that the experience witnessed by viewing observational film material about children living and learning is simultaneously and indivisibly both the result of the corporeal camera, that camera's interaction with the participants, and what they are in the midst of doing. It is in this way that observational filmmaking in this kind of research is a visible rather than textual form of thought.

Ingold (2011) wishes to create direct connections between anthropology and the living of life. Without that connection, he argues, much in the experiences of others is missed. Depth and fullness in understanding is unattainable. Ingold (2007, 2011, 2013) presents drawing as open-ended and improvisatory. Its strength is in leaving a tangible trace of experience. Grimshaw and Ravetz (2015) quote Ingold (2011) at length. Part of this passage is so applicable to the practice of observational filmmaking that I repeat it below. Ingold (2011) is not concerned with a distanced representation of the world:

> I refer rather to the intimate coupling of the movement of the observer's attention with currents of activity in the environment. To observe is not so much to see what is 'out there' as to *watch what is going on*. Its aim is thus not to represent the observed but to participate with it in the same generative movement. (p. 233, original emphases)

For Ingold (2011, 2013), drawing is a trace of the engagement of the senses and the body with media in experience. The trace is far more than disembodied descriptions and analyses; it shows a physical connection with the participatory artist, the situation and the circumstances in which the drawing was made. If knowledge is revealed in drawing, it is knowledge that is formed in *making*. The making of a drawing is "a continuous emergent practice [...] a knowing with rather than knowing *of* or knowledge about" (Grimshaw & Ravetz, 2015, p. 259). To complement their reading of Ingold (2007, 2011, 2013) and Grimshaw and Ravetz (2015) draw out the corporeal, experiential, experimental and opening qualities of drawing explored by Taussig (2009, 2011).

However, both Ingold and Taussig see the images a video camera creates in opposition to their argument about knowledge as revealed in the process of making drawings. Their mistake is to see the video image only as an image, rather than a *trace* of the observatory and participatory processes that produced it. In observational filmmaking as research, the processes of filmmaking form continuous, unfolding, temporal traces of experiences, which are valuable, not because they are fixed representations or narratives, but because they are generative, dynamic forms of direct, corporeal, sensory engagement in and with the situation within which they were made. I contend this helps reach a deeper understanding of those situations by opening, revealing and creating pathways to new knowledge about them.

Grimshaw and Ravetz (2015) show how Ingold's and Taussig's arguments about knowing through making can be drawn into the debate about how observational filmmaking can be a useful anthropological research method. They suggest that the embodied, corporeal camera of observational filmmakers generates a trace of their experience and those whom they film. As Ingold (2011) critiques the camera as a technological device that gets in the way of direct experience, he fails to recognise that the camera can be an extension of the body in similar way to a stick of charcoal or graphite pencil. Although the camera makes no physical marks—directly showing the results of how the body used media—the succession of filmic material in time forms fluid prints of the experience of the camera operator. The tool (the camera) moves, follows, gets closer or further away, takes up points of view and, through its human operator, decides what is included in the frame and what is left out. When filming, the camera operator improvises in and with the situation as that situation changes. All of those phenomena and decisions about a point of view are continuously moving in time and operate in and through changing spaces. This resonates with the kind of experience I have when drawing.

Unlike drawing, however, the process of making observational film material preserves every moment and movement as the camera records. In drawing, the product is frozen at the point the last mark is made and the process of making marks is implied by the trace left static and silent on the surface. If observational filmmaking is taken first as a process of experiencing, rather than as a method for constructing representations, consumers of research can share directly in that process of experiencing and so come to know more about the situation and the actors in it.

Technology, Tools, Craft and Stories

To build a critical discussion of an artist's drawing, both as outcome and process, the media used—ink, charcoal, pencil, blood, mud—is a vital component in any interpretive understanding. Understanding the tools and technologies used by artists to create with media is also part of art criticism and art historical discourse. The nature of the tools and technologies used in filming, including—but not exclusively—the cameras and the editing software, deeply affect the process of research and the nature of the filmic outcomes.

The sociologist Richard Sennett expounds on the relevance of concepts such as skill, 'craftsmanship' and the use of tools in his book, *The Craftsman* (2008). Sennett contributes to the 'material turn' in the social sciences and humanities, which has grown from an increasing recognition that the nature of objects and the material world must be central to understanding meaningful living. A focus on things and thingness is a reaction to post-structuralism's crises of the discourses of representation (Miller, 2013). Theorists who place materiality in the foreground consider how objects are part of human action and are central to the meaning making in much human endeavour.

If digital video cameras and editing software are tools central to the way that observational filmmaking as research or pedagogy works, then there will be skills and judgements associated with their use that deeply affect the outcomes. As these tools are used, there is an "intimate connection between hand and head" (Sennett, 2008, p. 9). MacDougall, during his *Childhood and Modernity Project* and I—as will be established in the subsequent chapters—teach or share skills in the use of cameras and software with participant children. The children practise ways of using these tools so as to observe what it is that is going on. In an important sense, and in way that requires much critical reflection, the child-with-camera also becomes a research tool, which an education researcher may develop a certain craft in using.

What I wish to draw out here, however, is that there is a "dialogue between concrete practices and thinking; this dialogue evolves into sustaining habits, and these habits establish a rhythm between problem solving and problem finding" (Sennett, 2008, p. 9). Tools and how their use is developed and adapted through the making of something is an example of the generative flux of inquiry that Dewey advocates. Knowledge is created not found. This suggests to me that knowledge is made using cognitive tools as humans make objects with physical tools. As I suggest in Chapter 5, there will be both cognitive and physical engagement in and with experience through specific use of specific research tools.

In the second part of *The Craftsman*, Sennett (2008) develops the notion of the use of tools with a focus on skills. He makes two arguments, "first, that all skills, even the most abstract, begin as bodily practices; second, that technical understanding develops through the power of the imagination" (p. 10). The first argument suggests that the deeply significant role of sensations as knowledge is gained in physical practice; the second investigates reflexivity implied by the interconnectedness of thinking and doing integral to making. Sennett draws out the necessary states of resistance and ambiguity—the use of a tool is contingent on each material circumstance it engages in and with—and therefore the "grounding of skill in physical practice" is essential (p. 10). I suggest that attention to the nature of research tools and the craft of how they are used anchors research in the material world in which researcher and participants are embedded. This is especially vital when the kinds of experience at the centre of children's living and learning in school, namely the affective, material and aesthetic experience, are in play.

In ethnographic filmmaking, the impact of constantly evolving technologies contributed to changing the potential relationship between the researcher and participants. It was not necessarily that the technology made a difference to the status of what was recorded as more or less truthful, but it transformed the way that the filmmaker could enter with the circumstances and engage with the participants' actions and interactions. Feld (2003) describes how Jean Rouch explained in his various writings that "the presence of the camera, like the presence of the ethnographer, stimulates, modifies, accelerates, catalyzes, opens a window" (p. 16). Therefore, it can be argued that the direct contact with people that Rouch advocated was catalysed as much by technological evolution as by film theory or personal preferences. Indeed, it is often impossible to extricate whether continuous technological developments led to new theory, or whether the development of theory suggested directions in which to develop technology (Feld, 2003).

In viewing the resulting observational filmic material, the filmmaker, participants and the viewer are not only watching and listening to what is going on, they are also watching the results of a corporeal camera in the setting. The nature of the camera and the way it is used deeply affect what is seen. In other words, the camera is not physically visible, but the choices and judgements made about where it is, how it is looking and how aspects of the technology are bought into play are very present. The craft of camera use forges the filmic outcomes in the media of experience. This form of media draws the consumers of research into the very circumstances of the research, which are absent in other methodologies. This, I argue, is a strength, especially when set against the temptation to construct stories using instrumental, didactic and documentary film techniques.

Arts-Based Research in Education

Elliot Eisner (1998) and Tom Barone and Eisner (2012) have opened a rich seam for those who argue that artistic practice and expression can lie at the centre of education research. At the core of this idea is that teaching and learning, as well as education research which examines teaching and learning, exhibit aesthetic qualities about which judgements should be made rather than explanations of cause and effect. A critical task of a researcher is to render judgements, based on an aesthetic sense of a whole (Eisner, 1998). Arts-based methodologies are needed to both reveal and express aesthetic values and judgements. Barone and Eisner (2012, p. xii) define arts-based education research (ABER) as "a process that uses the expressive qualities of [artistic] form to convey meaning". Research may show aspects of the social, emotional, sensory and aesthetic world to us through forms in the research that function beyond words.

Therefore, Eisner's methodologies, as with other arts-based methodologies like Saldaña's *ethnodrama* (2005) or Irwin's *a/r/tography* (2004), conceptualise aesthetic relationships at the heart of the researched situation. Felt experience must also be explored and expressed (Siegesmund, 2012). This felt experience will be situated in and between research participants, and between participants and the context within which they are communicating. It will also be situated in art that is made by a researcher during the research. I allude here to artistry in the making and aesthetic qualities in the outcomes of observational filmmaking. The danger, as Pariser (2013) argues, is that art and aesthetics are seductive terms, which allow the researcher off the hook of objectivity and replaces this with subjective self-centeredness, self-satisfaction, entertainment, and even complacency as possible outcomes.

However, despite these dangers, to chime with Siegesmund (2012), I wish to consider that artistic practice in observational filmmaking is a form of opening ways of thinking which are impossible with other methodologies. This does not necessarily mean abandoning other methodologies. On the contrary, observational filmmaking might become a component in pluralistic methodologies which, as Dewey (1938) advocated, interpenetrate science, language and art to open pathways to understanding which are far closer to life as it is lived. This suggests a potential amalgamation of qualitative social science methods suggested by ethnographic practice *with* observational filmmaking as an artistic practice. This is one area in which the integration of the craft of observational filmmaking with academic education research may be explored.

Rita Irwin (2008) describes a/r/tography as an arts and education practice-based methodology. Rather than design a research project with a set of methods and data analysis applicable to specific research questions set in advance of the research, a/r/tographers undertake research rather as an artist, writer or musician might create an artwork. So, researchers do not necessarily know the form of their research before they begin. The form is revealed—a/r/tographers use the term 'rendered'—in the research process, which is closer to an artistic process than a social science methodology.

Therefore, a/r/tography may offer another viewpoint on how observational filmmaking might function as education research from an arts and humanities rather than social science base. In the word a/r/tography, 'a' stands for artist, 'r' for researcher and 't' for teacher. The forward slashes indicate how these concepts are both separate and simultaneously folded into one word. Irwin (2008) believes that these roles are synthesised in an a/r/tographic project so that "artistic and educational practices inform, contradict, and complement one another" (p. 27). Irwin, who is one of the founding pioneers of a/r/tography, suggests this is research that is an act of living inquiry: "Knowing (theoria), doing (praxis), and making (poiesis) are folded together in a/r/tography to form rhizomatic ways of experiencing the world and creating the circumstances to produce knowledge and understanding through inquiry-laden processes" (Irwin, 2008, p. 26). Irwin (2008) and other a/r/tographers acknowledge that the conceptual underpinning for a/r/tography is found in the philosophy of Gilles Deleuze (Springgay, Irwin, Leggo, & Gouzouasis, 2008). I consider the example of Deleuzian thinking in Chapter 6. A/r/tographers continuously explore. Conclusions are not sought. They see research as a form of living life—of being in the world (Irwin, 2008). In this way, emotion, intuition, cognition, perception and the spiritual can all contribute to knowing more. However, it is difficult to pin down a critique of a/r/tography from a conceptual standpoint as a/r/tographers' conceptualisation of their practice emphasises *lack* of definition as a conceptual quality. It is a deliberately slippery practice. The ontological and epistemological frames for a/r/tography are alluded to rather than argued, as a/r/tographers tend to fall back on the status of research as art to justify their methodology. For this reason, it is more helpful to look at a specific example of a/r/tographic research to understand and critique the way in which a/r/tography works. However, if an a/r/tographic output is a one-off performance or physical artwork and consumers of research must be physically present with the art to fully appreciate arts-based forms of knowing, the potential impact of this form of research is severely limited.

This critical reflection draws out a number of pitfalls and problems for observational filmmaking as research. The researcher who is also an artist (a filmmaker) in the research is potentially split. These tensions are even more even more problematic if the artist/researcher is also a teacher in the research context. If art (filmic material) is used as part of the dissemination of research, the quality of that art (film) must be addressed. It is difficult to assess artistic quality with frameworks designed for academic writing in the social sciences. There are resounding dissonances between art (filmmaking) practice and most education research practice. There will be unhelpful conflict in how the research is designed and undertaken and how it is disseminated and critiqued if these disharmonies remain unacknowledged or unresolved.

Despite these pitfalls, this book is itself an example of a pluralistic methodology for research. This integrates filmmaking, which might be described in terms of arts based methods, with this academic text based argument. A film *together with* an academic text will open the possibility of a research method, which expresses a vivid, detailed and multilayered understanding of children's experience.

An acknowledgement of an arts-based approach to research through film is made here because artistic experience is, in part, ineffable. And, if not ineffable, then it is often very difficult to describe and interpret the fullness of experience with words. If that is so, then a research process will be more helpful if it is able to embrace at its core affective, material and aesthetic experience as children learn and live in schools. The nature of audio-visual recording and the products that result are a way forward; however, they also create further specific methodological dilemmas, which I open out in the following sections.

Video as Data

The Economic and Social Research Council (ESRC) in the UK supported the writing of a *National Centre for Research Methods* (NCRM) working paper (Jewitt, 2012), which offers an introduction to the use of video for research. The document "mapped the scope and use of video for data collection and showed that video is a significant resource for many contemporary researchers across a range of fields" (p. 21). There is no reference in Jewitt's report (2012) to the long tradition of film and filmmaking in anthropology. There is a very brief acknowledgement of participatory video.

In contrast to the spirit of researchers' use of digital video in an observational *filmmaking* process, in the field of education Goldman, Pea, Barron, and Derry (2007) edited a substantial number of chapters and papers, which as a whole were designed "to expand the horizons of researchers in the learning sciences conducting research using video-as-data [sic]" (p. x). They speak of ushering in an era of *video scholarship* to contribute to creating knowledge and understanding about teaching and learning. They use the term *video record* that chimes with their primary vision of *video-as-data*. In a subsequent paper, Derry et al. (2010) proclaim, "video offers a means of close documentation and observation and presents unprecedented analytical, collaborative and archival possibilities" (p. 5). On the face of it, this statement is something observational filmmakers might support. However, Derry et al.'s paper (2010), just as with Goldman et al. (2007), turns away from intrinsic qualities of the medium, as they demand that the complex kinds of information video records "requires thoughtful attention to the problem of how to extract data and meaning" (Derry et al., 2010, p. 6). The mining of video material for data is further confirmed as they attest that: "The vast majority of educational research using video has involved the detailed analysis of clips" (p. 9).

Where Derry et al. (2010) come closest to allying with observational filmmaking methods is in their description of how some researchers select video material using aesthetic criteria to illustrate an evolving interpretive narrative. However, even here, the motive is to assimilate "chunks and then contextualise them within a narrative thread" (Derry et al., 2010, p. 12). Narrative is the predominant and usually predetermined force that drives the research, and video is a tool to facilitate this. In other words, the circumstances themselves, especially their aesthetic and material qualities, are relegated to the role of servants of narrative and exposition. To confirm this, Derry et al. (2010) illustrate how teacher professional development videos take on a documentary form in order to advocate or illustrate a point of view. Just as with Jewitt (2012), this suggests video is additional rather than integral as it "adds value to learning research" (Goldman et al., 2007, p. xi).

The process of setting out to collect data for rigorous analysis later, regardless of whether this is using quantitative, qualitative or mixed methods, is designed so that findings can be 'written up' and conclusions drawn. These outcomes are conceptual representations that explain what was going on. A duality is created in the separation of the researched circumstance captured as video data and the research outcomes disseminated in an academic frame. Although Goldman et al. (2007) and Derry et al. (2010) acknowledge that video material is more visible than forms of written and coded forms of data, and that an advantage of this visibility is that data can be *seen* and video records can be viewed many times, they also hedge their bets and point to questions about whether the particularity of video records means that they are valid as data, or can be generalisable and so useful in research terms.

As I hope this then makes clear, although there are resonant overlaps between ethnographic observational filmmaking and *video-as-data*, researchers who use observational filmmaking techniques operate a digital video camera and use professional editing software from a premise that is different from research methods presented by Goldman et al. (2007), Derry et al. (2010), and Jewitt (2012). Instead of primarily seeking to generate data for analysis or material for the construction of expository narrative, observational filmmakers first and foremost wish to use observational filmmaking methods to look carefully. They visually explore and visually present aesthetic, embodied, and material qualities of the lived experience of others. At all times these remain in the foreground of the research process. Material and aesthetic qualities intrinsic to experience and essential to its understanding are present in the filmic outcomes; they will not be found if film clips are considered as data, coded and then analysed according to some external conceptual frame.

Video as Method

Sarah Pink (2013) has pointed out that opportunities for the use of video in research are constantly evolving and that fixed recipes for methods, or inflexible, dogmatic methodologies, will not cope with the flux and flow in an emerging potential for using an audio-visual way to research. The technological tools, in the form of digital video cameras, microphones and editing software, are in rapid, continuous development. The nature of these tools and how they were and are used deeply affects outcomes (Harper, 2012). If a researcher uses technological tools for research, those tools become as important a part of the research context as the researcher, the subjects and their situation.

Bearing in mind the diversity of ways in which researchers bring methods and theoretical frameworks to bear on the use of video, a researcher may only be able to fix the interrelationship of theory and practice in their particular circumstance at that particular time. However, Pink (2013) argues it is crucial to do so, in order that the theory and method and their relationship are transparent. This is essential so that knowledge produced in and through video is understandable.

Pink (2001), in the first edition of *Doing Ethnography: Images, Media and Representation in Research*, approaches visual methods from an ethnographic stance. In doing so she problematises representation and interpretation and the way that knowledge is created within the social sciences. In parallel to Pink, but from a sociological position, Banks (2001) also began to argue that the positivistic, realist and scientific paradigms for, for example, video-as-data, could not embrace the challenge presented by visual methods. In video-as-data, the process of the production of images and the images themselves are dominated by theoretical discourse that is seen as controlling the kind of knowledge produced, rather than potentially revealing what is yet to be known. Because of this hierarchy, an opportunity to sense closer connection to the circumstances of the research through audio-visual recording is reduced, if not lost. The video material is considered data to be analysed and consigned to the background rather than the foreground of the interpretive process. One crucial effect is that the visual is subservient to the written word, so that knowledge attained through an audio-visual research process is mostly shared by academic forms of writing. Much of the qualities inherent in the audio-visual are abandoned. They simply don't fit with text.

To deepen the thrust of that argument, Pink (2013) acknowledges that a number of social anthropologists were already arguing that ethnographic observational filmmaking had shown how different forms of useful knowledge may come through sensory experience shared by deeply situated filmic material. The video camera and editing software are not only tools within the research method, their use is able to bring into the foreground epistemology with means to grasp "taken-for-grated aspects of life; investigating the normal process of seeing and being in the world" (Harper, 2012, pp. 139–140).

For sociologist Harper (2012), visual methods are so evidently useful that he riles against the failure to teach university students to use audio-visual technologies. But, the rapid advances towards readily affordable, intuitive, yet deeply powerful technologies have left university lecturers behind. Harper (2012) writes about sociology, "there is virtually no training in graduate schools in filmmaking [...] it also reflects a mistrust of film as a legitimate way to express sociological ideas" (p. 233). I will add, it is not only the expression of ideas that is mistrusted, but also the function of filmic processes to open pathways to new knowledge.

However, I suggest audio-visual methods in education research, which are positioned from an observational filmmaking rather than video-as-data standpoint, bring into focus the deep-seated dilemma in locating such research as a social science. There is a difficult to reconcile dissonance between the method and paradigmatical base of most education research methodology. Anne Harris (2016) implicitly recognises this. In the conclusion of *Video as Method*, Harris (2016) attempts "to move from method toward methodology – that is, the integration of what you *do* with that tool in relation to theory" (p. 151). To aid her argument she quotes Gillian Rose (2012) arguing that her theoretical position is for "understanding visual images as embedded in the social world and only comprehensible when that embedding is taken into account [...] To do that you will need to have an explicit methodology" (p. xviii). I would add that audio-visual outcomes of observational filmmaking are embedded not only in the social world, but also the material, aesthetic and affective world of those participating in the circumstances of the filming. In relation to research and to learning, what the camera user does with the camera as a tool is melded with theories and theses of all kinds in the thoughtful processes of filming, reviewing, editing and sharing.

A sensitive awareness alone of personal, cultural, intellectual and ethical positioning does not address what Dewey calls *experience* and what Deleuze has termed *pure immanence*, a creative ontology of becoming, in which the very substance and flux of experience is part of the discourse (Deleuze, 2001). Both Dewey and Deleuze argue for the integration of being and meaning. Deep understanding of what others do in the world is not possible without sensing the qualities of experience (in Dewey's terms) as integral to what others mean. In social science based education research, as meaning is separated from experience, dualities are created—affect in experience is reduced and even discarded; and wholes are dived into parts to help analysis of those parts. All of this atomising and fracturing reduces the possibility of a fullness of understanding of what others are doing. Adapting Rose (2012) and acknowledging Harris (2016) and MacDougall (2006), seeing others through observational filmmaking is as much corporeal as cultural. Researchers are not limited to uncovering new knowledge through interpreting what an analysis of data might mean, they are exploring the very medium out of which meanings emerge. In research terms, this gives meaning traction and purchase in the medium of experience, as outcomes are more easily sharable and impactful, with a far greater reach than professional academic text alone. As Rose (2012) puts it, this is "perceptual, experiential and sensory" (pp. 7–8). To use a potentially disengaging academic term that is gaining currency, this is *postrepresentational*. In terms of my own research project, I suggest it is essential to an understanding of what is going on as children experience living and learning in school. Harris (2016) acknowledges Rose's prominent position in unfolding this argument and, I suggest, opens a route to understanding MacDougall's notion of the social aesthetic in anthropological observational filmmaking:

> [...] our recent attraction to the work of Deleuze (and Massumi too) is a synthesizing of affect, technology, creativity and a kind of enjoyment of the freedom of a *beyond-representational world* of both signs and signifiers, practices and artefacts - interrelationships that are not always contingent on the human. (p. 155)

More simply, the dynamic activity of observational filmmaking as research is a medium for the expression and understanding of Deweyian inspired conceptualisation of experience. This is a fluid epistemology where the methods used are the methodology and vice versa. In the empirical methods that I describe in Chapter 5, I will be, in effect, exploring pedagogy as the bridge between methodology and method.

Participatory Video in Arts Education Research

I have already described how in the learning sciences video material is most often viewed as data to be subsequently analysed (Derry et al., 2010; Goldman et al., 2007; Jewitt, 2012). I will now draw out some specific examples of participatory video in arts education research. Here it has been used as a component in pedagogy, an expository documentary form to represent ideas about social issues, and as a mechanism to give research participants a voice—see, for example, Barone (2003) and Stille (2011). As a contrast to video-as-data in education research, Wood and Brown (2012) provide a useful and nuanced review of the academic literature about art, science and documentary film. They echo, by reference to writers such as Sontag (1977), an argument that using a camera is necessarily a subjective participation and intervention in the world.

Barone (2003, p. 215) saw participant documentary filmmaking in an art education context as a process of enquiry, which can confront established educational imagery—"monolithic notions about schooling experiences". Barone (2003) describes the value of collaborative practices enabling participants to create documentaries that challenge accepted conventions. To do this, he sought to use formal narrative elements such as plot, characterisation and visual imagery to create film with participants, which was made to serve a significant, predetermined theme—for example, a challenge to dominant visual ideologies about school.

The narrative documentary approach is also adopted by Stille (2011). She describes how a documentary film process engaged elementary school pupils in portraying their local school community. Stille (2011) uses documentary filmmaking as a pedagogical tool that enabled pupils and their teacher to record children finding out about attitudes to the environment as they create a garden. There are interviews with the pupils, parents and teachers about the project. Just as with Barone (2003), the use of video is designed to produce outcomes that become a form of advocacy for a set of ideas the researcher wants to promote.

Barone (2003), Stille (2011), and Wood and Brown (2012) all present examples of *participatory* video research. This has been used as a methodology in different research disciplines for over twenty years (Milne, Mitchell, & De Lange, 2012). High, Singh, Petheram, and Nemes (2012) articulate the diversity of participatory video research by describing a number of research vignettes. However, they also restrict themselves to discussing documentary-style film and video making, which most often has the aim of addressing social issues (Milne et al., 2012).

However, there is an emergent challenge to participant video as a research methodology with an emancipatory agenda (Milne et al., 2012). Giving participants video cameras and respecting their agency within the research may be effective as an illuminating record of social issues. But when the researcher has a predetermined view on these issues and selects and edits material to reflect this view, the research outcomes are more likely to be reflecting the researcher's voice rather than that of the participants. This creates dissonance within the research methodology (Schuck & Kearney, 2006).

Pahl and Pool (2011) confront this methodological dissonance and the ethical concerns it highlights as they present an account that explores what happened when children were asked to enter an academic domain as co-researchers using video cameras. They discuss how participatory video is a way that children's voices can be represented in research but point out how children's epistemologies can be at odds with what adult researchers intended. The video material children shot and valued meant that, as researchers, Pahl and Pool (2011, p. 36) had to relinquish their adult qualitative methodological frameworks in favour of the children's demonstration of "living your life"—in other words, as researchers they had to "give up on our ideas" in order to respect the children's voices.

In the learning sciences, the predominant use of video material is as data for subsequent analysis. In a parallel tradition within education research, participatory video methods enable participants' voices to be heard. This material can also be analysed as data using social science techniques or used as evidence to reinforce documentary-style narratives that address social and political issues. The danger is that these methods tend to reflect researchers' pre-held views rather than participants' voices and the knowledge they may discover.

Concerning Children's Experiences

Sheila Greene and Malcolm Hill (2005) draw attention to potential paradigm clashes in how children are considered in a vast range of social scientific research: "It is evident that the predominant emphasis has been on children as objects of research rather than children as subjects, on child-related outcomes rather than child-related process and on child variables rather than children as persons" (p. 1). This indicates the wide range of potential research methodologies concerning children's experiences.

In this book, I am not focusing on methods that might be used to understand the rights, status or characteristics of children as individual people and how each person is part of a broader social dynamic. Neither am I looking in-depth at finding ways to understand the complex interrelated psychological experiences of *one* child in his or her experiences of his or her self, the world, and others. Although I am suggesting that observational filmmaking is helpful to explore children's experiences as they live an learn in school, I am not attempting to find methods to draw out the significance of children's experience in terms of developmental psychology, nor on whether, in a Goffmanesque sense, there are definable sociological forces underpinning the micro matters of how they get on with matters at hand. First and foremost, I am working out how best to research the 'child-related processes' of children's experience in school, keeping essential ineffable qualities in that experience alive and in the foreground throughout the research process. If I can do that well, those features of experience, such as the material and aesthetic, may become more available as researchable qualities across a broader spectrum of research concerning children.

Dictionary definitions of *experience* emphasise the consciousness of, or condition of, being affected by an event. If, as an example, children's learning in school is at hand, I am interested in children's experiences therein. These are circumstances that are inevitably sensory and material. Children are living beings in a physical word. Although there will be abstract thinking going on, it is clear, from an observational filmmaker's perspective, that there are forms of experience that cannot be satisfactorily constituted as a *discourse* of one kind or another. Therefore, forms of research that are limited to finding meaning through discourse analysis, for example, will miss much of the experiential force—and, therefore, the forms of thought—in how children are living and learning.

Social anthropologists argue that observation is a good place to start researching material qualities, which are part of children's experience. MacDougall's research demonstrates that children are able to share such experiential qualities in experience when it is they, rather than adults, who observe by operating cameras. Greene and Hill (2005) also appeal to observation as a starting point: "Thus observational studies may give us an entrée into children's experience if they show us ways in which children make efforts to understand and negotiate their worlds" (p. 6).

Through a review of film material presented in Chapters 1 and 2, it is possible sketch categories of children's experiences as they live and learn in school, which observational filmmaking is able to offer routes to new knowledge and understanding about, for example:

- Children's interaction with adults, including teachers.
- The made environment, especially schools, in which experiences take place.
- Interrelationships between children.
- How children's experience looks and feels whilst they are learning.
- Interplays between the natural and made environment as children live and learn in school.
- Experiences inside and outside.
- Children's relationships with objects, such as furniture and books.
- Communication, language and its interrelationship with material qualities of objects, the environment, other children etc.
- Playfulness and learning.
- Learning and living through time, such as the progression through a school day.
- Learning and technology.
- Children's experiences in respect of different teaching styles.

Children as Researchers

There is a significant body of education research in which children are active participants in the research because they have access to particular kinds of knowledge and experience; that is, the kinds of experience children have with which adults cannot easily directly engage (Alderson, 2008; Christensen & James, 2008; Kellett, 2010; Marsh & Richards, 2013). Within this body of work there are contrasting views about how to define degrees of children's participation in research. For example, Hart (1992) constructed a theoretical framework in terms of a hierarchical ladder. On the first rung, children are a token or decorative element in the research. However, as they, metaphorically speaking, climb the ladder, children may be increasingly informed and consulted about the research; until, on the final and eighth rung, they may initiate their own decisions in the research process and choose to share these with adults. On the other hand, Shier (2001) adopted a more flexible set of evaluative principles for children's participation by asking adult researchers to frame questions about openings for participatory research, opportunities for children in that research, and the obligations of adults. The definitional model advocated by Hart (1992) tends to pigeonhole approaches to researching with children. These might obviate the multi-dimensional slippage between the relative roles of adults and children that must be present. Shier's (2001) approach is adult focused in a way that diminishes a potential for agency, which might be present through children's voice as researchers. In contrast to both Hart and Shier, Lundy (2007) focuses on empowering children's voice and suggests that children can be offered space to express views, facilitated by adults, and listened to in a way that leads to action as appropriate. Marsh and Richards (2013) expand Lundy's empowerment framework by suggesting children should also be offered opportunities to reflect on the research process.

Kellet (2010) analyses such differences in conceptualising children's participation in research in terms of the relative forces of power and emancipation. Taking a social science perspective, she writes:

> The legitimacy of research into children's worlds and children's lived experiences where the research is conceived wholly from an adult perspective is open to challenge. The research questions they frame and the way in which they collect data are substantially different from adults and can offer valuable knowledge and insights. (p. 197)

In a paper which illustrates a number of opportunities and challenges that Kellet (2010) identifies, Marsh and Richards (2013) give an extended account of the use of video by one 11-year-old boy, a participant in their ethnographic study of children's playground games. This is set in the context of a number of different ways children used the 'Flip' camcorders. Children ran about wildly with the cameras, sometimes reflecting the excitement of taking part, at other times revealing nothing because the camera was pointing at the ground as they rushed about. On other occasions, brief portraits of a fragment of a game are recorded. The following researchers' comment reveals what they wished for: "some children's videos were also extremely informative as they consisted of extended observations of children's playground activities" (Marsh & Richards, 2013, p. 63). The camera also occasionally became an agent within the games and Marsh and Richards (2013) relate how the boy in question, Suavek, makes the camcorder an instrument of his play. He became absorbed in playing with the camera rather than using it to observe play as part of the collaborative research with the researchers. This, then, was not part of a remit to enquire into play, but a manifestation of play to share with the researchers.

The multifarious ways children used cameras in Marsh and Richard's (2013) project illustrates the potential for participant researchers and participants in the research to misunderstand each other. Consumers of the research are also likely to be less clear about what was going on and why. For example, the adult model of social science research may conflict with a view of children's right to express a view and take an agential position (Marsh & Richards, 2013). Whether children can be said to be 'experts' on their experiences or are simply conduits through which adults can gain expertise through sharing in those experiences is another open question.

There is a necessary reflexive complexity when considering children as researchers or participant researchers. To highlight three areas for consideration: first, there are ethical concerns in relation to the powerful role an adult researcher may have in relation to the children who are taking part in the research. In what sense children are free, or not, to take decisions within the research process was often blurred in practice. Secondly, the rights of children and the adult's responsibility to protect children can be in conflict. Thirdly, epistemologically speaking, children's experience can significantly inform research; however, it is not always at all clear in what sense and to what degree it is the child or the adult perspective that is present in the research outcomes.

Marsh and Richards (2013) publish a number (for example, MPJM2011-12-21) which, as Marsh (2012) notes in a sister article, "refers to the file name of the original data, which are stored at the British Library for researchers to access" (p. 520). Additionally, a few short video extracts from Marsh and Richard's project are available on the British Library 'Playtimes' website. The videos are presented as archival material about aspects of playground games. The status of the video material, who shot it and how, is not at all clear. This demonstrates that Marsh and Richards see the video material as data to support their research narrative and they deliberately place it at a distance from consumers of the research. They also control how the video material is interpreted through text.

In contrast, in the children's films referenced towards the close of Chapter 2, it is immediately apparent that the nature of the *collaborative* relationship between child and adult researcher is at the epicentre of the research practice. The adult researcher's influence is everywhere to be seen in the style of camera use and the choices made when editing. Yet, the underlying pedagogy that supported and enabled children to learn about observational filming as a practice has also liberated them to share with us powerful insights into their experiences. The child and the researcher have co-created a practice to which they both openly contribute. Notably, the researcher does not ask us to read any explanatory or interpretive text about the film material—the films are simply published as they are. Of course, other academic commentators write about what children have filmed and how they went about it. I have found it fascinating to witness how MacDougall's observational film outcomes generate a significant amount of related debate about children's experiences and the circumstances they show. If the research community wants to insist on labelling MacDougall's films as 'data', then this 'data' retains its integrity as film material. It becomes an essential and indissoluble component of knowledge creation as text based comment, critique and interpretation interrelate with it.

I suggest that the techniques of observation with cameras developed over decades within social anthropology, together with the most recent developments empowering children to be observational filmmakers, should impact on the work of any education researcher concerned with children's experience. This is especially because the potential of children as researchers and with the way digital video technologies are available as practical investigative research tools are intermeshed. This book intends to contribute to a process of drawing together the two separate research practices of observational filmmaking in social anthropology and audio-visual participant research with children in education.

Conclusion

This chapter has touched on a range of theoretical and methodological domains, which might inform and challenge observational filmmaking in education. Each of the sections highlights an area for critical discourse that might intersect with my adoption of experiential empiricism through research methodologies and methods encompassed by observational filmmaking. I suggest that the breadth of academic and intellectual practices found in this chapter is not surprising given just how varying notions of epistemology, experience and, now for over 100 years, the presence of audio-visual media as a form of representation, are pervasive in humanistic and artistic cultural forms.

The problem I have highlighted is that the use of scientifically orientated research methods, however qualitative, to explore essential material, aesthetic and affective phenomena in experiences as children live and learn are likely to miss those phenomena. Consequently, before I can begin to inquire into children's experiences, I needed to establish just how to go about the research so that material, aesthetic and affective phenomena are not lost or veiled. This book is partly about just how observational filmmaking might be developed as a potential methodology and method for education research to addresses that problem.

Therefore, a practical approach to observational filmmaking in schools and with children might be said to intersect in various ways with issues found within ideas about phenomenology, empathy, aesthetics, observation, ethnography, filmmaking, technology in research, arts-based research, video used as data, video as a method, participatory video research, children's experiences, and children as researchers. There will be other headings that other academics might prefer or demand, but these were the significant ones in developing my understanding.

However, if I am to remain close to a philosophy of inquiry founded in the experiential empiricism I set out in Chapter 2, then I must set prioritisation of those ideas well to one side and go on to what happens when observational filmmaking is explored as a method to research children's experiences as they live and learn in school. I suggest that it is only by collapsing theory into practice and practice into theory that it will be possible to more completely know and thoroughly understand how that might work.

However, before I set out a detailed example, in the form of a generalised guide, of a possible observational filmmaking practice for children, teachers and researchers, I now turn, in Chapter 4, to explore ethical dilemmas which surround such a practice, especially one in which children may be both the observed subjects and also the observers of their own and others' experiences.

References

Alderson, P. (2008). *Young children's rights: Exploring beliefs*. London: Jessica Kingsley Publishers.
Barone, T. (2003). Challenging the educational imaginary: Issues of form, substance, and quality in film-based research. *Qualitative Inquiry, 9,* 202–217.
Barone, T., & Eisner, E. (2012). *Arts based research*. Thousand Oaks, CA: Sage.
Bourriaud, N. (2002). *Relational aesthetics* (Trans. S. Pleasance & F. Woods with the participation of M. Copeland). Paris: Les presses du reel (Original work published in French in 1998).
Breyer, T., & Gutland, C. (Eds.). (2015). *Phenomenology of thinking: Philosophical investigations into the character of cognitive experiences*. New York: Routledge.
Christensen, P., & James, A. (2008). *Research with children: Perspectives and practices*. New York, NY: Routledge.
Coplan, A., & Goldie, P. (Eds.). (2014). *Empathy: Philosophical and psychological perspectives*. Oxford: Oxford University Press.
Dalston, L., & Lunbeck, E. (2011). *Histories of scientific observation*. Chicago: University of Chicago Press.
de Bolla, P. (2001). *Art matters*. Cambridge, MA: Harvard University Press.
Deleuze, G. (2001). *Pure immance*. New York: Zone Books.
Depew, D. (2005). Empathy, psychology, and aesthetics: Reflections on a repair concept. *Poroi, 4*(1), 99–107.

Derry, S., Pea, R., Barron, B., Engle, A., Erickson, F., Goldman, R., ... Sherin, B. (2010). Conducting video research in the learning sciences: Guidance on selection, analysis, technology and ethics. *Journal of the Learning Sciences, 19*(1), 3–53.

Dewey, J. (1931). Qualitative thought. In J. Boydston (Ed.), *John Dewey the later works, 1925–1953* (Vol. 5, 1988). Carbondale: Southern Illinois University Press.

Dewey, J. (1934). Art as experience. In J. Boydston (Ed.), *John Dewey the later works, 1925–1953* (Vol. 10, 1988). Carbondale: Southern Illinois University Press.

Dewey, J. (1938). Theory of inquiry. In J. Boydston (Ed.), *John Dewey the later works, 1925–1953* (Vol. 12, 1988). Carbondale: Southern Illinois University Press.

Eisner, E. (1998). *The enlightened eye, qualitative inquiry and the enhancement of educational practice*. Columbus: Prentice Hall.

Feld, S. (2003). Editor's introduction. In. S. Feld (Ed.), *Cine-ethnography—Jean Rouch* (pp. 1–28). Minneapolis: University of Minnesota Press.

Glock, H. (2008). *What is analytic philosophy?* Cambridge: Cambridge University Press.

Goldman, R., Pea, R., Barron, B., & Derry, S. (Eds.). (2007). *Video research in the learning sciences*. New York: Routledge.

Gombrich, E. (1961). *Art and illusion: A study in the psychology of pictorial representation*. Princetown: Princetown University Press.

Greene, S., & Hill, M. (2005). Why research children's experience. In S. Greene & D. Hogan (Eds.), *Researching children's experience: Methods and approaches* (pp. 1–21). London: Sage.

Grimshaw, A., & Ravetz, A. (2009). *Observational cinema: Anthropology, film, and the exploration of social life*. Bloomington, IN: Indiana University Press.

Grimshaw, A., & Ravetz, A. (2015). Drawing with a camera? *Ethnographic Film and Transformative Anthropology, 21*(1), 255–275.

Halpern, J. (2001). *From detached concern to empathy: Humanizing medical practice*. Oxford: Oxford University Press.

Harper, D. (2012). *Visual sociology*. London: Routledge.

Harris, A. (2016). *Video as method*. Oxford: Oxford University Press.

Hart, R. (1992). *Children's participation: From tokenism to citizenship*. Florence: UNICEF.

Hickman, R. (2008). The nature of research in art and design. In R. Hickman (Ed.), *Research in art and design education* (pp. 15–24). Bristol: Intellect.

Hickman, R. (2010). *Why we make art and why it is taught*. Bristol: Intellect.
High, C., Singh, N., Petheram, L., & Nemes, G. (2012). Defining participatory video from practice. In E.-J. Milne, C. Mitchell, & N. De Lange (Eds.), *The handbook of participatory video* (pp. 38–45). Lanham, MD: AltaMira Press.
Hoey, B. (2014). *A simple introduction to the practice of ethnography and guide to ethnographic fieldnotes*. Huntington: Marshall University Digital Scholar.
Hollan, D., & Throop, J. (Eds.). (2011). *The anthropology of empathy: Experiencing the lives of others in Pacific societies*. Oxford: Berghahn Press.
Iacoboni, M. (2008). *Mirroring people: The new science of how we connect with others*. New York: Straus and Giroux.
Ingold, T. (2007). *Lines: A brief history*. Oxford: Routledge.
Ingold, T. (2011). *Being alive: Essays on movement, knowledge and description*. London: Routledge.
Ingold, T. (2013). *Making: Anthropology, archaeology, art and architecture*. London: Routledge.
Iphofen, R. (2013). *Research ethics in ethnography/anthropology*. European Commission, DG Research and Innovation. Retrieved July 13, 2017, from http://ec.europa.eu/research/participants/data/ref/h2020/other/hi/ethics-guide-ethnog-anthrop_en.pdf.
Irwin, R. (2004). A/r/tography: A metonymic métissage. In R. Irwin & A. de Cosson (Eds.), *A/r/tography: Rendering self through arts-based living inquiry* (pp. 27–40). Vancouver, BC: Pacific Educational Press.
Irwin, R. (2008). A/r/tography. In L. Given (Ed.), *The SAGE encyclopedia of qualitative research methods* (pp. 26–28). Los Angeles: Sage.
Jewitt, C. (2012). *An introduction to using video for research* (NCRM Working Paper). London: NCRM.
Kellett, M. (2010). Small shoes, big steps! Empowering children as active researchers. *American Journal of Community Psychology, 46*(1), 195–203.
Kogler, H., & Stueber, K. (2000). Introduction: Empathy, simulation, and interpretation in the philosophy of the social sciences. In K. R. Stueber & H. H. Kogaler (Eds.), *Empathy and agency: The problem of understanding in the human sciences* (pp. 1–61). Boulder: Westview Press.
Kuhn, A., & Westwell, G. (Eds.). (2012). *Oxford dictionary of film studies*. Oxford: Oxford University Press.
Lundy, L. (2007). 'Voice' is not enough: Conceptualising Article 12 of the United Nations convention on the rights of the child. *British Educational Research Journal, 33*(6), 927–942.

MacDougall, D. (2006). *The corporeal image: Film, ethnography, and the senses*. Princeton, NJ: Princeton University Press.

MacDougall, D. (Director). (2007). *SchoolScapes* (Motion Picture). Australia: Centre for Cross-Cultural Research, Australian National University.

Margulies, A. (1989). *The empathic imagination*. New York: W.W. Norton.

Marsh, J. (2012). Children as knowledge brokers of playground games and rhymes in the new media age. *Childhood, 19*(4), 508–522.

Marsh, J., & Richards, C. (2013). Children as researchers. In R. Willett, C. Richards, J. Marsh, A. Burn, & J. Bishop (Eds.), *Children, media and playground cultures* (pp. 51–67). Basingstoke: Palgrave.

Miller, P. (2013). *Cultural histories of the material world*. Ann Arbor: University of Michigan Press. Retrieved November 21, 2016, from Project MUSE database https://muse.jhu.edu/book/25312.

Milne, E., Mitchell, C., & De Lange, N. (Eds.). (2012). *The handbook of participatory video*. Lanham, MD: AltaMira Press.

Pahl, K., & Pool, S. (2011). Living your life because it's the only life you've got. *Qualitative Research Journal, 11*(2), 17–37.

Pariser, D. (2013). Who needs arts-based research? In F. Hernández-Hernández & R. Fendler (Eds.), *1st conference on arts-based and artistic research: Critical reflections on the intersection of art and research* (pp. 62–69). Barcelona, Spain: University of Barcelona.

Pink, S. (2001). *Doing visual ethnography: Images, media, and representation in research*. London: Sage.

Pink, S. (2007). *Doing visual ethnography*. London: Sage.

Pink, S. (2013). *Doing visual ethnography* (3rd ed. expanded and revised). London: Sage.

Rose, G. (2012). *Visual methodologies: An introduction to researching with visual materials*. London: Sage.

Saldaña, J. (2005). *Ethnodrama: An anthology of reality theatre*. Walnut Creek, CA: AltaMira Press.

Sandall, R. (1972). Observation and identity. *Sight and Sound, 41*(4), 192–196.

Sennett, R. (2008). *The craftsman*. New Haven: Yale University Press.

Schuck, S., & Kearney, M. (2006). Using digital video as a research tool: Ethical issues for researchers. *Journal of Educational Multimedia and Hypermedia, 15*(4), 447–463.

Shier, T. (2001). Pathways to participation: Openings opportunities and obligations. *Children and Society, 15*(2), 102–117.

Siegesmund, R. (2012). Dewey through a/r/tography. *Visual Arts Research Journal, 38*(2), 99–109.
Sobchack, V. (1992). *The address of the eye: A phenomenology of film experience.* Princeton, NJ: Princeton University Press.
Sontag, S. (1977). *On photography.* London: Penguin.
Springgay, S., Irwin, R. L., Leggo, C., & Gouzouasis, P. (Eds.). (2008). *Being with a/r/tography.* Rotterdam, The Netherlands: Sense.
Stille, S. (2011). Framing representations: Documentary filmmaking as participatory approach to research inquiry. *Journal of Curriculum and Pedagogy, 8*(2), 101–108.
Strawson, G. (2011). Cognitive phenomenology: Real life. In T. Beayne & M. Montague (Eds.), *Cognitive phenomenology* (pp. 285–325). Oxford: Oxford University Press.
Stueber, K. R. (2006). *Rediscovering empathy: Agency, folk psychology, and the human sciences.* Cambridge: MIT Press.
Taussig, M. (2009). *What color is the sacred?* Chicago: University of Chicago Press.
Taussig, M. (2011). *I swear I saw this: Drawings in fieldwork notebooks, namely my own.* Chicago: University of Chicago Press.
Wolcott, H. (2008). *Ethnography: A way of seeing.* Lanham, MD: AltaMira Press.
Wood, M., & Brown, S. (2012). Film-based creative arts enquiry: Qualitative researchers as auteurs. *Qualitative Research Journal, 12*(1), 130–147.

4
Ethics

Introduction

Academic writers about education research and those who discuss pedagogy (particularly when adults teach children) address ethics. Indeed, they must, since teaching or researching others, especially children, often implies a difference in status and power. Power can not only be abused, freedoms curtailed and choices prescribed but research outcomes or what is learnt by pupils can be severely skewed by a failure to recognise the effect of the powerful position from which teachers or researchers are operating in respect of children.

Take the education researcher who places a video camera on a tripod at the back of a classroom to collect data about the interaction, say, between a teacher and pupils. Whether or not pupils are helped to sufficiently understand why there is a camera recording the lesson and what will happen to such recordings, there is an assumption that this is a form of science. The objectivity implicit in such scientificity is expressed in the researcher's intent to arrive at 'true' definitions of the pupils and teacher's behaviour and communication. This intended objectivity is powerful. Both the pupils and the teacher are objects of research. The data that is produced necessarily confines their behaviour and communication into analysable categories. In this case the powerful position the researcher assumes in respect of the objects (the humans) under research is less able to encompass lived qualities in their experience. This is because by using objectivity and scientificity to distance the researcher's subjectivity from those under examination, the researcher is less likely to understand the lived experience of others as humans. The researcher is too far away, both literally and metaphorically.

Of course, reducing experience to categories of analysable data may help answer certain kinds of questions. The point here is that an awareness of ethical issues tangential to the research processes are needed to appreciate the very narrow parameters of knowledge sought after asking certain kinds of questions. In my experience, such a limiting and objectifying of children's experience as they live and learn in school distances education research from what happens in classrooms. Most teachers, in practice, pay little attention to research. It has little to do with their experience of how children live and learn.

Video Ethnography and Ethics

I have already argued that from the standpoint of ethnographic observational filmmaking in social anthropology, the subjectivity of the researcher is not only welcome, it is essential. Moreover, an observational camera operated by a person is animal in origin (MacDougall, 2006). It looks at, adjusts its point of view, shifts attention and decides what to focus on with the perceptual and conceptual mind of the person (the animal) that operates it. The artefacts, the images that are made, embody thoughts, feelings and perceptions not only of the subjects portrayed but also the maker of those images. These, as MacDougall (2006, 2011) suggests, are corporeal images and are inherently reflexive. They are "not just the images of other bodies, they are also images of the body behind the camera and its relations with the world" (2006, p. 3).

But completed images are separated from us and have independence; they are deliberately made to be about something. This implies that decisions have been made *about* what is recorded (and then shown) and *how* that process has been undertaken. What was seen through the camera has been framed and organised and whoever views that when editing is also framing and organising what and how that image is seen. In other words, however corporeal filmed images may be, they must also, especially when produced for viewing, be cognitive. If MacDougall's challenge to filmmakers is to create structures "in which being is allowed to live, not only in isolated glimpses but in moments of revelation through the whole work" (2006, p. 5), then the power and status of the filmmaker who is able to allow a being to 'live' in filmic outcomes must be clearly acknowledged. Therefore, the shades of a reflexive awareness of the imbalance in relations between adult and child, in circumstances when children might be deemed to be co-researchers or co-filmmakers with adults or filming independently of adults, must be considered.

To put another way, the combination of record, embodied personality and communicability means the video ethnography of observational filmmaking must confront issues such as anonymity, privacy and exploitation. Digital video is readily sharable. There are obvious concerns about how children's video material is used. However, those same qualities of easily accessible representations in audio-visual form may also naturally be used to create communities of filmmakers and their audience, all of whom are able, in principle, to collaborate, review, analyse and interpret what they see and hear. Unlike text, there are immediate, tangible, material images to share, about which even very young children can readily engage and comment. This is useful. That benefit must be set in a positive balance against the inevitable dangers.

But in a broader frame, the more distanced treatment of video as data creates different ethical issues. Although an implicit objectivity might be a welcome outcome of data analysis, if outcomes are interpreted and represented in textual forms, then the distance between the researched circumstance and the consumer of the research is considerable, even if the intention is different. So, although outcomes from data-focused research processes may be understood by an academic reader, those outcomes are disconnected from real world circumstances for participants (especially children) and potential beneficiaries (such as teachers).

An ethical discussion must include the limiting exclusivity of the academic form of much social science research.

In another strand of argument, subjectivity is not solely a feature of observational filmmaking as a potential research practice, there is inevitable subjectivity in collecting *video-as-data* with ethnographic methods. Even placing a camera on a tripod at the back of a classroom is a subjective decision. This means it is essential to produce a multilayered reflexive and ethical discussion, which is opens the specific practice of using video in a particular project to scrutiny. This is partly so that the user of the research is able to grasp the nature of the knowledge that has been created, how it came into being and its relative objectivity and, partly, to protect participants from exploitation. A danger is that these discussions can become complex methodological nuances, which—if reflected in the methods and how these are described—mean that the research can be difficult to understand even within the academic community.

Ethical debates about using digital video, whether as research data for analysis or as part of an observational filmmaking process, ought to be bound into the status and characteristics of the knowledge—by whom it is made, how it is produced and how it might be used. That is, in relation to observational filmmaking, ethical debates might be best pragmatically located more in methods and outcomes and less in theoretical methodological discourse or sets of hard and fast ethical rules.

Ethical Principles and Video-Based Research with Children

There are two approaches whose strands inevitably interweave in both the theory and practice of research and teaching. It is possible to argue from a principled position—there should be a set of ethical principles that are followed. Or one can argue from a situated stance—in teaching or research—that what happens and why that happens should be addressed in terms of the unique situation that pertains in each case. Therefore, principles and the particularities of practice each bear on an ethical discussion of observational filmmaking for education, whether as pedagogy or as research, and whether it is children, teachers or researchers who are using cameras and editing films.

Here is one example of how academic writers attempt to generalise an ethical approach, which might be applied across varying research circumstances. This is a 'check list' but it is quite different from situated ethical issues about a particular visual based research circumstance. I have adapted it from Marion and Crowder (2013). There are quite a few other approaches. I personally found this slant a useful prompt when critically examining my own practice and the kinds of filmic outcomes exemplified in Chapters 1 and 2. This intersects with a more situated series of questions and answers, an example of which concludes this chapter.

- Who has authority in how children's experiences are represented in film? How is the triadic research relationship between filmmakers, subjects and audiences acknowledged?
- There may be a problem of a decontextualization of film material (and stills taken from that material) when viewed out of context. This raises the issue of an inevitable lack of control in respect of when and how filmic images are shown. Audiences bring their own values to viewing films, which clash with the values of the filmmakers.
- Certain outcomes may be presumed when sharing observational film of others but the actual effect of such sharing may be different than what was hoped or intended.
- What are the relations and responsibilities towards research, pedagogy, the communities and individuals taking part?
- Is it possible to balance privacy versus the general values of sharing video in public? What are the subjects' wishes? What are the camera users' wishes? Are children able to express what they feel about sharing video material they appear in or shot? Should children be able to veto the sharing of video material that was recorded during research or as part of a curriculum in school?
- That last issue illustrates the importance of communication with and consent of subjects/communities at every stage in the research process. How is communication between all participants established and maintained throughout the process?

- There are broader issues in the practice of working with the ubiquitous presence of digital materials. These intersect with general concerns about the collection and dissemination of visual materials about children within the context of globally expanding media savvy and experience.

There is a lot to consider. There is a danger that over thinking an observational film project with layers of nuanced ethical rumination may inhibit what happens. But the alternative is also problematic. For example, Ricki Goldman (2007) writing from a social science perspective, articulates a powerful reminder to balance any brazen advocacy of unfettered use of video in education research:

> As travellers and tourists in unknown classrooms, educational researchers are now armed with cameras and handhelds to explore every nook and cranny of the classroom, zooming here and there, observing the real lives of children and teachers in their habitat [...] based in a world view that encourages us to shoot, capture, dissect and organise. (p. 33)

In this way, and to cut through to an expression of ethical issues in a simpler from than my adaption from Marion and Crowder above, questions are raised about the kind of knowledge audio-visual recording facilitates in a research context. How and what is known becomes an ethical issue with questions about how video is recorded; how researchers interact with participants in the circumstances of the research; and how the resulting video material is used.

In the previous chapters cameras can be powerful, but also cameras can be an extension of the person using them. In that sense cameras are no more or less powerful than the person using them in relation to others in the same shared circumstances. Whether a researcher is the director and originator of an ethnographic project, as well as a camera user or trainer of camera users, inevitably, subjectivity is an overwhelming quality. This means that video-based ethnography "is personal, close-up and affected by the views of those who videotape and direct the video camera's lens" (Goldman, 2007, p. 26). This is the case no matter who uses the cameras. The connection between the filmmaker and those being filmed bonds both in a relationship in the shared circumstance where filming is taking place. It is personal.

That close-up and personal trait in video research about others does not sit so easily with a tendency to assume that being "ethically pure" is a welcome objective and best achieved by following good ethical principles (Hill, 2005, p. 65). Given the experiential empirical underpinning this book (inspired by the philosophy of Deweyan experience drawn out in Chapter 2) that observational filmmaking can contribute to education research and classroom pedagogy, then both the concepts of purity and a drive towards defining principles are definitely secondary concerns for my ethical position. Thus, I will go on further down to draw on the now well-rehearsed arguments in the field for a *situated* approach to ethics as this thesis unfolds.

However, when reviewing Hill's (2005) chapter outlining ethical considerations in researching children's experiences, I realised that his principled approach also provided (just as that of Marion and Crowder cited above) another very useful set of reminders and prompts which can begin to inform ethical practice during my research enquiries. In articulating his stance on ethics, Hill (2005) acknowledges Alderson (1995). Hill (2005) summarises his approach in terms of two very general principles to guide ethics for research that aims to explore children's experiences. Firstly, researchers should consider children's wellbeing, protection, and children's choices about participation. Secondly, children should be informed about the research and the contribution it intends to make and that their contribution matters.

One issue Hill (2005) examines in that context is should children have an equal voice in what happens in research about their learning experiences; if so, how are their interests best understood and incorporated into research practice? Or, should researchers acknowledge that children and adults are not equal and so accept that children's agency is limited in the context of research concerning their experiences? Traditionally, especially considering research *on* children, children may be objects or subjects of research. In contrast, more recent research has explored children as social actors and extended this to value children as active participants and co-researchers (Christensen & Prout, 2002).

The UN Convention on the Rights of the Child supports the view that children are social actors who have the right to participate in activities that affect them, including research. Children should be listened to, consulted, informed and, wherever possible, actively involved. If this ethical imperative is accepted, then this will influence the way an adult researcher conducts research concerning children's experiences and the relationship with children in the research process. This ethical position puts a further stress on the scientificity of education research, which is asking for a degree of objectivity, generalisability and replicability in order to satisfy the demands from politicians and policy makers for clear evidence to support, for example, classroom teaching practices. The welcome respect offered to children as they are increasingly invited to actively participate in research comes into a dissonant relationship with the scientificity of education research. As Christensen and Prout (2002) comment about the wide-ranging debates, "this does not merely *add* to the complexity of the field, but rather *multiplies* it" (p. 482, emphasis as in the original).

Children and adults as groupings of humanity have similarities but are also different from each other. Adults have responsibility for children's welfare and happiness, which will include understanding more about them and how they can better be supported in their learning and development. This is not a symmetrical relationship. Children are not responsible for adults in the same way. There are differences, not only in power, but status (Hill, 2005). Christensen and Prout (2002) reflect a broad consensus amongst those who research with children when they advocate a dialogue between researchers and children. They write: "Key to this is the challenge of taking responsibility for children [...] such a stance means entering a dialogue that recognises both intra- and intergenerational commonality but honours difference" (p. 495). In this context, although general ethical guidelines may have a role in focusing researchers' attention on elements in the wide-ranging ethical domain, in the end, the emphasis is on the "individual responsibility and personal skills of the researcher through developing a constant sensitive and reflexive approach in his or her practice" (Christensen & Prout, 2002, p. 495). So inevitably, general issues will always be coloured by the specific circumstance. For example, where research in school and classrooms is at stake there are many specific questions that might be asked about the research in respect of the school or the specific class. If the research is taking place in families, then how is the wider set of family members and friends included or excluded in considering the research? It is only within the specific circumstances of the research that talking and communicating with children and their adult carers, and listening to them and acting on what they wish for and advise, that an effective and ethical process is possible.

An Example of a Situated Ethical Practice

In this final section of this chapter, I will describe an example of a situated ethical practice in the particular circumstances of an observational filmmaking project in a Barcelona primary school. Previously in this chapter, I discussed research ethics with regard to video ethnography, participant research with children and a broader debate concerning power and responsibility regarding children in research. I will return to a series of ethical questions, which might be amongst those which researchers, teachers and, indeed children should be asking as they embark on a project which involves observing others with video cameras. Here, I will give a specific response to those kinds of question that my research colleagues, the school's teachers, the children and I all considered and talked about as we collaborated to share in a developing observational filmmaking project.

The project began in the autumn of 2017. I worked as a visiting researcher with the University of Barcelona Department of Fine Art to initiate an observational filmmaking project in a Barcelona city-centre primary school, *Escola Dovella*. The project set out to explore children's experiences as learners through observational filmmaking techniques. Inspired by David MacDougall's *Childhood and Modernity* project, and by my own experiences working with children in Cambridge (UK), we set out to introduce some of the principles of observational filmmaking to the Grado Sexto class (Sixth Grade). These children are between 10 and 12 years old. Part of the curriculum in Escola Dovella is a process of reflexion and self-reflexion on what it is to be a learner and how children learn. The project as pedagogy fitted with that aim. In terms of research, we wanted to explore what happens when children are enabled to use observational techniques to film, independently of adults, children's experiences living and learning, especially but not exclusively in school. An essential component of setting up the project was the discussion with children, teachers, parents and university-based researchers about ethical principles and practices. The questions that follow are examples of what was considered and were inspired by an approach adopted by Hill (2005).

If children are taking part in an observational filmmaking project, either using the camera or being filmed, then does the purpose of the project also serve their interests?

In general terms, if children participating as observational filmmakers for an education research method contributes to understanding more about children's experiences in school, then children's interests will be served. In specific terms, the whole of Grado Sexto (sixth grade) learnt about research and took part in observational filmmaking workshops. Children learnt about operating cameras and a technique of filming. They also learnt about qualities, strategies and responsibilities concerned with observing others and being observed. The teachers, children and I thought that this did serve their interests as children as they lived and learnt in school.

How do any risks for children stack up against potential benefits?

I judged that there were few risks to children in this project. Video material is easily shareable, but all the recorded material was stored on encrypted drives. For individual filming, children had charge of their own individual flash memory cards. These were labelled and stored in school. Filmic outcomes were uploaded to a secure on-line platform where it might be shared only with specific people and with password access. Children were also shown how to delete material that they were unhappy with directly in the camera. Any risks to the children were managed, there was awareness amongst all participants, including children, of risks and these were more than compensated for by the benefits as set out in the previous paragraph.

Are children able to choose to take part and can they withdraw from situations in the project without prejudice to their rights and opportunities?

Yes, all children could opt out of filming or being filmed at any time. Children talked about how it felt to be filmed and how it felt to be filming. They told the camera user if they felt uncomfortable being filmed. They looked out for signs of discomfort in others being filmed. If they were unsure, filming would stop, but in Grado Sexto, they would still continue benefiting from taking part in the project as a whole, even if they did not want to be in front of or behind the camera lens, taking an active role in filming. In practice, none of the children in Grado Sexto chose not to be filmed.

Are all children in principle included or if some are excluded, why is this?

All children were included. As this was initially a class project and considered a contribution to learning, and because children were in school and teachers organise the learning day, this class were obliged to take part at the start. In relation to both research aims and pedagogy the relative acquiescence of children to the power of adults, particularly in the context of formal education in schools, is a powerful factor in the nature of any outcomes.

Does the project draw on resources normally available to children, such as materials, time and energy? If so, are children aware of any 'cost' to them? Are they 'compensated'? Are any 'transactions' such as this open and acknowledged by all?

Cameras and other technology were provided by the researcher, the University of Barcelona and through the school's existing capacities, so there was no drain on school resources. The initial workshops took place in school time. Both the head teacher and class teacher were positive about the benefits to the children regardless of the research project.

Can children have an input in what happens during the project?

Yes, the children increasingly determined much of what happened during the workshop sessions. That is what they filmed and, increasingly, how they filmed was down to them. However, the overall structure of the first sequence of workshops and the structure of how each individual workshop unfolded (for example, the balance between, instruction, discussion and action was planned by the adults). The aim was to introduce observational filmmaking to children so that they might gradually be able to film independently in an observational style independently of adults.

Are any parents or carers and adults in loco parentis (such as teachers) able to voice opinions and concerns about what will and what does happen?

Yes, teachers and a researcher from the University of Barcelona discussed the project with parents and carers at a meeting before the project began. In this case, there was strong support for the initial workshops for the whole of Grado Sexto. However it was emphasised that any doubts or concerns arising as the project unfolded must be shared with the school.

What safeguards are in place to protect children?

The class teacher, head teacher and researchers from the University of Barcelona each took an overview of what was happening as the project unfolded from their perspective. There was constant and open dialogue with children who were encouraged to speak openly about any doubts or issues they might have. A line of communication was always open for parents and carers should they wish to raise anything about the project. Video files were kept on encrypted or password protected drives.

In deciding whether to take part in the research are children fully informed about the project? Does that also apply to everyone involved?

Yes, as the lead organiser of the project I visited Grado Sexto some weeks before the project began, specifically to talk at length with them about education research, observational filmmaking and to hear their opinions and views.

Who takes the final decision to take part – the child, the teacher, or the parent/carer? Is there any pressure applied, overt or covert, so that children take part?

The initial workshops were programmed as part of the curriculum in school lesson time. Therefore, for Grado Sexto as a whole it was the class teacher and head teacher who decided that the project would be of benefit to the class. Children could not opt out of the workshops as they were considered part of the school curriculum, although they could opt out of filming or being filmed. The subsequent use of video cameras by individual children to film their and others' experiences living and learning in school was voluntary. Children's rights to take part or not to take part either as camera users or when being filmed were respected. As the project progressed and video work happened outside of formal lessons, participation was voluntary.

Especially where video is concerned there are issues in terms of how any resulting material is used and disseminated. Are all the stakeholders aware of how the research might be used? Do they agree?

The parents and carers of children who were filming or being filmed were asked explicitly for permission to use any film outcomes in presentations and publications related to the project. I specifically returned to ask the Grado Sexto children and parents for permission to use material they shot. Any future outcomes for use as illustrations in conferences or publications would be on a secure password protected Vimeo platform. An option can be set to prevent any download of this material.

What is the impact of the project on children, both in the particular sense of individuals taking part and in the potential broader sense of practices and policy for classrooms, schools and pedagogical practice in the school in general?

The impact on individual children was strong. They commented on how they enjoyed and benefited from the project and about how much they had learnt about video camera use and the ethics of observing others with cameras. I and the class teacher believed that observational filmmaking, both in theoretical and practical terms, may be able to impact positively on children's experiences when learning and living in school.

Conclusion

The preceding ethical commentary raises issues about agency and power. Those issues lie at the heart of observational filmmaking both as research and as pedagogy. Questions arise. For example: Could methods of observational filmmaking, such as those advocated in this book, help children share knowledge about children's experiences, which are veiled by conventional education research practices and classroom pedagogy? Are children sharing their own and other children's experiences or merely sharing experiences that adults have generated especially for them to share? Although that last question may suggest a pressing critique, the special circumstances created by observational filmmaking methods may be more beneficial than harmful in respect of certain kinds of knowledge. For example, as children participate making observational filmmaking in school, pathways may open to understanding experiences, such as the affective, material and aesthetic experiences of others, which are largely inaccessible through other education practices. If that is the case, the development of this research craft—through understanding a tool and practising its use—may offer the deep penetration into certain specific contexts that case study advocates such as Flyvbjerg (2001, 2004) value so highly.

References

Alderson, P. (1995). *Listening to children*. London: Barnardos.
Christensen, P., & Prout, A. (2002). Working with ethical symmetry in social research with children. *Childhood, 9*(4), 477–497.
Flyvbjerg, B. (2001). *Making social science matter: Why social inquiry fails and how it can succeed again*. Cambridge: Cambridge University Press.
Flyvbjerg, B. (2004). Phronetic planning research: Theoretical and methodological reflections. *Planning Theory & Practice, 5*(3), 283–306.
Goldman, R. (2007). Video representations & the perspectivity framework: Epistemology, ethnography, evaluation, and ethics. In R. Goldman, R. Pea, B. Barron, & S. Derry (Eds.), *Video research in the learning sciences* (pp. 3–37). New York: Routledge.
Hill, M. (2005). Ethical considerations in researching children's experiences. In S. Greene & D. Hogan (Eds.), *Researching children's experience: Methods and approaches* (pp. 61–86). London: Sage.
MacDougall, D. (2006). *The corporeal image: Film, ethnography, and the senses*. Princeton, NJ: Princeton University Press.
MacDougall, D. (2011). Anthropological filmmaking: An empirical art. In E. Margolis & L. Pauwels (Eds.), *The SAGE handbook of visual research methods* (pp. 99–114). London: Sage.
Marion, J., & Crowder, W. (2013). *Visual research*. New York: Bloomsbury.

5

Camera Work and Editing for Children, Teachers and Researchers

Introduction

It is possible to view the Indian children's films (referenced at the very start of Chapter 1 and towards the close of Chapter 2) by considering how it was that these children came to film in that way. Clearly, the films exist because children collaborated with adults and other children. Equally significant is that they are using cameras in a particular way. An adult taught, demonstrated, discussed and challenged the child filmmakers. The children were asked to think carefully about what they wanted to film and why. Therefore, they had a definite subject in mind before they began filming. Children knew they were collaborating in a research project and that their work with the camera would likely add to knowledge about their lives and experiences as children. In order for them to understand that and in order to be able to film independently, the adult taught the children. Children practiced what they had learnt. This was not necessarily in a formal way within a curriculum structure, but nevertheless deliberate pedagogy was involved. This chapter unpacks ways in which pedagogy may aid researchers, teachers and children use cameras and editing software for research and learning.

An implicit theme that runs through this book is that pedagogy and research methods are inevitably interwoven. This chapter is orientated around pedagogy, firstly because what children chose to film and how they film is hugely influenced by any pedagogical intervention and secondly because how teachers and researches may embrace observational filmmaking will also depend on how they, as learners, come to learn and practise the craft needed to use cameras and editing software in an observational style. In other words, an observational film outcome for research or for learning depends on pedagogy as much as it is dependent on who was filming and what they were filming. The nature of the tools used, the ways those tools are used, the purpose they are used for, together with the thoughtful awareness's of the circumstances in which they are used—all of those aspects are introduced to children. Researchers and teachers will also gain from observational filmmaking pedagogy as they learn and practice this as a method. Therefore, in this book research and pedagogy fuse, whether that is for the benefit of objectives in education research and/or children's learning.

This Chapter sets out, in a matter of fact way, practical elements of such pedagogy. But there is a dilemma, a discordance, which I sense pervades the entire project of this book. In respect of the experiential empiricism which I introduced in Chapter 2 and which drives the nature of the knowledge observational filmmaking in education might attain, perhaps such pedagogy ought to be set in specific practices more than in generalised principles; in other words, pedagogy will situate itself in specific circumstances and should be drawn out in actual examples. Such an account might become a story about how certain children learnt to film in certain ways and how their films came about. However, this would be so specific to time, place, people and events that it might be unhelpful to researchers, teachers and, indeed, children who live and work in very different circumstances. Take, the issue of the video camera. I judge it is less helpful to explain the nature and workings of a specific camera and more helpful to speak about the nature and functions of video cameras in general. This has two immediate benefits; firstly sets of ideas about cameras become pedagogical headings for teaching strategies; secondly such a discussion will help orientate teachers and researchers about what kind of cameras they might use and why. If there is no choice in the cameras available, then the opportunities and limitations of those specific cameras become upfront in research and teaching, rather than left to one side or even ignored. I suggest that it is only in the melding of a generalised text such as this with experiential practice in the specific circumstances that a reader of this book is (or will be) part of that a deeper and more useful understanding is possible, both of this text and of the possibilities for research and learning.

Notwithstanding the argument in the previous paragraphs, as I write this text, I am developing a project with children in the Barcelona Primary School, Escola Dovella, which I introduced in the ethical discussion in the final section of Chapter 4. The school teaching team believe that observational filmmaking might, perhaps even should, become integrated into the fabric of teaching and learning. Children and teachers find that to film in this way is a powerful self-reflective tool. With the tools of a video camera and editing software, they observe, inquire, record, review, analyse and reflect experiences in school. They argue that the values and practices of observational filmmaking could be embedded in curriculum as a route to knowledge about learning and what is being learnt. I am grateful and I hope this will bring experiential knowledge about teaching and learning through a school's auto-ethnography of what is the aesthetic, affective and cognaitive fabric of participants' experiences.

Many of the theoretical and reflective aspects of observational filmmaking for education have already been broached in previous chapters. This chapter looks more specifically at practice. Thus, the nature of skills, techniques, tools, strategies and methods appropriate to observational filmmaking for education are the subject of this chapter. I have written this with teachers and researchers in mind as a set of prompts for what they may consider important, in their particular circumstances, to introduce to learners, especially children, who are new to observational filmmaking.

To do this, I have abstracted pedagogy for observational filmmaking for education into a set of headings. Under each heading there are suggestions about gaining knowledge and understanding of tools, techniques and relevant ideas. These are general and not specifically situated so they may be adapted to any particular learning or research situation.

Pedagogy for Learning and Research

Pedagogy is a sweeping term. It might be thought as synonymous with the word *teaching* in phrases such as pedagogical practices (teaching practices) or pedagogical theories (teaching theories), however it has a broader resonance. Definitions encompass the function of teaching, how teaching works, the science of teaching, the art of teaching, teaching methods, techniques and strategies. However pedagogy can also embrace: communication between learners and between teachers and learners, the way the physical environment affects learning, and how families and communities affect learning. Inevitably, cultural, societal, political and ethical forces are embedded in theories and practices of pedagogy. What happens when learners learn and teachers teach may be described in relation to pedagogy. All of the above domains contribute to pedagogically framed understandings about activities, experiences, interactions, events and routines, which are planned or unplanned in schools and other places where children learn. So, when adults conduct research with children as knowing participants or, to be more specific in the frame featured by this book (when adults support children to use cameras and editing software for observational filmmaking) pedagogy is fundamentally present. Therefore, it is not difficult to imagine that all or any of those aspects listed above will come into play to a greater or lesser extent if observational filmmaking contributes to either learning, education research or both.

Video Cameras and Other Devices

Which video cameras are best for observational filmmaking? At the time of writing in 2017, video can be recorded on mobile phones at one end of the spectrum to highly sophisticated cameras with television broadcast quality functions at the other. Cameras originally designed for still photography—digital single lens reflex cameras (DSLRs)—have powerful video functions. Outside of professional television and film production, video cameras range from the least expensive consumer cameras with basic functions to pro-consumer cameras with much of the functionality of professional equipment. Researchers, teachers and, indeed, children should take some time to understand the function of available cameras in relation to the circumstances and objectives of any particular project. What can a specific device do? What can't it do? How can that device be used and how does that functionality affect the possibilities for the research and/or the learning? I hope reading this chapter will help think about issues in understanding a video camera as a tool that impacts on both *how* research and/or learning happens through observational filmmaking methods and *what* the outcomes of those methods will be like.

Camera phones are commonplace but they have severe limitations in respect of observational filmmaking. Almost all the functions of mobile phone video recording are automatic. This leaves little room for thoughtful control by the filmmaker. Such absence of manual functionality hinders reflection about audio-visual qualities founded in practice. Significantly, phones have very basic sound recording functions. The microphone on a mobile phone will simply fail to cope well in busy environments such as classrooms. It is possible to use sound recording apps to improve the versatility of how phones deal with recorded sound, but these do not match the straightforward power and quality of a video camera with an external microphone recording into a dedicated channel aligned to video. Video quality on phones may be excellent for social media sites and sharing with family and friends, but comes under stress when examined carefully in editing software, especially when attention to aesthetic and material qualities in experience is sought. It is not easy to hold a phone still and steady whilst filming. The culture of mobile phone use may clash unhelpfully with the characteristics of observational filmmaking as described in this book. For example, many short videos clips shot for entertainment, rapidly shared and then forgotten is quite foreign to the nature of the observational films referred to in earlier chapters. Most of all, there are issues with the security of the video material. In considering who owns the phone being used, how is the video material controlled? Is it freely sharable via social media? What are the dynamics of the relationship between the phone owner and the project in respect of issues such as privacy, ownership and access to the recorded video? This book is advocating a particular approach to filmmaking for education. In my experience, and broadly speaking, mobile phones are less likely to be useful than other cameras. However, of course, there may be many ways that video shot on mobile phones can aid research and learning, but probably a very different research framework would be applicable.

The cameras on other mobile devices such as iPads and other tablets have similar issues with those on phones. However, there are some advantages to tablets. For example, they may be easier to hold. They have larger screens, which may help children frame shots. If a school owns the tablets, there may well be systems set up to securely manage anything that children record. Also, if a school uses tablets in classrooms, there may be plenty available for children to use, whereas video cameras may be more difficult to procure. But in other respects tablets may have the similar disadvantages as phones.

Amateurs and professionals alike use DSLR cameras to shoot video. Although designed initially for still photography, their internal software may offer much of the functionality of video cameras. There are advantages over video cameras. For example, users can easily change lenses to suit different subjects and circumstances. However DSLR cameras are not ergonomically designed for video work in complex situations and settings. For example, holding a DSLR camera steady whilst moving the camera to follow a process or person in a crowded classroom is difficult. Users often buy frames and grips to help with this. DSLR cameras are not primarily designed to record sound. Therefore to augment that capacity, additional kit is required so that external microphones can be added. In the end the whole arrangement can be cumbersome and awkward to use in an observational style. At the time of writing in 2017, many standard DSLRs limit the length of video clips a camera will record. Although that is changing as newer DSLR cameras simply record video until the memory card is full or battery runs out. Notwithstanding disadvantages, many professional video makers prefer DSLR cameras to video cameras. The same advice pertains here as throughout this chapter. Knowing about the camera in relation to what it will be used for and where it will be used, combined with the practical and real constraints such as budgets and availability, will help researchers, teachers and children make informed and thoughtful decisions.

Consumer video cameras come in many different forms. Technology is in constant development. At the time of writing in 2017, cameras marketed to consumers rather than professionals increasingly incorporate professional features at increasingly more affordable prices. The pace of technological change is breath taking. However, that must not be a reason not to engage with the camera as a technological tool; on the contrary it is even more important to understand the specific camera used in a project. Whatever cameras are available, an awareness of both their limitations and the opportunities they offer will build knowledge of the tool and thus contribute to understanding the effect that tool has on learning or research outcomes. To illustrate some of the factors in play when thinking about cameras, I will close this section with a brief account of our choice of cameras for observational filmmaking workshops at Escola Dovella in Barcelona.

As a researcher, I already had one pro-consumer video camera available, a Canon XA25. This camera has full manual control across a range of functions, which professional filmmakers might appreciate. It also had 'auto' features that can operate in varying ways. These offer choices in how a user might decide to automate some functions whilst manually setting others. The touchscreen menu interface on an LCD view screen is very intuitive. Despite the professional capability, children find the camera very easy to use and can actively choose various functions with ease. It can record sound onto two separate stereo channels. There are opportunities embedded in the design to mount external devices such as wireless microphone receivers, shotgun microphones and additional handles and mini-tripods. The camera has small powerful rechargeable batteries which last well. There are two slots for flash memory cards and the camera is versatile in how it can record video in different formats onto different cards. The camera can capture broadcast quality video, which offers maximum versatility when editing, as well as highly compressed video for small file sizes and easy sharing. The camera is ergonomically designed and can be held stably or moved appropriately in many different situations.

However, one camera was not enough for a series of workshops with Grado Sexto, a class of twenty-five 10–12 year-olds at Escola Dovella. The University of Barcelona and the school managed to borrow from education resource centres another 4 consumer video cameras. Three of these were Sony HD Handycams. They are smaller than the Canon and can be held in one hand. Apart from size, there were differences with the Canon. Most significantly for our project was that the Sony had a shoe on the top of the camera body that needed a special adapter to attach a non-Sony branded external microphone. These proved difficult to get quickly. Therefore, at the start of the project children practised filming without an external shotgun microphone attached to the camera. This severely limited their ability record sound well. The Sony has an autofocus function; manual focus is not possible. In other words the camera makes most of the decisions. Although this is fine when children are starting to learn about the craft of observational filmmaking, it will restrict their developing understanding as they become more proficient. The Sony records stereo sound from one microphone onto two channels, but the Canon can record stereo sound from two microphones onto two separate channels for each input. This increases the flexibility of managing audio in editing software. The LCD touch screen on the Sony is smaller and not as bright. Therefore it is not quite as easy to view framing and review shots played back in camera. Menus for controlling auto and manual functions are less intuitive in the Sony than the Canon. The small size of the body means it is less easily adapted for attaching external microphones, handles and mini-tripods. The sensor, which captures the visual signals, is not as sensitive on the Sony as in the Canon. The Canon has additional options for connecting to external devices such as monitors. The Sony Handycam might seem less intrusive in a setting than the larger Canon. However, the more obvious way the Canon was used (and could be set up) helped children more easily understand the camera as an observational tool. There are other differences. However, crucially, if buying new, the Canon XA25 might cost four times more than the Sony. The Sony can record video to almost the same quality as the Canon. Almost all basic functions are available on the Sony as they are on the Canon, even if they are not as easy to intuit. The point to be made after such an extended discussion is that the type of camera used directly impacts pedagogy; it directly impacts how children may use cameras in situations; it also will impact on the audio-visual outcomes. These considerations, therefore, directly impact research process and end products. Nevertheless, factors such as cost and availability may trump the best intentions of researchers and teachers. Which camera is used in a project may well be the result of compromise.

To return to arguments made at the beginning of this sub-section, a form of observational filmmaking is possible with camera phones, but an awareness of the limitations of that tool in respect of other possible tools is a vital component in understanding qualities in the knowledge being created. To use a very blunt metaphor as an illustration: imagine teaching children to cook two meals. Firstly they must set about preparing a meal outside with no knives, pots or pans and using an open fire. Food will be cooked and eaten. It may be nourishing and delicious. The experience may be memorable. But contrast that with preparing a meal in a fully equipped kitchen. A very different kind of meal is possible. A very different experience is in play. In certain circumstances it may be more valuable to learn to cook a meal outside, in other circumstances more valuable to learn to cook in a fully equipped kitchen. Reflecting on the difference may offer a powerful way to come to a better understanding of what is done and how the outcomes come into being.

Tools and Equipment in the Camera Bag

Introducing Tools and Equipment in the Camera Bag

If there is a camera bag! The question is designed to establish, with all those participating in an observational filmmaking project, what tools and equipment are available to use. Each item is there for a reason. As well as simply knowing what is available, children can be helped to understand what those items are used for, and why those items are part of the project. Understanding how the various pieces of equipment interconnect and work together should also be highlighted. My own approach is to unpack the actual (or metaphorical) camera bag with children and assemble and then disassemble the various components with them as I go. A learning outcome might be that children can demonstrate that they can unpack and pack away the equipment independently, explaining what each item is and why it is there and what it is used for.

As each element of the camera bag is metaphorically unpacked in the sub-sections that follow, I have noted a number of essential features and examples of further opportunities for learning or reflection that might be appropriate. Note please, it may well be that in many circumstances the very first activity is to introduce some very basic ideas (such as holding the camera steady and deciding when to record and when not to record) and then let children explore those concepts by using the camera right away. Such an immediate hands on activity may well excite children's interest and bring the principle of a thoughtful practice into immediate play. In other words, there is no intention here to suggest that these following paragraphs are a list set out as a pedagogical plan to be followed in its entirety in the order it appears.

I suggest that teachers and researchers might benefit most whilst reading this chapter by having the specific cameras and microphones they are using alongside the relevant manual. The camera manual will have diagrams and much detail specific to that camera. The manual index will help teachers and researchers find the relevant features referred to here but in the context of how *their* camera works. The thrust of this book is to meld theory and practice, concepts and material experience together. Reading the text, referring to relevant parts of the manual and seeing and practicing how those elements, controls and functions operate in an actual camera will illustrate just how powerful such an approach to gaining knowledge is.

A Lens

Lenses let light in to the camera. They focus the image onto an electronic sensor in the camera. Different focal lengths are possible from a wide angle to telephoto. This allows a closer up view on an element in a setting in more detail or a lens can open out the angle of view. This flexible functionality helps the camera user to decide what to include in the frame. Light, focus, and framing are all factors in how an image appears in resulting video material. There may be a lens cap to protect the lens (it is easily damaged). There may be a lens hood to help stop very bright light (such as direct sun light) hitting the lens and causing 'flare'. Different camera lenses have different attributes. It is valuable to know what those are.

Batteries

A battery powers the camera. Batteries run down and limit the amount of time a camera can be used without recharging. It is useful if children can quickly understand how to manage batteries. How long will batteries last without recharging? There may be two batteries so that one is always available charged and ready to use.

Memory Cards or the Equivalent

At the time of writing in 2017, many video cameras use flash memory cards to store the audio-visual recordings. These cards are small and easily mislaid. An immediate question is who responsible for the cards and the content saved onto them? Who manages and decides how the audio-visual material is looked after will not only become part of the ethical practice in each project, it will also determine outcomes. If children are really filming independently, they ought to have control. For example, if children are not able to access the audio-visual recordings after they leave the camera they will not be able to view or edit those independently of adults. Conversely, what protections are in place to prevent participants from disseminating video recordings outside of an identifiable group? These issues pertain both in respect of any cards used in the camera and what happens after video is copied or transferred onto a computer. It is vital to organise a system for managing how video material is recorded in the camera. The amount of storage space available on a memory card or other portable device limits the amount of recording possible (in relation to the digital resolution used) without changing the card. Just as in learning about managing batteries, children should quickly learn about the capacity of memory cards and related issues of file sizes and image quality and resolution.

Microphones

The quality and nature of the recorded sound and what sound can and cannot be recorded is as important as the nature and quality of the video images. There are different kinds of microphones. Knowledge about the limitations and opportunities of whichever microphones are available is very valuable.

The internal camera microphone: In less expensive cameras these can often reproduce sound poorly. For example, it may be impossible to hear what is being said unless the camera is very close to the speaker, especially in situations such as busy classrooms.

A 'shotgun' microphone: This can be fitted onto a 'shoe' on top of the camera body and connected to the camera. These are directional microphones. They record sound from whatever the microphone is pointing towards. They may record some limited sound from behind the camera. There are many variations in the sensitivity of different shotgun microphones.

A wireless microphone with a transmitter and a receiver: The receiver may be fitted onto the camera shoe and connected to the camera. A person wears the transmitter (often clipped to a belt or elastic waist band) and a very small microphone is clipped onto clothing, often onto a lapel and connected by a wire, which can run inside the wearer's clothing to the transmitter. Demonstrating how to set up a wireless microphone, including working out how children can attach the transmitter and microphone themselves will be part of any pedagogy. There are additional ethical and privacy issues associated with wireless microphones. Wireless microphones will record what an individual is saying regardless of where the camera is pointing. The advantage is that conversations between children may be recorded even if the camera is the other side of a classroom. A disadvantage is that anyone may quickly forget they are wearing a wireless microphone. So conversations, which are normally private, are automatically shared with whoever is listening to the recording.

Other kinds of microphones: For example: A *cardioid* microphone records sound from a wider and less concentrated sound field in front than a typical shotgun microphone. Such a microphone might also be attached to a pole and held by a sound recorder away from the camera. However extra cables, equipment and people may be impractical and even disruptive to the smooth process of filming. A *boundary* microphone might be used to record sound with a 360-degree coverage.

Headphones

Headphones are essential. They can be attached to almost all video cameras. Children need to listen to what is being recorded through the headphones and replay clips to check that the sound is recorded well. Poor quality sound is the most common cause of frustration and disappointment when reviewing video material. Using headphones identifies problems whilst filming. These can often be corrected there and then. For example, a common cause of hiss or crackle is a poorly inserted microphone jack. This is easily solved. Using headphones helps focus a reflexive attention on sounds. These recorded sounds encompass much more than human voices talking.

Tripods, Handles and Grips

Handles and grips on the camera: Most cameras have a handle of some kind 'built in'. It is worth pausing to reflect on how these might be used to help hold the camera in different situations. However, the handle or grip that is part of the camera may not be the best way to hold the camera in the varying circumstances of many observational filmmaking situations. I have found, especially when children are using the cameras, that it is very useful to add an addition aid which helps hold the camera in differ ways.

Mini-tripods: Children find at least one version on a mini-tripod very helpful. Cameras can be quickly and spontaneously set on items of furniture or the floor. These small hand size tripods collapse into a handle.

Additional handles and grips: There are many versions of these. I used one with a shoe that allows a microphone to be connected a little away from the camera body. The principle is that any way of improving how the camera is held in a flexible and stable way in different kinds of situations will be beneficial. Each camera user will have their preference for what works well for them.

Full size tripods: I do not recommend these for observational filmmaking. They are cumbersome and tend to fix a camera in one position so it is unable to easily react to what is happening. However, tripods may be useful in certain situations, such as a video diary box where children can come and talk to the camera; or in a more formal interview situation.

Cables and Connectors

There will be a power cable to connect the camera to a mains supply to recharge batteries. There may be a separate battery charger. There will be cables to connect the camera to a computer to download recorded video material. External microphones will have cables to connect them to the camera. There may be cables to connect the camera directly to a monitor, a digital projector or TV to view video directly without downloading to another device. The function of those cables needs to be understood. They are designed to help the whole process of camera use run smoothly from powering the camera to managing the video outcomes. All connectors and cables should be well managed. When working with children, I recommend they keep each cable separately in the camera bag in its own small, labelled see-through bag.

Cleaning Materials and the Camera Bag

A lens cleaner and a soft brush with tiny bellows attached to clear dust from the lens surface will be useful. Lenses are delicate. Realising the need to care for the camera as a tool helps users reflect on the nature of the relationship between the tools, techniques and outcomes as a craft. What happens if the lens is dirty or damaged?

Caring for and managing the camera bag, whether an actual bag or some other container such as a travel bag or storage box is also a helpful way of reflecting on the relationship between the tools and the filming process. Losing items or a disorganised approach to storing the various pieces of equipment listed above will not be helpful.

Observational filmmaking works best when researchers, teachers or children can film spontaneously. Feeling at ease with the management of the equipment so it is increasingly used spontaneously without hesitation is a quality gained with practice.

Getting to Know the Camera Controls

Power On and Off and 'Record' On and Off

Obvious, yes, but leaving the camera powered up unnecessarily will reduce battery time. Conversely, if the camera is not on and ready to record, it may be impossible to respond intuitively to a new situation. Does the camera shut down automatically after a set period of time?

It is easy to forget to stop recording when an event ends when everybody is still in the midst of an on-going situation. If that happens, pressing the record button as the next opportunity to film presents itself will stop rather than start recording! Most cameras indicate when they are recording. Attentiveness to this is important. What affects decisions about when to record and how long to record will have a huge influence on the audio-visual outcomes. Children can reflect on this as they review their clips. Was it necessary to keep the camera running all that time? Did they stop recording too soon and miss an interesting part of a process?

The Zoom

This is often a rocker style switch. Many cameras have zoom settings that adjust the speed of the zoom and the sensitivity of the zoom control. Using the zoom too often and without thinking of the effect it has on the video material frequently creates almost unwatchable film. I often suggest that children do not use the zoom when they are filming, especially as they are learning about the camera and observational film-making techniques. Observational filmmakers, Ulla Turunen and Ilkka Ruuhijärvi, whose films are discussed in Chapter 1, used a fixed focal length. They did not use the zoom at all. The focal length has a strong effect on depth of field. For example, at the fullest extent of a camera zoom the amount (the depth) of a scene that is in focus is very narrow compared to using the widest angle available. Issues about depth of field and focal lengths are more advanced concerns, but children will benefit from understanding what is happening when deciding on whether or not to use the zoom control to help frame a shot.

Sound Input Controls

Most cameras will set audio recording levels automatically but more advanced cameras will have a manual controls to adjust the recording levels and decide which microphones are recorded onto which channels. Understanding and altering these settings after listening through the headphones to recorded clips may help achieve better quality sound. It might be a good idea that different microphones record onto separate channels—say a wireless mic recording the interaction of one pupil with others in class no matter where the camera is and a shotgun mic recording what is immediately in front of the lens—each channel can then be treated differently in editing software. It is also worth noting that some microphones take their power from the camera and that others have batteries. Knowing which microphone is powered in which way and knowing the relevant camera settings is important.

Focus

Almost all video cameras have an auto focus function. This is very useful as children begin using the camera, but auto focus can limit the way a shot works. For example, one frame might include objects in the close foreground whereas a child, who is at the centre of what is going on, is in the background. The auto focus may choose the foreground objects, leaving the child, who is the main subject of the shot, out of focus. The reverse can also be true. It may be that it is more appropriate to have the foreground objects in focus. Some cameras have a focus feature, which automatically tracks faces. It may be that this is activated and so the face of the child in the background is in focus when it was the intention to concentrate on the foreground objects. In that circumstance, the auto focus control might be helpful. It is worth noting that it is more difficult to maintain focus manually in an active scene, perhaps where children are moving about, and when the depth of field is narrow. All in all, in many circumstances an autofocus setting will work well. However, learning to control focus manually will aid reflexion on how choices are made about what is important in a frame and so extend the craft of observational filmmaking. The discussion of the zoom control above introduced how using a telephoto lens affects depth of field, and so what is in focus.

Aperture

Adjusting the aperture will let more or less light into the camera through the lens. Therefore, adjusting the aperture changes the amount of light reaching the camera's sensor. Almost all cameras will do this automatically so that the video is correctly exposed. But, just as with focus controls, sometimes an auto-aperture setting will not cope well in certain situations. For example, if you are filming in a classroom and the light levels are set automatically for an interior, as you pan towards a window, the camera will automatically adjust the aperture to correctly set the exposure for the bright light outside. When that happens, everything in front of the window inside the classroom is dark, silhouetted against the window. A viewer might not be able to see any detail inside at all. If children are filming in classrooms with many large windows, it might be much better to manage the aperture manually, setting it so that the interior of the classroom is correctly exposed no matter if the camera is pointing towards a window or not. Aperture also affects depth of field. When the aperture is smaller the depth of field is greater. But, less light enters the camera. The widest aperture setting lets lots of light in but the depth of field is narrow. Again, the point here is that through appreciating *how* the amount of light that enters a camera is controlled and *how* light affects what is seen in the video outcomes, researchers, teachers and children can be aided to reflect attentively on the nature of light and its qualities and effects in respect of the camera as a tool. Researchers may argue that correctly exposing a scene will enable them to see more detail in the recorded outcomes. If the scene is underexposed or overexposed, less detail is visible. This may restrict what the researcher may see and therefore discover.

A Camera LCD Monitor and Eyepiece

These are often hinged from the body of the camera so that the angle and direction of viewing can be altered. Camera users can see what they are filming. This will show what is being recorded in a very similar way to using the eyepiece of a viewfinder. The advantage for observational filmmaking is that the LCD screen allows the camera can be held in many different ways (for example at waist height) and the user can still easily see what is shown in the frame.

If the camera is held at shoulder height, then using the eyepiece can be very helpful. It is also often better to use an eyepiece in bright sunlight, when using the LCD screen may be difficult.

Touch Screen Menus

These are accessed from the LCD monitor. In 2017 many video cameras have touch screen menus. The menu functions are also often accessible via controls on the camera and visible through the viewfinder. The menus offer a structured and accessible way to change various settings and camera controls. This will include changing from auto settings to manual settings for example. Children will learn the basic functions of these menus very quickly indeed. As they become familiar with the camera, it is valuable to discuss what it is helpful to be able to change and what should remain untouched. More sophisticated cameras will have a set of additional functions. Some of these might be particularly helpful in specific circumstances. A teacher or researcher must first discover these for himself or herself before deciding how to incorporate knowledge of these tools into pedagogy. Some typical ones include:

Focus functions: Many video cameras offer different ways to aid or automate focus. The camera may be set to focus on facial features and to follow those features as the person moves in a scene. It is often possible to press the touch screen to choose which part of the image should be in focus. This might be particularly helpful to children filming in busy classrooms. There may be other focus functions such as adjustments to the speed at which the auto focus will respond to changes in the scene. A camera manual and practice will identify which are useful and appropriate in any particular project and circumstance.

Exposure functions: Note the discussion about aperture above. Many cameras have touch screen options to help set a correct exposure for a particular part of a scene, in a similar way to the way focus functions work.

Gain: This is a function that digitally enables the camera to boost the incoming signal to brighten an image in low light. Applying *gain* may reduce image quality.

White balance: This enables the camera to adjust to different light conditions. A white surface will appear different when recorded by a camera depending on whether it is illuminated, for example, by florescent light inside or bright sunlight outside. Cameras will adjust the white balance automatically. It is sometimes preferable to manage the white balance manually to prevent the camera changing the white balance frequently in a situation such as classroom with large windows. The colour cast apparent on the recorded image near a sunny window will be quite different from one under artificial light in the corner of the room.

Image resolution: In digital video cameras image resolution is measured in terms of the number of pixels the sensor records in a given area. The more pixels, the more detail there will be and the higher resolution of the image. Cameras can often offer a wide range of potential resolutions. An appropriate resolution can be selected taking into account the practicalities and the objectives of the project. One advantage of higher resolutions is that very high quality still images can be made from individual frames revealing great detail in a scene. Another advantage is that video outcomes can better reflect aesthetic qualities such as subtle variations in colour, light and texture. Higher resolutions improve the quality of video projections on large screens. The disadvantage in a project where a great deal of recording is happening is that high-resolution video will gobble up storage space very rapidly. High-resolution video will need more powerful computers to process and edit. Children using school computers may more easily manage smaller file sizes from low-resolution recordings. All the circumstances and objectives of an observational filmmaking project need to be considered when making technical choices about image resolution. As with other decisions suggested in this section, an awareness of how these affect research and learning is a valuable reflexive tool.

Microphone controls: For example, some cameras may allow the sound levels to be automatically limited to avoid distortion. It may be possible to vary the way the signal from different microphones is treated in different channels.

Image stabilising functions: Many cameras can automatically reduce the effect of camera shake and smooth out camera movements. Applying these may affect performance of camera as the images are processed in camera. But they may help improve the watchablity of video images.

Other functions: Check through the in camera menus and the manual to find out other functions particular to your camera and whether or nor they are helpful tools for the circumstances and objectives of a particular project.

Considering the Person-with-Camera and Who Is Being Filmed

How is it that one person gets to know another person so that they can understand more about them? Spending time with others, talking, interacting and sharing experiences helps. Look back at the films discussed in Chapter 1. When David MacDougall filmed *Gandhi's Children* (2008) he lived in the Prayas Children's Home for Boys for three months. Although he was an outsider, he got to know the children and the institution well. Nicolas Philibert who, together with his crew, made *Être et Avoir* (2002) and Ulla Turunen and Ilkka Ruuhijärvi, who shot the observations films for Finish television from the mid 1980s, all spent weeks and months alongside children as they filmed. Common sense might suggest that the more familiar a filmmaker is with the circumstances they are filming and the better filmmakers are known, trusted and accepted by those they are filming, the closer the film material will feel to those circumstances and the people therein. In contrast, there is an inevitable disconnect between objectives and outcomes, if a researcher turns up at a school, for example, and expects to immediately be able to film children in classrooms in a way which reflects those children's experiences. The quality and roundedness of any knowledge and understanding of children that results is likely to be improved by getting to know those children well.

Therefore, taking children in a school as an example, how well does the camera user know the people and the circumstances they are filming? How well do the people being filmed know and trust the camera user? What is the relationship between the camera user and those being filmed? For example, is the children's class teacher filming them? Is it another teacher in the school? Will the authority of a teacher in respect of children affect the outcomes? How long has a researcher been able to spend with children before filming starts? In what sense will building familiarity and trust make a difference? Adults have power over children. Children know this and will adjust to that relationship. But what if it is children who are the camera users filming other children? What are the power relations that one child may have as they interact with another?

The observational filming technique applicable, then, might usefully be addressed in response to this question: How does the pedagogy, which envelops the particular project in hand, encompass the building of understanding and trust between the person with the camera and those being filmed, and an appreciation of how a person-with-camera has power or not over those being filmed? What are the responsibilities of the person-with-camera to others in the circumstances of the filming?

In Chapter 1, I wrote about the corporeality of the camera, as it becomes an extension of the camera user's body and mind. A researcher, teacher or child is a human-with-a-camera. It is as such that they are creating and developing human-with-camera relationships with those they are filming. In my view, if there is openness, honesty and care for others, the researcher-with-camera, teacher-with-camera, or child-with-camera will build close and productive relationships with those being filmed. These qualities will be reflected in the filmic outcomes. Getting to know children's experiences better as they live and learn in school is then more likely. It is worth noting here, that the children's observational films referenced in Chapter 2 offer powerful insights into the child filmmaker's lives because those who are filmed knew, trusted or accepted the child-with-camera as a *child* with a camera. If an adult had attempted to film the same people in a similar way the results would, I contest, have been very different. Time may be needed to facilitate the building of trust and openness in relationships, no matter who is filming. Time may not always be easily found, but educators are equipped with experience to develop strategies to help in this vital, ethical, and inevitably methodological objective.

Because how the researcher-with-camera, teacher-with-camera or child-with-camera interacts with others who are sharing in the circumstances of the filming is fundamental to what is seen and heard in the resulting video material, it is therefore fundamental to the knowledge of those circumstances that results. There are many ethical nuances in the relationships between someone with a video camera and those being recorded and the how the resulting video material is used. Here are examples of the kinds of questions which will help reflect on the way interacting with others becomes part of the practice.

- How much time is there to prepare for the project and talk to everyone involved? How important is that to the nature of the outcomes?
- Do you know the people you are filming well? What difference might that make?
- Do the people you are filming know you as an observational filmmaker? Have they become accustomed to seeing you with a camera? What difference does it make if the people being filmed know about the reasons you are filming and the reasons why you film in a particular way?

- Do you have any power or authority over whom you are filming? For example, you may be a researcher working for a university and the school managers have given permission for the project. The class teacher may feel they have little say in whether this happens in their class. A child-with-camera may be several years older than other children they are filming in school. What difference might that make?
- How can you help build trust, mutual respect and understanding with those you are filming? How do those qualities affect the outcomes of the filmmaking?
- Can the people you are filming talk to you as you are using the camera? How might talk between you and those you are filming affect the video outcomes?

At the close of Chapter 4 there is an account of a range of situated ethical issues that were considered for an observational filmmaking project with children in a Barcelona primary school. The introduction to and discussion of ethical concerns is an essential component in pedagogy for observational filmmaking in education. This will apply whether it is researchers, teachers or children who are using cameras. The approach to pedagogy for appreciating ethical dilemmas in observational filmmaking will depend a great deal on the age of participants, their experience and the circumstances of the project. As an illustration, what follows is a list of headings, mostly phrased as questions for talking points, discussions, and potential activities. I have used these with children aged 10–12 years old.

- What is observation? Who observes? What is observed? Talk about scientists, artists and journalists for example.
- What does it feel like to be observed? Have you ever been observed?
- What does it feel like to be looked at? Have you ever been looked at?
- What does it feel like to do the observing?
- Observe each other's faces. Make observational drawings and take still photographs. Talk about the sensations of attentive looking and being looked at carefully.
- Where are video cameras used in society? Who uses video cameras? Why are they used?

- What are the positive and negative values that arise in different cases? For example: video monitoring in a city centre; video streaming in social media; using a video camera on holiday. Who controls the cameras? How does that make a difference?
- Look at some examples of extracts from observational films involving children. What can you see happening? Talk about where the camera user was? How was it that they were able to be there?
- Talk about the concept of permission. Do you always need permission to film other people? Who has authority to give permission in any given circumstance? How do you get permission from others to film them?
- How does it feel to be filming other people with a video camera? How can you recognise when people feel uncomfortable when you are filming them? What should you do if you see someone is uncomfortable being filmed?
- Should you film with a telephoto lens? Is it ever okay to film others from a hiding place?
- Think about different kinds of microphones. Many of the talking points above also come into play when recording what people say. What do filmmakers and participants need to think about when using wireless microphones?
- How should the video clips you have recorded be managed and looked after? Who has the right to delete clips? Who has the right to share clips with other people? Which other people can see clips and when might clips be shared?

After a number of workshops have taken place so that children have had opportunities to film and be filmed, discuss some of these issues again. It is valuable to alert them to differences between ethical principles and what happens in practice. The concept of judgement will come into play. There will not often be simple right and wrong answers to the kinds of questions drawn out above. For example, it may be useful to share comments about what happens when other children are being filmed. Did they playact or play up to the camera? Did they ignore the camera? Did they accept you with the camera? Did they talk to you as you were filming? Did you reply?

Camera Techniques for Observational Filmmaking for Education

Previous sections set some of the most important characteristics of the camera (and associated equipment) as a tool that a learner or a researcher might use to observe others living and learning in the kinds of circumstances to be found in schools. The previous section then considered the person-with-camera as relating to others in the circumstances of the project. There is a powerful need for pedagogy which catalyses reflection on these issues, not only for ethical reasons, but also because the nature of the relationships and the behaviours profoundly affects the generation of knowledge.

This section and its component sub-sections consider the kinds of techniques and skills that are particularly helpful for observational filmmaking. That is, the way the tool is used forms (or crafts) the audio-visual outcomes of the filming for learning and/or research in the circumstances of the encounters between camera users and other participants. Because the capabilities of the tool, together with its limitations, have a profound effect on the knowledge gained from how it is used, the way the camera is used as a tool is partly determined by the relationships between the camera user and those being filmed. Therefore, the following discussion of camera techniques should not be considered in isolation of the human circumstances in which the various methods are practiced.

To revisit the experiential empiricism discussed in Chapter 2, the tool as it is used in the circumstances it is used becomes a way of thinking formed in and of experience. Through thoughtful tool use, aesthetic, material and affective experience are not only present but foregrounded as experiential qualities in thoughtful filmic outcomes. In attending to such material, participants, be they children, teachers or researchers, get to know more about the circumstances as children live and learn in school. From such knowledge and reflexion about it, a better understanding of children's experiences is possible.

Setting Up the Camera Ready to Film

One useful way to introduce and develop awareness of the camera as a tool is to share ways of getting the equipment ready to film. This might be via a demonstration. For example, unpack a camera bag and assemble the various components whilst talking about each and the role they play in the filming. Equally useful is to explore carefully what happens at the end of a filming session by dismantling the camera, looking after the various components and packing these away. For example, learners and researchers must consider how the memory cards are dealt with. What happens to the recorded audio-visual material? What is a useful and practical way to look after batteries, cables and other accessories? A checklist of the contents of the camera bag (that is all the equipment a camera user will have available) plus a checklist of necessary actions might be valuable. As part of a practice routine, I discovered that asking children to film other children setting up the camera and packing it away again, explaining what they were doing as they went was a useful reflexive exercise (Fig. 5.1). Use the password *951159* to view video illustrations in this section.

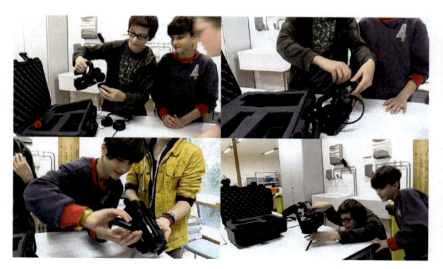

Fig. 5.1 Setting up the camera (https://vimeo.com/296849556)

Preparing to Record Sound

How might researchers, teachers and learners come to understand more about different kinds of microphones and the affect those differences have on outcomes? It may be worthwhile planning some exercises that highlight the issues and effects of using the different microphones available. At the very least, reflexion on any microphone the camera user has available and the way it records sound is important in building understanding. Before filming begins in earnest, whoever is using the camera should practise assembling and setting up external microphones feeding into the cameras. This is especially important for projects using wireless microphones. Camera users should check recorded sound levels using headphones attached to the camera. A common problem is static noise or hiss. Sometimes this is simply a result of a poor connection between a cable and the microphone (or the connection to the camera) and can easily be solved. Without checking, a great deal of filmmaking might take place with sound that is difficult to use. It is also worthwhile checking the quality sound after the audio-visual files have been downloaded and opened in software on a computer. Many cameras will set audio levels for the incoming sound automatically but if there are manual controls these may be useful in certain circumstances. The bottom line here is that focusing on pedagogy for practical and ethical issues surrounding recording sound (especially what people are saying) will bring this vital function in filming into the foreground. This means there will be a heightened awareness of the way sound and image are inextricably related in the processes of observational filming and in how the results are viewed and understood.

Holding the Camera Steady

In documentary and fiction filming, deliberately using a hand-held camera may create a sense of immediacy. As a camera user moves through a scene, the camera shakes and sways. The result could be a sense of nervousness, panic or perhaps a complete immersion in the dramatic circumstances unfolding in the on-going narrative. Such handheld techniques are designed to generate certain kinds of emotional responses. So, although a shaky camera may occasionally be valuable to filmmakers who wish to author an expressive narrative, in general, in observational filmmaking, it is almost always to be avoided. This is because one objective of the observational style is an attentive awareness of how people are, in the circumstances they are in, without imposing how a viewer should or should not respond. Simply in physical terms, camera shake can be very distracting. It is more difficult to pay attention to what the scene is revealing. Shaky shots are less comfortable to view. In contrast, attentive awareness is aided by a calm a steady camera. There are a number of techniques that researchers, teachers and children can practise to help achieve steady shots.

- Use external grips and handles to help hold the camera.
- Rest the camera on furniture such as tables and chairs, the floor or any other stable surface.
- Hold the camera into the body rather than at arms length.
- Hold the camera whilst leaning against a support such as a wall, doorframe or table.
- Use a device such as a mini-tripod.
- Relax whilst filming. Find a comfortable position. If standing, think about the best ways to stand in a stable, relaxed and comfortable way.
- Look at and talk about the results of filming after practicing these techniques—compare those outcomes with shaky camera shots (Fig. 5.2).

Sometimes the speed at which events unfold in busy classrooms, for example, might mean that it is very difficult to always achieve a steady camera. The camera user might be in the midst of what is happening and this will be reflected in a natural camera movement. That might help a viewer sense the person with camera and where they are in the setting. As in all these examples of pedagogy, it is awareness of the effect of technique, which is the most important outcome. All camera users, including children will develop a personal style of how to hold

Fig. 5.2 Holding the camera (https://vimeo.com/296850103)

the camera. As they develop some filmmakers may prefer to allow more camera shake than others because it reflects a fluid, less static style.

Staying Still and Waiting Patiently

Learning about holding the camera steady aids an awareness of the broader value of stillness and patience. Filmmakers who are aiming at entertainment, be that via fiction or documentary narrative, often move quickly from one shot to another and from one scene to another. If story telling is the aim then the benefits of stillness and patience are often put to one side in favour of driving a narrative momentum.

To foreground qualities such as the aesthetic, material and affective—those less linear but contingent elements of any circumstance—the person-with-camera must often stay still and wait patiently in a setting. Sometimes it is uncertain what will happen and the filmmaker must wait and see. At other times, holding one frame for a long time (or perhaps not moving away from a setting) will give time for sensations of colour, light, surface and sound to sink in. When a constant drive for narrative is set aside, a heightened awareness of sensations and perceptions of a place or of a person may be more profoundly revealed through attentive observation.

Researchers, teachers and children can practise staying still and waiting patiently with a camera. This does not necessarily imply the camera shouldn't be moved at all. As I will point out further on, the purposeful movement of a camera may help record a process or connect different elements in a scene together. Here are some ideas, which may help foster an awareness stillness and patience through practicing camera technique.

- Children are working in small groups. Each group chooses one camera position; say in a classroom during a lesson. They choose a frame (see next sub-section below) and hold this frame, recording video for an extended amount of time (say five minutes). Children make notes whilst they are filming about what they notice. They then watch the video clip and talk about what they can see and hear. Groups compare what they have discovered.
- This time children choose three different settings to film. These include inside and outside locations. They hold the frame still for three minutes in each location and use a review of the clips to draw up a comparison between the three places.
- The child-with-camera waits in a setting for, say, twenty minutes. The camera is in one position and they don't move it. They press 'record' when they sense something is happening they wish to film. They stop recording when that 'event' has stopped or passed through the frame. Children review the results and talk about issues faced when starting and stopping recording and what it was like to wait patiently.

Framing and View Points

What the camera user sees in the frame of the viewfinder will also be seen on screen when a viewer is watching the recorded video. In other words, what the researcher-with-camera, teacher-with-camera or child-with-camera chooses to include in that frame at the moment they are filming is shared with whoever is viewing the recording later. This connects the perceptions, sensations and cognition of the person-with-camera to a viewer. Qualities, which come from attentive looking, can be shared.

Researchers, teachers and children might explore framing in this way. Cut a series of rectangles from stiff cardboard that have the same proportions as, say, the LCD screen on a video recorder. These can be different sizes. Use the cardboard frames in different settings in the school. First hold them at arms length and move the frame from side to side and up and down to help choose what to include within the cardboard viewfinder and what to leave out. Also explore changing stance. For example sit on the floor or climb onto a table to get a point of view. Talk about what happens. Next move the cardboard viewfinder closer to the face so that more and more of the scene is included with the frame, then ask a helper to hold the frame several metres away. Talk about what is happening. After practicing with the cardboard viewfinder, children can practise with the camera, recording their decisions and reviewing the results.

Filmmakers might reflect on what kinds of decisions are involved in deciding what to include in the frame and how wide or narrow an angle of view to take? Here are some examples of points to consider:

- Are you concentrating on one person? If so, do you need to move the frame to follow them? Do they always need to be in the middle of the frame? What or who else needs to be in the frame? What are the differences between showing all of the person in the frame, part of the person, or perhaps details of that person such as a face or hands?
- What objects are you including in the frame? What do the objects tell the viewer of the video about the circumstances you are recording?
- Can you see what someone is doing in the frame? For example, someone might be making something? You are there and know what is going on, but can you see this in the frame? You may need to move the camera and reframe another shot to help the viewer understand what is happening.

- What is in the foreground and in the background of the frame? Are you more interested in what is in the foreground, the background or both?
- When filming in a building, what elements of the architecture and furniture are included in the frame? What is the effect of this? For example, when filming inside are there very bright windows in the frame? Are you looking through a doorway into a room, or perhaps down a corridor or up a staircase? Can you see the whole room in the frame? Is that important?

After such a discussion and some practice exercises with the camera it will soon become apparent that more than one frame will probably be needed to take in what is happening in a scene (Fig. 5.3). For example, it is possible to frame a child getting on with an activity in the classroom. But a different frame might be needed to show the objects the child is using and how they are handling those objects. A third frame might be needed to show their facial expressions whilst they are working. A fourth frame might take in the whole scene in the classroom. Each new frame may well demand a new shot. But, there is a danger in prescribing, in advance of being in the setting, the way a scene ought to be put together by certain kinds of shots the filmmaker takes. One of the most useful qualities of the observational filmmaking style is how an attentive absorption in the circumstances allows the filmmaker to reflect through using the camera what it is like to be there. The benefits of that intuitive response are easily frustrated by too much structure imposed in advance. Nevertheless, thinking through what is going on when choosing how to frame a scene will help develop a thoughtful approach. This thoughtfulness helps in sharing both the experience of the person-with-camera and the experience of whoever is being filmed. In pedagogy for framing, as in drawing out all the different elements of the observational style, there is a balance to be struck between planning in advance, thinking about what is happening in the moment and then responding based on intuition and perceptions at the time.

Fig. 5.3 Framing

Moving the Camera with a Purpose

A person-with-camera will often have to move the camera to follow what is happening, especially when close up to what is going on. Another good reason to move a camera is to connect two parts of a scene, which cannot be viewed simultaneously in the same frame—for example, two people talking on opposite sides of a table. Qualities that arise out of steadiness, stillness and patience are not helped if the camera is moved frequently and thoughtlessly—an effect which is sometimes known as 'hoovering up' a scene. It is often tempting to move the camera from side to side and up and down just to make sure that everything in a setting is recorded. The problem is that viewing the result of this can be disconcerting as there is no time to actually look at anything.

Researchers-with-camera, teachers-with-camera and children-with-camera can practise moving the camera from one spot with a purpose. It is useful to be able to hold the camera steady and to be able to move it smoothly. A certain amount of anticipation may be needed to follow a movement, process or conversation well. Here are some examples of scenes where it may be possible to practise this.

- Eating food by following the actions of a person from the plate to mouth and back again.
- Making something during a craft activity where the camera follows the hands of a person as they pick up different tools and use these on different materials.
- A conversation between two people sitting opposite one another.
- When filming from a distance, the camera follows a person, an animal or a vehicle moving through or across a space.
- Follow a housekeeping chore such as washing the floor as the mop moves from bucket to floor and back again to the bucket.
- There will be numerous other examples.

Here are some basic techniques about physically moving the camera that researchers, teachers and children can practise:

- Pan horizontally from left to right without moving the camera up or down. If the camera is resting on a hard smooth surface, or if a mini tripod is being used, it is possible to find a stable point from which the camera can be rotated to make this movement.
- Tilt the camera up and down with out panning from left to right. As with a pan, if the camera is resting on a hard smooth surface, or if a

mini tripod is being used, it is possible to find a stable point from which the camera can be tilted up and down smoothly.
- Physically move the camera up and down without tilting. For example, begin with the camera on a table top where it can see a child's hands and gently lift the camera vertically without tilting until the face is visible in the frame.

Camera users will naturally and spontaneously combine the three vectors suggested above to move the camera to follow what is going on. Practice improves the smoothness and appropriateness of these movements. In observational filmmaking the camera movement is responsive and a result of the camera-users thoughtfulness when looking attentively at the scene. In narrative focused documentaries and fiction filming the camera movement may be used for expressive reasons for example, to build tension and create emotional suggestions enhancing the story.

Using the zoom whilst filming can be very problematic. The zoom does not physically move the camera but adjusts the focal length so that the camera can seem to move much closer or further away from detail than it really is. The zoom is very easily overused. With a hand held camera, as the camera zooms in, the effect is to amplify shake. Until camera users are more practiced, if the zoom is ever used within a shot, rather than simply to frame a shot, it is best when the camera is stable. However when children have had some practice with the camera, I suggest the zoom may be helpful for framing purposes.

Moving with the Camera to Follow a Process or a Person

Often, the person-with-camera will have to move with the camera to follow a process or another person getting on with what they are doing. For example, the filmmaker would like to share experiences as children eat at lunchtime. There is a school canteen and children line up to collect food from the kitchen, find a table with friends and then eat. One option might be to follow one child through this process. The camera user may not only have to move the camera as, for example, the child asks for a main course and then collects the filled plate from a member of the kitchen staff, but also physically move with the camera as the child walks to a table and sits down.

Developing anticipation of what is happening and awareness of the objects and people around and about will help camera users move smoothly and purposefully without too much disruption to either the filming or to others. This can be practised. The results of filming in various circumstances where the camera user has moved with the camera can be compared and talked over in relation to technique.

An aim is, bit by bit, to sense that the camera as simply an extension of the body. It is as if the camera is physically part of the person using it. It is also cognitively inseparable from that person's thoughts and responses to their perception as they film. As with all learning any skilful craft, this takes time. In my experience, children are often much faster at progressing in this direction than adults, as they are more open to working intuitively and naturally with the camera. Camera users generate an awareness of space and the way space is filled with objects and people as they get on with what is at hand. How the person-with-camera moves in and through space with a camera to follow a person or process is shared with a viewer in the recorded video outcomes.

Thinking About Light and Colour

The function of the aperture control and other ways the camera sensor's exposure to light might be adjusted in response to different light conditions was discussed above. There was also a brief discussion how adjusting white balance adjusts the different effect of light sources (such as florescent light inside and bright sunlight outside) has on the outcomes after the camera sensor records colour. Both the aperture and white balance functions in a video camera are often set as automatic. This is helpful as less experienced users practise camera technique. But looking at and practising using the various settings and manual functions associated with both aperture and white balance will help build a much deeper understanding of the phenomena of light and colour and how those affect the video outcomes. Knowledge of those aspects of how to control light that enters the camera and how that affects how the resulting video images are exposed and display builds a technical awareness of light and colour. But these are experiential phenomena, and just as the sound that is recorded deeply affects the resulting film, so the camera user's awareness of colour and light in a setting, along with materials and textures, affects choices made about what to include in a frame. These choices are shared with viewers. Here are some ideas about exercise to focus researchers, teachers and children on these experiential qualities.

- Decide on five different frames, which demonstrate different qualities of colour in different settings in, say, a school.
- Record these for a short period, perhaps one minute. Replay on a monitor or screen and talk specifically about the nature of colour.
- Look out for colours used for decoration, colours in natural materials, colours in clothing, colours in different kinds of objects used in school. For example, compare colours of containers in a classroom as opposed to colours of containers in a kitchen or office.
- Repeat this focusing on differences in light. For example, sunlight coming in through a window, the light at the back of a cupboard, light under furniture, light in classrooms which have few windows, light from directional lamps.
- The same idea can be repeated with materials and textures.

Such an approach will build an awareness of these phenomena in experience. David MacDougall (2006) writes about how observational filmmaking is a research method that reveals the *social aesthetic*. The nature of the environment that surrounds and encompasses the practice of teaching and learning in school has a profound and usually unacknowledged effect on children's experiences as they live and learn in such places. Observational filmmaking can help unlock access an awareness of these socially aesthetic qualities.

Thinking About Focus

What is in focus and is not in focus affects the outcomes in several ways. For example, a person-with-camera has decided to include items in the foreground of a table in the classroom in the frame. They show a selection of items, such as pens and pencils, which children are using. However the filming has been following what one child is doing as they are learning. This child is now in the background talking to the teacher. The auto-focus decides that the objects in the foreground are the feature of the frame that should be in focus, so that the child talking to the teacher is actually out of focus. Understanding and practising adjusting the focus manually will give the camera user more control and an understanding about how focus works so that they can more easily share with viewers what it was they were concentrating on. A method that children find helpful is to rapidly zoom in to the maximum telephoto capacity of the lens, manually focus on a detail which is part of what should be in focus, and then zoom back out to the framing needed for the shot. Many camera tutorials talk about the importance of someone's eyes being in focus, if that person is featured in a shot. That tactic helps children know how to achieve that manually.

Thinking about focus technique also can catalyse a more general but deeper awareness of what is important in a filming sequence and what is less important. Which elements of a process need to be shared so that what is going on is better understood? Is it important not only to see a learner doing something but also what they are using, how their hands are moving, the expression on their face and how they are sitting or standing? If the focus is on a learner doing something, both in terms of a that learner being in focus and in terms of the person-with camera's focus on the learner as a subject, then is it important to show other children around them and their interaction with those children? Does the set up in the classroom affect what the child is doing? Deciding what is important in the scene as well as what to focus on, both technically and metaphorically, is how the person-with-camera can share with any viewer their attentiveness in a particular circumstances.

Speaking to the Camera, Video Blogs and Video Interviews

These are not necessarily observational filmmaking techniques, but each might have a role to play in how researchers, teachers and children use video cameras and microphones to share their experiences. The films discussed in Chapter 1 demonstrate the boundaries are not fixed and that the observational style is a fluid one which has influenced different ways of filming documentaries, and, indeed, fiction films.

In Anshu Singh's film, *Why Not a Girl*, described in Chapter 2, the 12-year-old Anshu, ends her film by talking directly to the camera. In *My Funny Film*, also discussed in Chapter 2, shot by 11-year-old Aniket Kumar Kashyap, the boy sings to the camera. In each case, children are holding the video camera in front of their face and talking (or singing) to it. This is an intimate way of sharing experiences and ideas. This form of camera work is not necessarily welcome. Especially in the context of a school, are children able to understand the implication of opening up their emotional response to situations and circumstances in ways that are recorded and then shared? However, talking to a camera is a technique worth exploring by researchers, teachers and children. In the cases of Anshu and Aniket, the children reacted spontaneously and naturally to the camera as they spoke and sung. That is a quality worth drawing out and comparing with something more scripted, planned or stylised interviews.

At the time of writing in 2017, video blogging (vlogging) is an established tradition in social media. There is a difference between vlogging in order to entertain others and garner 'likes' on one level (or money from advertising revenue on another) and using the technique as a method to create knowledge for learning or research. This kind of reflection ought to feature as researchers, teachers and children explore how video blogging could be useful in the quest to share knowledge about children's experiences. However, there may well be situations in which children decide that vlogging on a regular basis might help share kinds of experiences which observational filmmaking techniques inhibit.

There are on-line tutorials about interviewing others with video cameras, however most look at a set up that professional filmmakers might use on location or in a studio. There may be additional lights, a camera on a tripod and a formal and fixed relationship between the filmmaker as interviewer and the interviewee. Interviews shot on the fly, outside, by news reporters are more helpful examples to study. However, one way or another, it is possible to learn a great deal about video interview techniques by searching on-line and viewing video clips. Researchers, teachers and children might consider some of the following kinds of questions as they decide if interviewing is going to be a part of their observational filmmaking project.

- Has the interviewer built up a rapport with the interviewee? Do they know each other? Is that important?
- Does the interviewee understand the circumstances of the interview? For example, why is it happening and how will the video material be used?
- Where is the interview taking place? Who decides? What are the reasons for choosing one location over another?
- Is the setting formal or more relaxed? Is the interviewee sitting or standing? Have they practiced what they might say or is this more casual?
- The viewer will want to see the person talking, but are there other objects in the frame? What is in the background or on the wall behind? Are other people in the frame?
- How is sound being recorded? Are children interviewing other children in a busy classroom? If so what kinds of microphones are most useful?
- Think about light? Where is the light coming from? Are their shadows or bright sun throwing the interviewee into shadow or high contrast?
- Who is asking the questions? The camera user? Someone else? Can the questions be heard clearly? Is that important?
- Should the questions be planned in advance?
- Is the interview spontaneous, perhaps more like a conversation between the camera user and interviewee?

There are tips and techniques for asking interview questions on line (Fig. 5.4). For example the *East Midlands Aural History Archive Centre for Urban History* at the *University of Leicester* in the UK publish an on-line sheet called *Interviewing for Research—Asking Questions*. This document, or similar ones, will offer advice about learning to listen, keeping eye contact, asking open questions (not questions with 'yes' or

Fig. 5.4 Interviews

'no' as an answer), asking follow up questions to build on ideas or go deeper, and the pros and cons of asking leading questions which already suggest a direction for a response. Other tips may include keeping questions short, asking questions to clarify something which is not so clear, not butting in and interrupting, and showing respect for the person talking even if you don't like their answer. Look out for how they are feeling; it may be time to stop. Don't forget that if an interview is part of an observational film, then a viewer will almost certainly want to be sure who it is that is talking. Has this person already been seen in the film or do they need to be introduced (or allowed to introduce themselves)? Regardless of any research or learning project, practicing interviewing others and reflecting on the outcomes is a very useful for researchers, teachers and children.

Concluding Remarks

This section has sketched out a cluster of related possible techniques for using a camera in an observational style. The overriding intention is to show that this experiential way of generating new knowledge is attainable not only by researchers and teachers, but also by children. The intention is to be able to share ideas with others. In the case of observational filmmaking ideas are replete with material, aesthetic and affective experiences of both the person-with-camera and those in the film. Ineffable qualities in human experiences are at the heart of research and learning. In the following section I will discuss how editing software will take the recorded audio-visual material into a designed audio-visual software environment set up precisely to allow further analysis. This software facilitates different ways of organising and sharing filmic sequences as products of research and/or learning. Therefore, the following section of this chapter describes editing tools for observational filmmaking in an education context.

Editing Tools for Observational Filmmaking in Education

Introducing Editing

Filming and recording audio-visual material in an observational style will result in individual files—clips. These will be stored in the camera's internal drive and/or on a storage device such as a small flash drive inserted into the camera. How those files are managed and, subsequently, how they are treated in video editing software is part and parcel of observational filmmaking for research and/or learning. However, although making a film might seem to be a natural and overarching objective for observational filmmaking, each clip may have value, even if it is viewed in isolation, untouched and unedited. Children can immediately reflect on what the recordings show, and what the person-with-camera was doing and thinking when they were filming. They can do this right away, in camera, by using headphones to listen and the LCD screen to view individual clips. Researchers, teachers and children may also find value in playing clips on an external larger screen (either directly from the camera or after downloading to a computer). Viewing clips, together with other children and adults, catalyses talk about what has been recorded. Some researchers and teachers may argue that that alone is sufficient reason to film, so that deeper reflexion on the circumstances of filming are possible without a need to ask formal questions in an artificial research or learning environment. In other words, observational filmmaking may be very worthwhile without any editing taking place at all. This immediately differentiates observational filmmaking as an educative process, be that for research for learning or for both, and observational filmmaking as a research method that creates cinematic outcomes in social anthropology.

Having said that, functionality available in video editing software offers researchers, teachers and children a very powerful tool to organise, review, tag, select from, and adjust clips within an audio-visual setting. From within this environment clips can then be assembled into filmic outcomes. Thoughtful decisions are made with the very qualities in experience, which word based and data-driven analysis simply cannot encompass. That is, the fundamental value of an experiential empiricism in learning and research has a vehicle from within which visceral analytical thinking, which is aesthetic, material and affective, thrives. Even if final films are not produced, working within a video editing software environment allows such thinking to take place.

I recommend that researchers and teachers become more familiar with digital video editing software, not only so that they might use that tool themselves, but also so they can help children understand the value of such software as a vehicle for thinking and expressing ideas, which are not dominated by words. In my experience children (say between 10 and 12 years-old) will discover the basic functionality of editing software very quickly indeed. They happily think visually. This thinking is often very intuitive. Pedagogy for editing is less a matter of training (although that has a role) as pointing out the underlying reasons behind why the software functions in the way it does and how that functionality can be used to respond in depth to what had been filmed. One caveat, which I draw children's attention to right away, is that software is likely to have an array of tempting technological effects and transitions. For example, a transition may spin one clip into another or an effect may reverse colour in the entire clip. There are hundreds of other, often flashy, possibilities available just one or two clicks away. These are entertaining and often used to help market the software. This, however, may not help attentive looking and listening, for example.

The children's films made as part of the *Childhood and Modernity* project, which can be found in Chapter 2, were crafted by the social anthropologist David MacDougall. However, the child camera user made many of the editing decisions sitting alongside MacDougall as he worked. Both adult and child, looked at the clips the child made, the child selected the kinds of shots they wanted to use. MacDougall and the child decided the rough edit of the final film together. Such collaboration in a research context may be valuable. The conversations, thinking and decisions a child makes as they share ideas and work with an adult whilst editing their film about, say, an aspect of living and learning in school, may offer a richer and deeper source of information about a child's perception and experience in those circumstances than any simple series of interview questions or attempts to code and analyse children's experiences at a distance.

In the end, the same clips, whether shot by a child, a teacher or a researcher, are readily available to be imported into editing software and organised, reviewed, tagged and assembled into filmic outcomes by children, teachers and researchers working alone or in any form of collaboration. A researcher from another university in another part of the world might be asked to review clips. One child may work on another child's clips in the software environment. These are all examples of powerful opportunities that the audio-visual software environment offers for the creation of knowledge. In my own work, I found filming children as they worked with editing software on their own clips offered me an immediate insight into their thinking about what they filmed and why they filmed in that way. A researcher may adapt this potential in light of the kinds of questions they are asking in their research. Or, perhaps a researcher might use these techniques to explore children's responses to their experiences in order to discover the kinds of questions that need to be asked. Pedagogy for digital video editing will not only help children reflect on what they filmed it may well allow them to first analyse and then construct thoughtful, aesthetic, material and affective responses as filmic sequences. It will also open children's eyes to how media based audio-visual entertainment and reporting is constructed. With no other objective in mind, I suggest this is worthwhile learning in a digital age.

Just as with the camera, understanding the software as a tool, which can be used in various ways, draws out video editing as a craft. Each function contributes something to a research and/or learning process. I am writing this at the end of 2017. One feature of earlier discussions in this book is the effect of changing technology on the nature of the tool and the way those tools are used. This is inevitable. For that reason I have not chosen one particular software package to describe in detail, but after reviewing a cross section, I distilled their basic, common and essential functions for learning and research. I recognise that in five or ten years from writing these words in late 2017, there will certainly be new functions and the ones I write about will have changed in the way they work. It is therefore even more vital that whichever software a researcher, teacher or child uses as a tool for learning and research, becoming familiar with it and practising its use, in the context of the particular circumstances of that time, is essential. There are many on-line video guides. The software tutorials provided by the software makers are worthwhile. Bearing that in mind, the following sub-sections present in a pedagogical frame (although not as a training program) the fundamental components in a video editing software package. The objective is to understand more about how editing might function as a tool to aid learning and research.

Storing, Backing Up and Naming Audio-Visual Files

This process begins in-camera. As shots are recorded the camera will automatically assign a file name. However, this name can easily be changed in the process of manually copying a file to a computer or external drive. Editing software may import files directly from a camera and file names can also be changed in that software environment. There are essential methods in play. Does the camera user know where the original digital video file is stored? How is it named and is the process of naming files both consistent and useful? Is the file backed up? How does the software manage work on the file? Is there an advantage in changing the video file names? If so, are the changes made within a consistent framework for naming video files? Storing and naming the files (individual shots) is a fundamental first step in reflecting on and analysing the results of observational filming. Researchers and teachers will need to understand how files are named and stored.

Importing Shots and Organisation in the Software Environment

Video editing software offers a powerful audio-visual environment for review and analysis of filmed material for researchers, teachers and children. Although words offer useful tools for naming clips and the folders they are stored in, the way clips are discovered, presented and reviewed is audio-visually focused. A sensory fluidity in the way good video editing software works allows judgements and decisions to be made intuitively, often with aesthetic, material and affective qualities in the foreground. However, to help users organise ideas with audio-visual qualities up front, each software environment has a systematic form for organising access to individual shots, any 'tagging' of those shots, and their subsequent use in 'projects' (the results of assembling clips when editing).

For example, there may be 'libraries' within which all media relevant to a project can be found. Inside the library there are sub-folders. These may be termed 'events'. In each event sub-folder shots might be saved together that are linked by, say, a specific place or time. In editing, the selected shots (and parts of shots) are often situated sequentially in linear bands, say on a timeline; this is the place in which edited filmic outcomes take form. Each research or learning project will have different objectives and each in case the decisions about how audio-visual material is organised within the software environment will be a fundamental part of the analytic process. A researcher or teacher, especially those who are collaborating with children, will need to become familiar with these structural and organisational features in editing software.

Reviewing

How does the software allow its user to review the clips? One function I have found invaluable in my own form of research is the 'skimmer'. This allows a rapid viewing of clips' contents by skimming through frames very fast. It is possible to have a rough idea of what the clip contains quickly. The skimmer speed is controlled by the mouse or touch pad, so it is possible to slow down, pick a point and play the video at normal speed from there. A researcher might use the skimmer to look for moments when two specific children are communicating. They may want to select those moments from the wealth of material to analyse further. Alternatively, for an observational film, a researcher may wish to explore framing that especially reveals the aesthetic qualities in the classroom and school. The skimmer will help quickly locate the most promising shots from hours of video. A child might be interested in how adults and children interact in different ways. The skimmer will help that child find shots that are likely to show that. Whether or not the software possesses a skimming function, finding out how clips can be reviewed and considering techniques for that, is a vital part of this aspect of the research and learning methods. In the process of review most software will allow researchers, teachers and children to select, organise and 'tag' the chosen material (Fig. 5.5).

Rejects and Favourites, Tagging, Using Notes and Metadata

In the process of filming and editing *SchoolScapes* and *Gandhi's Children* (the two films are described in Chapter 1), David MacDougall compiled catalogues, in tabular form, of shots and their content. The tables and notes were either word processed and then printed or handwritten. They were organised in physical folders. MacDougall's factual notes become a record of both what had been filmed and, subsequently, how thematic components might be organised in editing. As he compiles this catalogue, the names he gives to various scenes become basic textual labels attached to the audio-visual material. This way of working embeds

Fig. 5.5 Reviewing video clips

access to detail with in a structural overview. Rather than paper based cataloguing, video editing software may offer that functionality in a way that also offers immediate access to audio-visual material. This simultaneous awareness of general themes, the sensations and perceptions offered by audio-visual recordings, and access to great detail in each circumstance and filmic sequence is a very powerful route to both intuitive and analytic knowledge. Children may not need to be as exacting as an anthropologist in keeping detailed records of what they film in order to benefit from observational filmmaking as pedagogy. Indeed, it will be difficult to persuade children to do that. However this 'tagging' and keeping track of scenes, shots and parts of shots is an organisational tool in dealing effectively with a lot of video material. In some video editing software environments, not only is it possible to name, and tag clips, it is also possible to add notes to an audio-visual file. These become embedded with the clip. The words and terms in those notes can be searched for later, bringing into the visual software environment only material 'tagged' in that way. Video editing software will also offer access to file metadata. This may present information such as the date and time the clip was made, the length of the clip and other useful data embedded in the clip by the camera. This information may be searchable and underscores any tagging of clips (or parts of clips) in the review process.

As children review video, perhaps using the function of a skimmer, they may be able to make two fundamental decisions as they go. Firstly they may be able to tag clips as 'rejects'. Or conversely, they may select a clip as a 'favourite'. The software may then be able to present only 'favourite' clips and hide everything that has been rejected. If children collaborate with other children or adults in this process, the talk about what is a 'favourite' or 'reject', in and of itself, can be both reflective and revealing. This opportunity is deepened if children are talking about tagging clips in more subtle ways. For example, perhaps reviewing and tagging material which shows talk between children in class on the one hand, and talk between a teacher and a child on the other.

Sound and Talk

Notwithstanding the obvious role of dialogue, sound is vital to the experience of video. To illustrate the powerful effect of coupling sound and image, consider how music soundtracks are a pervasive feature of feature films and television series made for entertainment. The music suggests an emotional ether suffusing experience. Music may convey doubt, dread, hope, relief, peace and so forth. Sound is also fundamental to how observational filmmaking works. Observational filmmakers do not use music to back their films. That would tend to dictate to viewers emotions the filmmaker suggests they should be feeling. But all manner of recorded sounds give a material quality to filmic experience. It is instructive to go back and view the observational film material suggested in Chapter 1, but this time focusing on the sounds and what they bring to the experience of the unfolding scenes. Editing software may allow researchers, teachers and children to consider organising, reviewing and tagging clips considering sound alone. What may seem, at first glance, a poor sequence in terms of image, might be powerful in relation to sound. Sounds may be separated into stand-alone tracks and overlain onto another part of the filming in editing.

Many video-editing software packages will show the waveforms from the recorded sound in a visual way. Editors can use these as visual prompts to help find precise moments when talk starts and ends. Editing software may allow the user to increase or decrease the sound levels in a particular sequence or perhaps apply filters to reduce unrelated noise such as hiss. The sounds of voices can be processed to prioritise clarity. This may be a great help, if talk is a vital component in the approach to research and learning. An image may be unusable if it shows two children talking, for example, and the recorded sound is poor so what they are saying cannot be made out. Curiously, an out of focus clip of the same children talking may be perfectly acceptable to a viewer, if they can clearly hear what the children are saying. When talking is a feature of the circumstances, sound frequently trumps image. Sounds and talking can often help link one shot to another in a scene, as an audio track is left to run into the subsequent visual material. This can suggest a continuum from one part of the scene to another even if, in fact, they were separated in time.

In short, the way a software package processes and edits sound is an important consideration in how the software might be used for research and learning. Adult users will benefit from familiarising themselves with these functions. Children can be helped to grasp the way sound and images work together in the editing software and the opportunities that software offers in terms of crafting an end product to share. At the very least, a review of the filmic material should encompass a consideration of the recorded sound.

Thinking About Assembling Shots into a Filmic Form

After organising, reviewing and tagging clips (or parts of clips), a software user will have an idea of what has been filmed. I suggest there are two distinct approaches to filming in an observational style. The first is to film with a purposeful and defined project in mind. For example, to observe how five-year-olds interact with adults in various different circumstances in school; the objective is to learn more about that. The second approach is to enter a setting not at all sure of what will be found and what might be going on and to use the camera to explore, observe and record to help think about that setting afterwards. It is only after such thoughtfulness that questions may form which will guide further study. In the latter case, a simple 'portrait' or 'landscape' of the setting and circumstances, without an overtly defined agenda or objective, might be very useful. In contrast, in the first instance, assembling clips into film sequences will likely be set up in order to build on the intuitive analysis the person-with-camera made as they decided what to film and how to film (in our example, as five-year-olds interacted with adults in school). Editing will then be a considered audio-visual response, continuing to develop a thoughtful analysis instigated because of the initial objective. In deciding which clips to show and in which order, the editor will represent how five-year-olds interacted with adults in a very deliberate way.

The point to takeaway from this short discussion is that not only is video editing software an excellent audio-visual environment for organising, reviewing and tagging clips, an initial and essential process in analysis, the same editing software is also a powerful tool for constructing research or learning outcomes designed to share knowledge with others. Whist I was a doctoral candidate I was trained to write academic text. The essays, papers and final thesis I produced were each written with differing objectives for different academic audiences. My intensive training, and a great deal of practice in appropriate writing techniques, helped me learn the craft of academic writing so that I could share my empirical research and theoretical ideas with others. Observational filmmaking is available to education researchers as a very powerful route to knowledge. But as in learning the craft of academic writing, researchers should accept that a craft of both camera use and editing would be needed to both analyse what is recorded and share audio-visual constructed outcomes with others. A parallel argument can be made in respect if learning. A great deal of time is spent in school training children to write. If children are to also benefit from audio-visual learning using cameras and editing software and to communicate ideas in an audio-visual form, they will need support, via pedagogy, to achieve those goals. Children will benefit from being able to communicate and share ideas in a thoughtful, carefully constructed audio-visual forms.

Assembling and Adjusting Selected Shots into Sequences

Selected clips, and parts of clips, can be dragged onto and then organised in a linear space, often called a timeline. Researchers, teachers and children can decide on the order of clips, reorder them, and adjust the start and point of each clip in relation those that precede it or follow it. Many software packages will allow sequences of clips to be banded one above another so that an editor might explore, in an audio-visual environment, how material from one filming session might be inserted into material from another. Editing software sometimes allows the audio channels to be disconnected from the clips. This means an editor can combine audio from different sessions or run a sequence of sound, such as a conversation, over images from another shot.

So the editing environment allows users to construct audio-visual outcomes, selected and then ordered, from the filmed material. The resulting filmic sequences are not only representations, which reflect a multitude of decisions; they are also further evidence of analytic thinking. Thus, the analysis the person-with-camera made, evident in choices made whilst filming, combined with the analysis of those shots as they are reviewed, organised and tagged in the software, is further enhanced by the reconstruction of material as it is further selected from and combined into filmic outcomes. As I suggested in the previous sub-section, this mirrors the kinds of processes a researcher might use to produce academic text after gathering data, organising, analysing and then constructing an academic outcome. The difference is that, with observational filmmaking, the whole procedure is primarily audio-visual. It is thus perceptual, corporeal, material, aesthetic and affective before it is word based. Kinds of knowledge that are gained intuitively and perhaps ineffably come to the fore. This is particularly valuable when getting to know and understand more about other people's experiences and especially so when children's experiences as they live and learn in school are at hand.

I have seen 10 and 11 year-old children pick up the most basic functions of a professional editing software package in a few minutes. The processes are intuitive. Children who have grown up using and communicating in digital environments find using editing software quite straightforward. I realise many children do not have that advantage, but even so, the functionality is very easy to learn. Of course, learning and practicing how to craft highly resolved outcomes as finished films takes time and experience. But a high level of finish is not always a desired outcome; children are very capable of producing roughly edited film sequences. I have found watching and listening to how two children collaborate to construct an edit of the material they shot very helpful in coming to understand their decisions they made as they filmed. In observing what is going on as children are working inside the software environment, there is a great deal to be learnt. For example, how they are now considering what is important and what is less important about what they originally filmed? How are they intuiting and conceptualising the decisions they are making about what to share with others and why that is important to them?

Beginnings, Cuts, Transitions and Ends

The information a filmmaker shares as a film opens will help orientate a viewer. This might be presented in text form. For example, short written information about 'who' 'where' and 'when' might immediately answer many straightforward questions. Observational films are characterised by an absence of a narrator. This is so that viewers are able to engage with the filmic material without being directed by the filmmaker as to what it is happening and what that means. But one or two sentences, which relay a little more information about the circumstances, could be very helpful. For example, if the film shows children learning to read, announcing their age and a statement about the time scale encompassed by a film could shortcut potential misunderstandings. For example it might be useful to state at the start that children are 4 and 5 years old and that older children from that particular school shot the film over a period of 6 weeks.

If there are significant changes in circumstances as the film progresses, it might be welcome to introduce brief orientating text within the film as one circumstance transits to another. The age of children might have changed or perhaps the film continues but now the material was shot in a different school. At the end of the film, it is possible to show a list of who took part and acknowledge the support they, and relevant institutions, offered. Although introducing text into a beginning, end or transition within observational film is worth considering, other forms of transition are both ubiquitous and powerful constructive tools.

Most software packages offer a range of ways of audio-visually transiting from one shot to another or from one scene to a next. The simplest way is to cut from one shot to the following shot. These standard cuts, or 'hard' cuts, are used in almost all fiction and documentaries made for entertainment. Take a look at an example of your favourite TV box-set drama or feature film and count the amount of time each shot is held before there is a cut to another. There are statistics available which show a variation in average shot length per genre. This ranges from 4 seconds for action films to just over fifteen seconds for horror films. Documentaries come in at an average of around thirteen seconds a shot (Follows, 2017). Observational films operate in a very different way. Immersion in a scene might mean that shots are held for much longer with out cuts from one shot to another. In David MacDougall's *SchoolScapes*, discussed in Chapter 1, many of the shots last for several minutes, some as long as five minutes. MacDougall is not driving a narrative forward, nor is he attempting a form of entertainment, he is calmly sharing with viewers what it was like to be observing and sensing the experience of the Rishi Valley School. Rapid cuts from one shot to another would not help that aim.

However, in *SchoolScapes* one scene inevitably ends before another begins. MacDougall shows this transition by fading the shot to black, holding a black screen for around two seconds and then fading from black into the new scene. The effect suggests a change in place and perhaps time. It also shows that the film material is but a brief window on the continuity of unfolding experiences of pupils and adults in the school. Those experiences began before the filming started and continue after the shot ends. Thus viewers sense the experiences of others in flux rather than in a contained or delineated form. Software will offer a wide range of transitions between shots. Some if the effects are very entertaining. Children will certainly have very different ideas about the value of these effects than adults.

Another basic cut used ubiquitously in fiction and documentary films is the cut away. This may insert a detail from another shot from the same scene to help show context or give the viewer more information. In the example of a child learning to read, it might well be helpful to insert a shot of the pages the child is reading, perhaps filmed from over their shoulder. The voice of the child continues unbroken over the cut away until the film returns to show the child reading with the adult. Many software packages make this very easy to do. In this way an observational filmmaker might construct a scene in which: the general circumstances of the reading lesson are shown, the body language of the relationship between adult and child is visible, the expressions on the child's face reveal something of the nature of the reading experience, the design and layout of the book can be seen, and it may well be possible to follow the words in the book as the child reads them. The whole process of the reading lesson might begin with a look at how the adult and child settled down. It might end with a conversation between them about what the child will be doing next and then how the adult or child puts the book away. Thus, the filming of the process allows the filmmaker, as they edit, to share different aspects of their own experience as they observed the experience the child and adult when reading together. Clearly, hugely significant qualities of these experiences could never be rendered in words alone. Or at least, any attempt to do so would be very inefficient.

There is a wealth of advice online and in books on the different kinds of ways filmmakers can put shots together to make a film. Objectives and intentions vary hugely and these are revealed in how the end products appear. It is very likely that an action sequence in a police drama will be edited very differently from an observational film about children learning to read. In the simplest terms, researchers, teachers and children can easily explore how transitions, cuts, beginnings and endings will help them assemble their film material in a coherent and purposeful way. Researchers and teachers should explore pedagogy to enable this. Collaborations in editing, between children and researchers, teachers and researchers, children and other children, whether or not all were involved in the initial filming, can be powerful reflective tools. An enormous benefit to education research is that the original observational film material, shot at the time and in the specific circumstances pertaining, is always easily available to whoever wishes to review again or make a new edit from those original shots. Unlike other forms of coded data used by education researchers, observational material can be viewed, commented on and discussed by children themselves. They have an even greater interest in this, if it is they (or children they know or relate to) who filmed the material in the first place. During these processes of collaborative review and editing of observational film material, children can more easily share knowledge about their experiences living and learning in school, about which they are expert.

Fine Crafting

Observational filmmakers in social anthropology usually take great care to craft finished films. These might have refined aesthetic qualities. Filmmakers want to share their work and it is natural that they want the forms those works take to be thoughtful, communicative and professional. In research, there is a long running and an on-going debate about how film can convey anthropologic knowledge. On the one hand when film is artfully crafted, the social scientificity of anthropology is threatened. On the other hand, experiential knowledge about material, aesthetic and affective qualities in the circumstances of others' lives does not fit at all neatly into scientific method. The careful construction of film with those ineffable qualities in the foreground may be quite unscientific but benefit the successful sharing of qualities in experience, which are very hard to pin down in other ways.

Jay Ruby (2008) argues that anthropological filmmakers should be very wary of the conventions of documentary. He goes as far as stating: "The need to make something the film world calls 'a good film' with commercial potential and that qualifies for the increasingly common market-based festivals should be abhorrent to scholars" (p. 4). I would add that the ethnographic film festival circuit, which may be less driven by prospects of financial reward, but is clearly part of a market in prestige, respect and intellectual capital, has parallel dangers attached. Yet, just as with academic writing, the ability to craft a finely rendered outcome is helpful in conveying ideas. If those ideas are better communicated via bringing into play artistic rather than scientific sensibilities, it might be because such sensibilities are, as Dewey (1934) argued, inseparable from thought. The craft of the filmmaker may make the sequence of edited filmic images not only easier to watch but more effective in conveying those experiences which words cannot deal with well. The films of David MacDougall (see Chapter 1) are finely crafted but they are far from the narrative driven, entertainment orientated films of TV documentary makers for example. They avoid the danger Ruby (2008) sees.

But, if children are using video cameras in an observational style and then rough editing their results so that they can take charge of sharing their experiences with others, is it necessary that they also learn to craft fine looking end products? The Indian children's films referred to in Chapter 2 were collaboratively edited. The child sat alongside the adult filmmaker and the adult used the software. The adult crafted the subtlety of certain juxtapositions and transitions. The child would not have known how to do that. There is no doubt the films are easier to watch because the editing is well done. I suggest that, whether or not children do more than rough edit their films, will depend on the circumstances and the objectives of the observational filmmaking project. The age of children will be a factor, the time available to teach children editing skills is a vital consideration, and availability of software and access to computers immediately comes into play and much else besides.

Having said all that, it is fundamental that researchers, teachers and children come to understand what it is to edit the audio-visual material they shoot and how that might be achieved. The basic functionality of software to support deep and collaborative forms of reflection on both the filmic material and the original circumstances in which it was shot can be summarized in terms of those functions that allow users to:

- store, back up and name audio-visual files
- import shots and organise these within the software environment
- review audio-visual material

- tag files and parts of files
- use notes and metadata
- be aware of editing sound and talk
- think about assembling shots into filmic form and why that is useful
- assemble and adjust selected shots into sequences
- begin, cut, transit and end filmic sequences
- export and share filmic sequences
- view and talk about what can be seen and heard.

These functions can be assimilated by researchers, teachers and children and used to deepen knowledge within the research processes, even if they do not go on to craft highly finished films.

Exporting and Sharing

Most software packages will allow the filmic material to be exported in different forms for different purposes. These can vary from the most compressed and therefore smallest files ready for social media platforms to the largest files for high quality broadcast video. Free and less expensive software will focus on the smaller file sizes, which are easily sharable via the Internet. There is significant loss of quality of both sound and image with highly compressed video. If an objective is to share video in a form which does justice to the subtlety in phenomena such as colour, texture and sound, then it is worth planning for the larger file sizes which will retain more digital information closer to, if not exactly as, it was recorded.

How secure is the video that is shared? Who owns the video material? What permissions are in place to share it? Is it appropriate for video material shot by children in school to be freely available? Adults may baulk at the idea that children might record audio-visual material, have control over it and then disseminate the video outcomes as they like. Yet, a child may argue that they shot the video with permission of the school and their parents. The child filmmaker's friends, who are seen in the film, also gave permission. The film excites everybody. They should be able to share it with whom they choose.

But, children grow quickly. They may be much less sure when they are eighteen about material they were happy to share when they were twelve years old. But if the adults have control over the film material and teachers, parents and children all gave permission in fill knowledge of the project at the time, should participants still have a veto on how the film is shared six years or more after the film was shot? These kinds of questions are only answerable in the specific circumstances of the project, and as I argued in Chapter 3, judgements rather than rules pertain. Ethics are situated. In one recent project I took the decision, with the participants, that the audio-visual files were only to be used in relation to that project and would not have a life outside of the project and its specific and pre-determined outcomes. That decision was appropriate to that project. It may not appropriate in others.

In my own research, to help manage how video is used, I have used a security enabled online platform to both store and share high quality video. This means I can set parameters to limit viewing and downloading to selected people (or nobody at all). But the platform also allows videos to be streamed on-line in a form compatible with the devices and Internet connections the viewers are using. So, if they know how to access the video, children can see it on the kinds of devices they are likely to use. Also, teachers may be able to share video in class on older computers, which may not cope well with data heavy files. On the other hand the online platform stores video in its original form and it is available, with permission, for downloading to use in a theatre style screening. I also have a back up of all the relevant files (both in their original form and in edited versions) on an encrypted, password protected drive. It is possible that very large volumes of video are generated by quiet a few camera users. How that video is stored and accessed must be considered, not just at the start of filming but throughout the editing and exporting process. These considerations are vital in the planning stage of the project, but any project will benefit from a built-in flexibility to respond as the work develops and needs change.

Viewing and Talking About Observational Film

In Chapter 1, I introduced Jean Rouch, the originator of *Cinéma Vérité*. Rouch explored how a cinematic form was created through improvisation, collaboration and performance as, for example, people could describe their own lives and memories stimulated and provoked by the presence of a film camera. The camera becomes an instrument of exploration. This was opposed to the idea of a camera recording an objective reality, which was somehow already out there waiting to be apprehended. In collaboration with sociologist Edgar Morin (b. 1921), Rouch also discovered that eliciting views of those he filmed when they saw themselves in the film produced new knowledge about their lives. At the start the film, *Chronicle of a Summer (1960),* the filmmakers are on screen as they began by talking about whether it is ever possible for people behave with sincerity knowing a camera is filming them. Rouch and Morin film people talking about a range of topics, some profoundly moving, that affect people and how they live together. Rouch and Morin then film the same participants again as they view the film and talk together as they see themselves on camera. Amongst many questions, this begs the question about where authenticity lies? In Rouch and Morin's first ruminations on the project, in the initial film of the participants as the discuss a range of issues, or in the film of the participants reacting and talking as they view themselves and listen to what they said to each other recorded on film? Or are those questions about authenticity (and related ones concerning sincerity and truth) simply unhelpful questions. Writing in the *New Yorker*, Richard Brody (2016) eulogises *Chronicle of a Summer*:

> It's one of the greatest, most audacious, most original documentaries ever made, one that poses—and, what's more, responds to—questions of cinematic form and moral engagement that underlie the very genre, the very idea of nonfiction film. Its ingenious reflexivity isn't the essence of its importance but is merely its source.

In Rouch's film participants discuss how conversation and performance—acting out and acting up—can reveal realities, emotional states triggered by memories, feelings and sensations. My own experience tells me that looking and listening to what has been filmed in a reflective and collaborative way, generates a further layer of meaning which is very useful in creating a deeper understanding of the experiences in play. Children may talk more freely and with greater insight when discussing film, which they might have shot or in which they are seen. On this bearing, not only is it the cameras, microphones and editing software that are tools catalysing research and learning. The projectors, screens, monitors, computers and the internet etc., through which and on which film material can be shared, are also tools which open pathways to useful knowledge and understanding of children's experiences as they live and learn in school. The way film is shown, the circumstances in which it is shown, and how the equipment and technology changes experiences of viewing film are also factors in the generation of any new knowledge.

Children can review shots in camera using the LCD screen or viewfinder and headphones to listen to what was said or sounds that were recorded. As has been set out in this section, children can easily review film material in the software environment, playing back shots, perhaps many times. I have noticed just how animated and thoughtful these conversations can be as they use editing software with film material they shot or appear in. However, in neither of these two previous cases are children viewing and talking about a deliberately constructed film sequence, or even, perhaps, a finished film.

If an observational film is edited, it has been constructed through a process that melds thoughtfulness, perceptions, sensations, feelings and an elusive but pervasive sense of an aesthetic into a product. The final film, even a rough edited final film, is much more than a record, it is the editor's experiential response to the experience of the person-with-camera and those who's experiences we see and hear in the film. This film, if it is shown, creates new experiences for viewers. The form in which researchers, teachers, children and other participants might talk about, discuss, write about and respond is highly relevant to the observational film experience. If through constraints such as time and availability of technology observational films are seen on older computer monitors in bright rooms and from quite a long way away, then it cannot be a surprise that viewers may not understand and respond to the experiences of others created in the circumstances of the filming, as well as they might. Researchers and teachers should acknowledge the conditions in which film is viewed openly and help children to understand more about how the form in which creative outcomes are shared is inextricably bound into ways in which those outcomes are understood.

Conclusion

This chapter has set out a generalised pedagogical framework for supporting children, teachers and researchers use video cameras and editing software appropriate for the task of observing and sharing children's experiences as they live and learn in school. This encompassed learning about:

- The varying nature of video cameras and other devises which record video
- The tools and components needed to film, including microphones
- Typical controls and functions on a camera
- A consideration for people being filmed
- Camera techniques for observational filmmaking
- Using video editing software tools from the perspective of observational filmmaking
- Fine crafting finished films
- Ways of sharing film material
- Viewing and talking about observational film.

A feature of observational filmmaking for education is how cameras are used. As techniques for observing with cameras are explored, a craft of observational filmmaking develops. This is extended by learning how video editing software can be used with the shots and clips from filming to further enable learning and research.

The question, which I will address in the rest of this book, is: How is it that observational filmmaking for education is research? In Chapter 3, I introduced ideas about phenomena, empathy, aesthetics, children's experiences and children as researchers. I critiqued a social science predilection to see video only as data for analysis and interpretation. But I also critiqued researchers who use video to create narratives, which support arguments for political and social change. In that case, video is the mouthpiece of the maker may be dominated by their ideology. In every case, the influence of ever changing technology on video cameras and editing software is always present. I have suggested throughout this book that material, aesthetic and affective experience should be centre stage. If all of that pertains, it is very hard indeed to see observational filmmaking as a scientific process of inquiry—even in the most open of qualitative processes located in social science domains. Therefore, to conclude this chapter and then fill out in Chapter 6, I will round off this book by exploring if it is helpful to see observational filmmaking for education as arts-based research and arts-based learning and whether that may or may not beneficially intersect with the predominance of scientificity in education.

In a chapter about arts-based research in education written by James Haywood Rolling Jr. (2017), there is an attempt to justify how art and design practices build theories via definable and theoretical representative tools. The problem is that Haywood Rolling Jr.'s (2017) insistence on an arts-based research (ABR) "inquiry architecture" refers to addressing research problems via science-orientated concepts such as data sets, even if those 'data sets' have artistic forms. It is as if, despite a passionate plea to acknowledge how knowledge can be constructed via artistic making, he has to return to a kind of scientificity in his language of theory, research questions, hypotheses, data collection, systematised analyses and so forth. The reason for this may be due to the struggles any arts based research discipline has to assert itself in a competitive world of university based research structures and funding. Education's allegiance to social science is much preferred before say, an allegiance to fine art, because how else might education take its place around the social science table? However, despite my misgivings, Haywood Rolling Jr.'s chapter (2017) includes an introductory account of 'thinking', which I reproduce here in full, as it captures something of the spirit of the process and practices of observational filmmaking, as I have described them in this chapter.

> In her influential book *Thinking in Systems*, Donella H. Meadows (2008) defines a system as a "set of elements or parts that is coherently organised and interconnected in a pattern or structure" that becomes more than the sum of its parts and "produces a characteristic set of behaviours" classified as "function" or "purpose" (p. 188). Ultimately the purpose of any research is to illuminate and activate the systems that sustain you – organising what you know so you can grow – calibrating your position and agency in the present world, as well as your fulcrum points for leveraging and unpacking prior knowledge into future possibilities. (Haywood Rolling Jr., 2017, p. 492)

It is perfectly possible to substitute the word 'research' with the word 'learning' in this extract. Using Haywood Rolling Jr.'s (2017) text as a model, observational filmmaking is valuable for both learning and research in schools because it actively illuminates the systems of living and learning in an organised way so that researchers, teachers and children can calibrate their position and agency in the present world. They can then grow, via understanding more, into future possibilities that are catalysed via the generation of new knowledge in this audio-visual form. Observational filmmaking for education is dynamic, experiential, experimental, explorative and deeply observed. It is one model, with unique characteristics that are especially accessible and valuable for children, for understanding human interrelationships with others, the natural and made worlds.

Running through the practical sub-sections of this chapter, it is clear that there are sets of interconnected and interrelated elements, which are coherently organised in ways that can generate structures that are more than the sum of their parts. This is thought manifest. But it is not thought formed in the abstraction of theorising, utterly dependent on words; it is thought formed in the flux of the visceral qualities of living and learning. **For children, teachers and education researchers,** the observational filmic materials' expressions of ineffability are only possible via pedagogy, which allows one person to learn with another in a craft of tool use and technique. Thus the structures, systems and processes of observational filmmaking are scaffolds for thoughtful manifestations of material, aesthetic and affective experience.

References

Brody, R. (2016). The extraordinary "chronicle of a summer". *The New Yorker*. Retrieved December 30, 2017 from https://www.newyorker.com/culture/richard-brody/the-extraordinary-chronicle-of-a-summer.

Dewey, J. (1934). Art as experience. In J. Boydston (Ed.), *John Dewey the later works, 1925–1953* (Vol. 10, 1988). Carbondale: Southern Illinois University Press.

Follows, S. (2017). *How many shots are in the average movie*. Retrieved December 28, 2017 from https://stephenfollows.com/many-shots-average-movie/.

MacDougall, D. (2006). *The corporeal image: Film, ethnography, and the senses*. Princeton, NJ: Princeton University Press.

MacDougall, D. (Director). (2008). *Gandhi's children* [Motion Picture]. Australia: Centre for Cross-Cultural Research, Australian National University.

Philibert, N. (Director). (2002). *Être et Avoir* [Motion Picture]. France: Maïa Films, Arte France Cinéma, Les Films d'Ici, Centre National de Documentation Pédagogique.

Ruby, J. (2008). Towards an anthropological cinema. *European Association of Social Anthropologists E-seminar Series*. Retreived December 29, 2017 from http://www.media-anthropology.net/index.php/e-seminars.

Rolling, J. H. (2017). Arts-based research in education. In P. Leavy (Ed.), *Handbook of arts-based research* (pp. 492–510). New York: Guilford Press.

6

Epilogue

Experiential Empiricism and Ethics

How do human beings actually make sense of tangled circumstances in living and from that knowledge create useful ways of acting that make that living better? Taking Fesmire's (2003) interpretive account of Deweyan ethics as a guide, Dewey's deeply empirical and pragmatic approach was social (humans share circumstances and experiences with others), imaginative (humans constantly generate new ideas and experiences to make progress through the flux of living) and artful (aesthetic and material experience underpins all meaning in what humans say and do). Therefore, Dewey (1931, 1934) argued that attention to experience should lead all inquiry. That is, rather than always seeking to impose a relational matrix of theory onto human experience, it is often more productive to attend carefully to experience through experience. To put this another way, just because experience seems a multifaceted, muddled and confusing phenomenon, it is all too tempting to impose theories onto experience to categorise and define just how humans live lives. However, such an approach to theorising first, may obscure—even deny—the very qualities through which learning about experience is possible. Therefore, it might be ethically preferable for education researchers to engage in meaningful ontologies before meaningful epistemologies. That suggests, in researching children's experiences as they live and learn in school, that knowledge gained via seeking definitions should be placed behind knowledge gained by attentiveness to living and learning.

In terms of observational filmmaking as a research practice, whether or not adults or children are the filmmakers, I suggest the way that both filmmakers and viewers come to know more about the experiences of those filmed is via attentiveness to emotional, material and aesthetic qualities—very human qualities which are part of how anyone comes to know more about others. Consider how one comes to make a friend and then come to know them better. If one person is describing that friend to another, such experiential knowing will be at the core of what is said. Knowledge of another is bound into experience of them. It seems almost a tautology to say that knowledge of children's experiences as they learn and live in school is bound into how those that come to know them experience them.

Taking a view that the processes of filming and editing an observational film are inclined more to the arts than the sciences, then I argue it is appropriate to return to Dewey who is forthright about how experience might be approached through art: "art is the most direct and complete manifestation there is of experience *as* experience" (p. 301). This implies that, to reveal the nature of children's experience in depth, researchers must embrace aesthetic and material experience, because "esthetic experience is experience in its integrity" (Dewey, 1934, p. 278). This is a significant challenge for education researchers, who set out to understand more about children's experiences as they live and learn in school. How can research respect and value the uniqueness of aesthetic and material experience and still draw out relationships with cognition, conceptualisation and interpretive analysis which humans use to structure useful ways of living and learning—in schools, for example?

Critics might suggest that the inherent and inevitable aesthetic self-consciousness of edited film material as a research outcome is too subjective to be appropriate in a research discipline—which should be orientated more towards science than art if it is to be useful. Another danger is that researchers who turn to observational film to express knowledge about ineffable qualities in living may unsuspectingly conflate outcomes with process—the filmic object with the work making the film (research outcomes with research processes). That is, researchers who commit to observational filmmaking *only* as outcomes, may miss the very thrust of an experiential research endeavour located in the working process of observing with video cameras. It is the working in and through aesthetic and material experience that useful understanding and, therefore, paths to new learning and knowledge will be found. This process is visible in observational film material whether or not it has been edited into a finely crafted finished film. That should alert education researchers to a danger of any approach that relies on highly crafted and beautiful observational films as research outcomes. Such artistic 'fineness' in presenting the experience of others might obscure just as much as disengaged theorising obscures through strict adherence to academic conventionality. In terms of my adoption of observational filmmaking as an education research method, I moved away from producing highly crafted edited films as constructed aesthetic research outcomes. Instead, I suggest that outcomes can remain embedded in the process of filmmaking, both camera work and software review. Therefore, new understanding is located within the processes of research rather than solely dependent on either refined filmic outcomes or academically framed definitions. That understanding is found within the craft and the pedagogy of filmmaking as applied in the specific circumstances of the research situation. Characteristics of this craft and its associated pedagogy were drawn out in Chapter's 1, the close of Chapter 2 and throughout Chapter 5 of this book.

There is no claim here that observational filmmaking offers some kind of enhanced and idealised 'realism'; on the contrary, the claim is that the deepest understanding is located in the nuanced sharing of subjective points of view within the specificity of the particular circumstances at hand. The observational sensibility that a process of filmmaking engenders, both camera work and editing, is explorative and experimental first. If definitions are sought out of interpretive commentaries on the research process, then those are built out of experience, which is retained as the bedrock to understanding.

Just as Dewey (1934) might have hoped, this kind of research is not valuable because it weaves a convincing narrative or engages consumers with a powerful and moving aesthetic, rather it is because aesthetics, ethics and epistemology are melded together and constituted as a meaningful expression of experience as useful research, engagement with which engenders understanding. That is, research about experience—in this case children's experience living and learning in school—is most useful when it draws that experience into the research frame without veiling, distancing or denying experiential qualities because of an artificial duality demanded by social science forms of analysis and subsequent academic representations in text.

Dewey and Deleuze

In her paper for the journal *Educational Philosophy and Theory*, Inna Semetsky (2003) posits that both John Dewey and Gilles Deleuze offer conceptual frames which re-position knowledge as inseparable from experimental and experiential processes of living. Semetsky (2003) draws out a sweeping conception of *thinking* that she finds in Deleuze, in which knowledge is generative before it is defining, always in flux, and is inevitably imbued with experiential qualities such as affect, the material and the aesthetic. She illustrates how the same sweep of thought occurs in Dewey. The view that Dewey and Deleuze inhabit similar ontological domains has other proponents. For example, Semetsky (2003) begins her paper by referring to Richard Rorty's (1982) claim that Dewey is "waiting at the end of the road which, for example, Foucault and Deleuze are currently travelling" (p. xviii). Rorty (1982) implies a possible convergence of Deweyan and Deleuzian theories of knowledge in both their pragmatism and their deeply empirical insistence on the primacy of experience.

I am briefly drawing attention to a Deleuzian view in the final chapter of this book, because a post-modern conception of philosophy he represents has become embedded in influential aspects of education theory and in practices in contemporary arts, including film. In arts education, for example, the a/r/tographers led by Rita Irwin (2004, 2014) have sought an organic, rhizomic process of non-definitional arts-based education research (ABER), which draws its inspiration from Deleuze. In contemporary visual art, Bishop (2012) charts the many forms of collaborative and relational visual art practices, which have abandoned fixed forms of images as representation. A key early theorist for these still unfolding practices in contemporary art was Nicolas Bourriaud (2002) whose articulation of relational aesthetics owes an acknowledged debt to Deleuze and his co-philosopher Guattari. Although philosophers may baulk at too close a comparison between Dewey and Deleuze, two very different thinkers in time, place and intellectual antecedents, illuminating a number of core Deleuzian tracks on the centrality of experiential process confirms the validity of my own conceptual frame for the developing methodology I am exploring in this book. It is within the flux of an always-inquiring experience that knowledge is, or *becomes*, as Deleuze (1994) terms it.

Colebrook (2002) demonstrates that "Deleuze took nothing for granted and insisted that the power of life … was its power to develop problems" (p. 2). This restless, constant state of inquiring is, in Deleuzian terms, a *becoming*—a constant state of evolving change. Colbrook (2002) puts it like this: "Instead of providing yet one more system of terms and ideas, Deleuze wanted to express the dynamism and instability of thought … the aim of writing should not be representation but invention" (p. 4). What are usually accepted as norms for rational argument and theorising inhibit access to knowledge in life-fullness, a becoming into an "open and creative whole of proliferating connections" (Colebrook, 2002, p. 5). This is a philosophy that intends to open new knowledge rather than enclose knowledge with definitions—a liberating and plausible route towards artistic forms of knowing that artists and arts educators intuitively and willingly follow.

Deleuze (1994) frames his philosophy as a synthesis of the sensible. This is an attempt through the medium of philosophical language to grasp in language something of the nature of the sensation of being, which as Deleuze is attempting to articulate, is at the fundamental heart of all knowledge. Without recognising this, by leaving experiencing being out of our frames of understanding, we know less. Attending to what is going on in the processes of making and consuming observational film can take us closer to this Deleuzian philosophical vision. The notion of the aesthetic, so vital in Dewey's conception of *Art as Experience*, is set in the beingness of art rather than in separating out judgements about art. As Rajchmann (2001) puts it, "through affect and percept, artworks hit upon something singular yet impersonal in our bodies and brains, irreducible to any pre-existent 'we'." (pp. 9–10).

For Deleuze, then, attending to beingness is acknowledging a permanent state of immanence as sources of all we know. Connecting in spirit to the same sources in William James that Erving Goffman (1974) cited, Deleuze (1977) asks for a "plane of immanence" to be considered as a "radical empiricism" (p. 49). It is in this sense that Rajchmann (2001) draws out of Deleuze the same collapsing of dualities, the energy of continuous imaginative inquiry and the demand to attend first to experience, even in respect of our own lived experience, that I have seen in Dewey:

> For immanence is pure only when it is not immanent to a prior subject or object, mind or matter, only when, neither innate nor acquired, it is always yet 'in the making'; and 'a life' a potential or virtuality subsisting in just such a purely immanent plane. (p. 13)

In terms of research and learning, when exploring much of what we do and say, humans can step outside of this sensation of being and get on with using all sorts of analytic frames to get at what is at hand. But I suggest that this is less acceptable for research about children's experiences as they live and learn in school. Here an exercise in thought is required, which allows the knowing ego of the researcher to dissolve into the material situation at hand. In this sense, the merging of the human holding the camera within the situation being filmed suggests that observation filmmaking can become a multilayered, multifaceted form of experiential thinking. This is generative thought as an essential precursor to any possible defining thought.

Such Deleuzian inspired appeals to experience have found a home in debates about qualitative and post-qualitative education research methodologies. For example, MacLure (2013) argues for materially informed research processes that are "non or post-representational research practices, drawing in contemporary materialist work that rejects the static, hierarchical logic of representation, and practices such as interpretation and analysis as conventionally understood" (p. 658). Searching for alternatives to realist and constructivist research ontologies, Fox and Alldred (2015) draw out new materialist forms of social research. Using conceptual frames drawn from Deleuze and Guattari (1977) they conflate components of research such as the researcher, data, methods and contexts and present these as 'research-assemblages'. The intention is to de-privilege research as creating knowledge through social construction and to promote research as a form of social production. Affect, rather than deliberate agency is the force at the centre of the research impact: "There is no subject and no object and no single element possesses agency. Rather, an affect is a 'becoming' that represents a change of state or capacities of an entity: this change may be physical, psychological, emotional or social" (Fox & Alldred, 2015, p. 401). They describe their ontology in this way:

> It shifts from conceptions of objects and bodies as occupying distinct and delimited spaces, and instead sees human bodies and all other material, social and abstract entities as relational, having no ontological status or integrity other than that produced by their relationship to other similarly contingent and ephemeral bodies, things and ideas. (p. 401)

There is a plethora of highly theoretical writing about education and social science research methodology in this materialist, affect driven vein. Much of the underlying intellectual impetus is found in post-modern, post-structural, and post-phenomenological philosophies of theorists such as Deleuze.

My problem with this strain of education research theorising, exemplified by the two articles cited above, is that it places ideas rather than experience centre stage. It does not do what it says on the tin. Such research is either dominated by an overt (or covert) political intention to bring about social change or by an adherence to theorising first. In other words, ideas, even idealism, dominate. That is precisely the effect of seeking knowledge via either learning or research *only* in ideas that Dewey's pragmatic philosophy and educational progressivism rejected.

Observational Filmmaking for Education and an Arts-Based Paradigm

I thought it valuable to make a connection between my own theoretical inspirations for this work, which I found in Dewey and particularly in *Art as Experience* (1934), with a post-modern frame. The philosophy of Deleuze provides an appropriate post-modern example. Looking further, within education research there is a pocket of arts-based researchers conducting ABER. As I have already pointed out, a/r/tographers, exemplified by the work of Rita Irwin (2004, 2008) are an example of this. Deleuzian inspired theoretical sentiments are found throughout a/r/tographers' academic writing on their methodology. Both inside and outside of the domain of education, thinkers such as Michel Foucault, Guattari and Bruno Latour have also inspired post-structuralist academics. For example, non-representational theorists in Geography might give a flavour of academic domains, which I suggest chime with the underlying theoretical currents of observational filmmaking methodology I am advocating. For example, Dewsbury (2003), Thrift (2007), and McCormack (2017) suggest how social theorists might go beyond representation and find geographical knowledge and meaning in embodied experiences. These thinkers emphasise experiential practice as a route to knowledge over theory building solely located within the abstracted scientificity of the social sciences.

But, just as with the post-qualitative education research theorists mentioned in the previous section, it is dangerous to go too far down this cul-de-sac of theorising which distances thought from experience. The practices of observational filmmaking for education that I have described in this book are valuable precisely because they do not abandon experiential thought for overtly intellectual abstractions. Because observational filmmaking is a form of thinking that is manifest in experience, it is available to children, teachers and researchers regardless of their academic training or intellectual interests and capacities.

Throughout this book observational filmmaking for education has been presented as a methodological tool. The methods employed depend on the use of various items such as cameras, microphones and editing software. These are physical and digital tools, which demand a craft in how they are used. Learning to use a tool effectively requires getting to know its capabilities well through practice. As observational filmmaking also engages directly with others, coming to understand the ethical implications of the craft are inseparable from the use of its tools. Because of all that, observational filmmaking for education must be pedagogical in its origin and as such, research and learning coincide. This is undeniably evident when researchers and teachers collaborate with children, who become camera users and film editors. But pedagogy sits at the root of how adults learn to use these tools as well. The generation of knowledge is dependent on the transmission of knowledge about the methods used to discover that knowledge.

Social scientists often start from a belief that research must be led by one or several research questions. These define the parameters of an inquiry. The aim is to answer the question. To do that a conceptual frame is explored which underpins the gathering of data, the organising and coding of that data, its analysis and interpretation followed by the dissemination of the new knowledge gained. By leading social research with a definitive question and by containing that research in a conceptual and theoretical frame, researchers can easily miss the overarching goals that drove their research in the first place. In this book, I have suggested that in education research such scientificity can privilege data collection and analysis in a way that irreversibly separates the outcomes of research from its subjects and consumers. To be specific, in order to come to understand more about children's experiences as they live and learn in school, teachers and researchers will need to engage with pervasive elements of that experience which are inevitably material, aesthetic and affective. Children experience school with their bodies and their minds. Their sensations drive their perceptions and their experiences are filled with thoughts and vice versa. There is no sense in leaving material, aesthetic and affective experience out of any research frame that has an overarching goal of understanding more about how children experience living and learning in school. If we are to improve the quality of children's learning and living in school, we should try to understand the fullness of their experience not limit our understanding to only that which can neatly fit into a social scientific frame.

Should all that imply that observational filmmaking for education, as it has been presented in this book, might best find a home in the arts and humanities rather than the social sciences? The very existence of that question, and the inference for funding and academic status that it might imply, shows the limitations of our academic categories. If observational filmmaking helps learning and research about children's experiences in schools should it not be valuable, even if it straddles established disciplines and defies neat categorisation? In her introduction to her edited *Handbook of Arts-Based Research* (ABR), Patricia Leavy (2018) argues that ABR is paradigmatically separate from qualitative and quantitative methodologies. This is because ABR assumes artistic practices and outcomes create and convey meaning. This meaning has aesthetic form. It has to have, because it is via aesthetic sensibilities that the making and consuming of artistic products engenders reflexivity and empathy and so builds a caring and compassionate understanding of others' experiences. Aesthetics, writes Leavy (2018, p. 5), "draw on sensory, emotional, perceptual, kinestheic, embodied and imaginal ways of knowing". I suggest Dewey (1934) would absolutely agree. I also suggest that this is an explanation of why viewers can learn so much about the circumstances and experiences from the children's observational films I cite in Chapter 2.

I have shown that observational filmmaking is not a discipline only accessible university-based academics. It is a transdisciplinary way of knowing and communicating that is available to every person as a way of thinking about different kinds of situations in different kinds of circumstances in order to come to know these and understand them better. Observational filmmaking is a craft and camera users and video editors, be they adults or children, will benefit from practice. But this is, in essence, no different from how skills in communicating through written language are a craft. The advantage, for both for children as participant researchers and for research about more ineffable qualities in children's experiences living and learning in school, is that observational filmmaking is corporeal, based in sensations and feelings and eminently sharable throughout the processes of learning and inquiry. That makes it very different from word-based and text-based forms of thinking.

McNiff clarifies ABR as "a process of inquiry whereby the researcher, alone or with others, engages in the making of art as a primary mode of inquiry" (2018, p. 24). He continues, "Art is a way of knowing and communicating [...] it is the artistic process of inquiry that can be used to explore [...] the totality of human experience" (p. 24). Building from that and distilling the impetus of this book, I suggest that an operational definition for observational filmmaking for education for research and learning could then be described as *a process of pedagogy and inquiry whereby the researcher, teacher and learner, alone or with others, engages in observational filmmaking as a primary mode of learning and inquiry.*

Then, is observational filmmaking for education an arts-based form of research? In respect of learning, should it be found in an arts education curriculum frame in schools? These questions reflect paradigm conflicts. These are especially noticeable, as social science patterns of inquiry tend to narrow into formats that are not receptive to artistic thinking and artistic experience. Indeed, "Staying close to artistic ways of knowing [...] goes against the grain of prevailing institutional mind sets and values" (McNiff, 2018, p. 22). So, McNiff (2018) acknowledges that there is conflict as artistic-based research processes abut social science-based research processes. This need not be a negative phenomena as different paradigms of knowledge creation offer to each other insights into how conceptual frameworks and resulting methods of inquiry deeply affect the possible parameters of knowledge and therefore the possible usefulness of research outcomes. They can, McNiff (2018) argues, compliment each other. I agree, the processes of observational filmmaking can work independently as learning or research, but this can intermesh with academic text, forms of analysis, or simply written and spoken interpretations to create a deeper, more rounded and more human knowledge about circumstances such as children's experiences in school. There is an advantage in opening research and learning to the widest possible spectrum of thought that encompasses the artistic, scientific and linguistic. Believing in science or believing in art is not at all mutually exclusive. Dewey would argue the reverse is true. What is dangerous and limiting is absolutist thinking which denies the one or the other or attempts to assimilate the one inside the other. That latter condition affects a great deal of art-based education research. If the only home education research seems to have is as a social science, there is a temptation is to shoehorn ABER practices into a social science paradigm; somehow looking for ways of categorising, qualitatively measuring or objectivising the arts-based processes and outcomes. But a neat fit is simply impossible. Trying to do so just misses the point of experiential empirical knowledge. It flies in the face of common sense to argue that the only way of understanding others is to measure their behaviour, however lose and qualitative that measuring is. A human comes to understand another human by getting to know them and experiencing them in a myriad of ways. Social science may offer routes to specific areas of knowledge about others but it can never encompass all possible forms of knowledge.

To reflect on where a disciplinary home for observational filmmaking for education might be, I suggest observational filmmaking shifts across paradigms of knowledge generation and expression. Or it may simply operate in its distinctive way. It may aid learning across curricula categories. But it may be a form of learning valuable in itself. Most of all, as I demonstrate throughout this book, the processes within observational filmmaking for education are a powerful method for thoughtful experience of others, so that qualities in material, aesthetic and affective are not lost. These are qualities that a dominating scientificity will miss. Therefore, observational filmmaking for education is a transdisciplinary process dealing with human experience and understanding. It cannot be completely circumscribed as a social science discipline, nor is it entirely artistic in its processes and manifestation. It may be a partner to social science research methods about children and schools, it may also become a beautiful expression of children's experience as they live and learn in school from which a great deal of understanding results. The bottom line is that observational filmmaking is a useful method to deepen both learning and research.

Some Advantages of Observational Filmmaking for Education Research and Learning

Some of the advantages of observational filmmaking for education in terms of education research and learning might be summarised as follows. I am grateful to the example of Leavy (2018) who used a similar approach to argue for the advantages of ABR.

Exploration and discovery. The thoughtful use of the camera as a tool supports one person in how they can observe what it is that is going on in different circumstances in schools and classrooms. That person can be a child, a teacher or a researcher. The outcomes of the looking and listening carefully are recorded and easily shared with others. This enables viewers not only to share in the experience of those being filmed but also to share the experience of the person-with-camera. This can be a powerful way to explore circumstances. New discoveries will be made. Reflection, review, and discussion with others may generate vital questions to explore further.

Generating new perceptions and opportunities for research and learning. The processes and outcomes of observational filmmaking will allow children, teachers and researchers to collaborate and create new viewpoints on children's experiences in school which are very difficult to access using text based methods. These are eminently sharable. This sharable experiential audio-visual media opens opportunities for research learning, via talking, reflecting and interpreting what observational filmmaking material shows.

Connecting the general with the particular and vice versa. Observational filmmaking can reveal a general context quickly and almost simultaneously show how detailed elements within that context are interconnected. For example, a process, such as learning to read, happens in the general environment of the classroom and school, and is deeply affected by that. But within that process, turning pages, tones of voice, words and pictures, how children are sitting (and much else besides) all interrelate to contribute to how the reading works. Observational filmmaking is able to make those connections without losing the sense of the whole process. That interconnectedness of the physical and cognitive in the reading process is almost impossible to render with words alone. Academic research outcomes as academic text cannot connect others, such as teachers and other children, with the experiences of children as they live and learn in school.

Empathetic and emotional routes to understanding more. Observational filmmaking can catalyse an empathetic engagement with the experiences of those participating in the filming. This opens the possibility of building an emotional understanding of the lives of children in school and how emotions affect learning. Without an emotional understanding, research can become dry, remote and disconnected from the lives of those it seeks to improve. This is especially pertinent when children are learning. The revealing of children's emotional experience whilst learning offers children, teachers and researchers opportunity for critical engagement with the sensation of learning. This is valuable knowledge and supports the development of a deeper more human understanding about children's experiences in school. Academic text is unemotional, usually unapproachable, and deeply un-empathetic in its intentions. It does not engage with the phenomena of material, aesthetic and affective experiences. It therefore denies access to many, especially children and teachers, so that they cannot directly benefit from a critical engagement with the research.

Participation, collaboration and multiple perspectives. Observational filmmaking for learning and research is necessarily participatory and collaborative. A person-with-camera becomes a very visible part of the circumstances of the filming and engages directly with others in that circumstance. The outcomes of filming depend on how both the observer and those who are observed by the camera interact with each other. This participatory sharing in the circumstances of the filming extends to the circumstances of editing and viewing. Here, as recorded experiences are reviewed, analysed, assembled and shared in an audio-visual form, the experience of those being filmed, the person filming, the software user and any eventual viewers coalesce. Observational filmmaking for education depends on all agreeing to share these experiences with each other. New knowledge is thus generated by all from multiple perspectives, not only from the perspective a researcher, a teacher or just one child. A wide range of people can readily share in the outcomes of observational filmmaking and will bring their own perspectives to bear. In this way, a research or learning process naturally generates dialogue. It is open to multiple ways of interpretation, decentralising and democratising the value of research and ways of learning so that a more open access to better understanding is available to more.

Melding of research, learning and pedagogy. Observational filmmaking for education depends on pedagogy. Craft is needed to use the filmmaker's tools of cameras, microphones and editing software, together with many additional components and internal functions. There are varying filmmaking styles and techniques, including how different relationships between filmmakers and participants are generated and develop. All can be learnt about and practiced in a myriad of different ways. Each affects both the processes and outcomes of observational filmmaking for learning and for education research. Pedagogy also facilitates the sharing and transmission of knowledge that results. In observational filmmaking for education, especially when children are the filmmakers, pedagogy remains upfront and in the foreground throughout.

Foregrounding experiential meaning before narrative meaning. Even in academic papers in the social sciences, narrative is present. Story telling is ubiquitous. For example, a research journey may move through exploring the intellectual background to the research, the discovery of a research question, accounting for the methodology used to answer that question, a description of the methods used to gather relevant data, an account of the analysis of that data, the interpretation of the results and a conclusion which returns to address the original question. In television and cinema the quality of the story telling and how narrative is driven often determines the success of the media, at least in terms of entertainment. In both these academic and media based examples, the drive is towards a coherent and complete end product. Observational filmmaking is different. Although narratives may help create a structure for a filmic sequence, as a process is followed for example, and although highly crafted and aesthetic end products are possible, in observational filmmaking qualities such as patience, stillness, and an awareness of the aesthetic and material in the circumstances of the filming are often dominant. Overt narrative is secondary. This means that roughly edited films or simply a review of individual clips from a filming session may be quite sufficient given the objectives of the research/learning. That does not mean that the craft of editing will not usefully construct deeply thoughtful and felt products from the shared experiences of person-with-camera, those being filmed, and the editing software user. Often, a filmmaking project will begin with a particular objective in mind (for example an audio-visual exploration of a child learning to read). The way the camera is used in the circumstances of the classroom as, perhaps, a child and adult interact in the reading lesson, is a first layer of experiential analysis of what it is that is going on. The filming may return over several weeks or months to follow the progress of the child. In the editing software environment, the material will be reviewed, organised and tagged and a succession of clips and parts of lips may be assembled into a complete film. In each part of that process much will be discovered.

Conclusion

Observational filmmaking places experiential meaning before narrative meaning. The act of filmmaking and viewing, and the processes of editing are visceral, aesthetic and affective. There is direct engagement with our material world as filming records phenomena such as colour, light, texture and sound. This is not overtly intellectual although it is very thoughtful. In camera use and editing observational film techniques are naturally analytic, but rather than text and word based, these analyses foreground qualities such as the material, aesthetic and affective. Experience is never abandoned in a quest to discover and articulate its parts. It remains ever present. Researchers, teachers and children can return again and again to filmic material in its raw unedited form or as the constructed products of edited filmic sequences. Observational filmic outcomes can leave a lasting impression, even a sensation of having been alongside the filmmaker in the specific and situated circumstances they were filming in. This depth of a shared experiential engagement both in the making and in the consuming of filmic products is powerful fuel for learning. It is in the pedagogical interaction between researchers, teachers and children that the processes of observational filmmaking are shared, practiced and crafted into filmic outcomes. I suggest that this *pedagogical mode* of audio-visual thinking is the reason why observational filmmaking can be research in education and about education and why it provides enormously rich and catalytic material for that research. Observational filmmaking for education can generate experiential knowledge of children's experiences in schools and catalyse a more rounded, deeper and more human understanding of those experiences.

References

Bishop, C. (2012). *Artificial hells*. London: Verso.
Bourriaud, N. (2002). *Relational aesthetics* (Trans. S. Pleasance, & F. Woods with the participation of M. Copeland). Paris: Les presses du reel (Original work published in French in 1998).
Colebrook, C. (2002). *Gilles Deleuze*. London: Routledge.
Deleuze, G. (1977). *Qu'est-ce que la philosophie?* Paris: Minuit.
Delueze, G. (1994). Chapter V: Asymmetrical synthesis of the sensible. In *Difference and repetition*. New York: Columbia University Press.
Deleuze, G., & Guattari, F. (1977). *Anti-Oedipus* [in the English language translation]. London: Viking Penguin.
Dewey, J. (1931). Qualitative thought. In J. Boydston (Ed.), *John Dewey the later works, 1925–1953* (Vol. 5, 1988). Carbondale: Southern Illinois University Press.
Dewey, J. (1934). Art as experience. In J. Boydston (Ed.), *John Dewey the later works, 1925–1953* (Vol. 10, 1988). Carbondale: Southern Illinois University Press.
Dewsbury, J.-D. (2003). Witnessing space: 'Knowledge without contemplation'. *Environment and Planning A, 35*, 1907–1932.
Fesmire, S. (2003). *John Dewey and moral imagination*. Bloomington: Indiana University Press.
Fox, N., & Alldred, P. (2015). New materialist social inquiry: Designs, methods and the research-assemblage. *International Journal of Social Research Methodology, 18*(4), 399–414.
Goffman, E. (1974). *Frame analysis: An essay on the organization of experience*. London: Harper and Row.

Irwin, R. (2004). A/r/tography: A metonymic métissage. In R. Irwin & A. de Cosson (Eds.), *A/r/tography: Rendering self through arts-based living inquiry* (pp. 27–40). Vancouver, BC: Pacific Educational Press.

Irwin, R. (2008). A/r/tography. In L. Given (Ed.), *The SAGE encyclopedia of qualitative research methods* (pp. 26–28). Los Angeles: Sage.

Irwin, R. (2014). *Radicant teacher education.* Paper delivered at the 2nd Conference on Arts Based Research and Artistic Research, University of Granada, Spain, 29 January 2014. Retrieved August 20, 2017 from http://art2investigacion.weebly.com/uploads/2/1/1/7/21177240/spain_final_new.pdf.

Leavy, P. (Ed.). (2018). *Handbook of arts-based research.* New York: The Guilford Press.

MacLure, M. (2013). Researching without representation? Language and materiality in post-qualitative methodology. *International Journal of Qualitative Studies in Education, 26*(6), 658–667.

MacDougall, D. (Director). (2008). *Gandhi's Children.* [Motion Picture]. Australia: Centre for Cross-Cultural Research, Australian National University

McCormack, D. (2017). The circumstances of post-phenomenological life worlds. *Transactions of the Institute of British Geographers, 42*(1), 2–13.

McNiff, N. (2018) Philosophical and practical foundations of artistic inquiry: Creating paradigms, methods, and presentations based in art. In P. Leavy (Ed.), *Handbook of arts-based research* (pp. 22–32). New York: The Guilford Press.

Rajchmann, J (2001). Introduction. In G. Deleuze, *Pure immance* (pp. 7–23). New York: Zone Books.

Rorty, R. (1982). *The consequences of pragmatism.* Minneapolis: University of Minnesota Press.

Semetsky, I. (2003). Deleuze's new image of thought, or Dewey revisited. *Educational Philosophy and Theory, 35,* 17–29.

Thrift, N. (2007). *Non-representational theory: Space, politics, affect.* London: Routledge.

References

Alderson, P. (1995). *Listening to children*. London: Barnardos.
Alderson, P. (2008). *Young children's rights: Exploring beliefs*. London: Jessica Kingsley Publishers.
Alexander, T. (1987). *John Dewey's theory of art, experience, and nature: The horizon of feeling*. Albany: SUNY Press.
Alexander, T. (1998). The art of life: Dewey's aesthetics. In L. Hickman (Ed.), *Reading Dewey* (pp. 1–22). Bloomington: Indiana University Press.
Alexander, T. (2013). John Dewey's uncommon faith: Understanding 'religious experience'. *American Catholic Philosophical Quarterly, 87*(2), 347–362.
Andrew, G. (2003, June 11–18). Massive hit. *Time Out*, p. 2.
Balázs, B. (1970). *Theory of the film: Character and growth of a new art*. New York: Dover Publications.
Baldacchino, J. (2014). *John Dewey: Liberty and the pedagogy of disposition*. Dordrecht, The Netherlands: Springer.
Banks, M. (2001). *Visual methods in social research*. London: Sage.
Barone, T. (2003). Challenging the educational imaginary: Issues of form, substance, and quality in film-based research. *Qualitative Inquiry, 9*, 202–217.
Barone, T., & Eisner, E. (2012). *Arts based research*. Thousand Oaks, CA: Sage.
Bishop, C. (2012). *Artificial hells*. London: Verso.

Bourriaud, N. (2002). *Relational aesthetics* (Trans. S. Pleasance & F. Woods with the participation of M. Copeland). Paris: Les presses du reel (Original work published in French in 1998).

Bregstein, P. (1986). (TV Film). *Jean Rouch and his camera in the heart of Africa*. Documentary Educational Resources.

Breyer, T., & Gutland, C. (Eds.). (2015). *Phenomenology of thinking: Philosophical investigations into the character of cognitive experiences*. New York: Routledge.

Brody, R. (2017). The extraordinary "chronicle of a summer". In *The New Yorker*. Retrieved December 30, 2017 from https://www.newyorker.com/culture/richard-brody/the-extraordinary-chronicle-of-a-summer.

Chriss, J. (1995). Some thoughts on recent efforts to further systematize Goffman. *Sociological Forum, 10*(1), 177–186.

Christensen, P., & James, A. (2008). *Research with children: Perspectives and practices*. New York, NY: Routledge.

Christensen, P., & Prout, A. (2002). Working with ethical symmetry in social research with children. *Childhood, 9*(4), 477–497.

Clifford, J., & Marcus, G. (Eds.). (1986). *Writing culture: The poetics and politics of ethnography*. Los Angeles: University of California Press.

Colebrook, C. (2002). *Gilles Deleuze*. London: Routledge.

Colleyn, J.-P. (2009). *Jean Rouch. Cinéma et anthropologie*. France: Cahiers du Cinéma.

Coplan, A., & Goldie, P. (Eds.). (2014). *Empathy: Philosophical and psychological perspectives*. Oxford: Oxford University Press.

Dalston, L., & Lunbeck, E. (2011). *Histories of scientific observation*. Chicago: University of Chicago Press.

de Bolla, P. (2001). *Art matters*. Cambridge, MA: Harvard University Press.

Deleuze, G. (1977). *Qu'est-ce que la philosophie?* Paris: Minuit.

Deleuze, G. (1994). Chapter V: Asymmetrical synthesis of the sensible. In *Difference and repetition*. New York: Columbia University Press.

Deleuze, G. (2001). *Pure immance*. New York: Zone Books.

Deleuze, G., & Guattari, F. (1977). *Anti-Oedipus* (in the English language translation). London: Viking Penguin.

Depew, D. (2005). Empathy, psychology, and aesthetics: Reflections on a repair concept. *Poroi, 4*(1), 99–107.

Derry, S., Pea, R., Barron, B., Engle, A., Erickson, F., Goldman, R., …, Sherin, B. (2010). Conducting video research in the learning sciences:

Guidance on selection, analysis, technology and ethics. *Journal of the Learning Sciences, 19*(1), 3–53.

Dewey, J. (1896). The reflex arc concept in psychology. *Psychological Review, 3*(4), 357–370.

Dewey, J. (1931). Qualitative thought. In J. Boydston (Ed.), *John Dewey the later works, 1925–1953* (Vol. 5, 1988). Carbondale: Southern Illinois University Press.

Dewey, J. (1934). Art as experience. In J. Boydston (Ed.), *John Dewey the later works, 1925–1953* (Vol. 10, 1988). Carbondale: Southern Illinois University Press.

Dewey, J. (1938). Theory of Inquiry. In J. Boydston (Ed.), *John Dewey the later works, 1925–1953* (Vol. 12, 1988). Carbondale: Southern Illinois University Press.

Dewsbury, J.-D. (2003). Witnessing space: 'Knowledge without contemplation'. *Environment and Planning A, 35,* 1907–1932.

Doran, A. (2014). Deciphered by children: The city's view from below. *The Asia Pacific Journal of Anthropology, 15*(5), 470–473.

Eisner, E. (1998). *The enlightened eye, qualitative inquiry and the enhancement of educational practice.* Columbus: Prentice Hall.

Falcon, R. (2003, July). Back to basics. *Sight & Sound,* p. 38.

Feld, S. (2003). Editor's introduction. In S. Feld (Ed.), *Cine-ethnography—Jean Rouch* (pp. 1–28). Minneapolis: University of Minnesota Press.

Fesmire, S. (2003). *John Dewey and moral imagination.* Bloomington: Indiana University Press.

Fesmire, S. (2015). *Dewey.* New York: Routledge.

Flyvbjerg, B. (2001). *Making social science matter: Why social inquiry fails and how it can succeed again.* Cambridge: Cambridge University Press.

Flyvbjerg, B. (2004). Phronetic planning research: Theoretical and methodological reflections. *Planning Theory & Practice, 5*(3), 283–306.

Follows, S. (2017). *How many shots are in the average movie.* Retrieved December 28, 2017 from https://stephenfollows.com/many-shots-average-movie/.

Fox, N., & Alldred, P. (2015). New materialist social inquiry: Designs, methods and the research-assemblage. *International Journal of Social Research Methodology, 18*(4), 399–414.

Gabriel, T. (1982). *Third cinema in the third world: The aesthetics of liberation.* Ann Arbor: University of Michigan Research Press.

Gentleman, A. (2004, October 3). Film's fallen hero fights on for his class. *The Guardian*.

Ginsburg, F. (2014). Chronicles of the ephemeral: Some thoughts on Delhi at eleven. *The Asia Pacific Journal of Anthropology, 15*(5), 455–457.

Glock, H. (2008). *What is analytic philosophy?* Cambridge: Cambridge University Press.

Goffman, E. (1974). *Frame analysis: An essay on the organization of experience.* London: Harper & Row.

Goldman, R. (2007). Video representations & the perspectivity framework: Epistemology, ethnography, evaluation, and ethics. In R. Goldman, R. Pea, B. Barron, & S. Derry (Eds.), *Video research in the learning sciences* (pp. 3–37). New York: Routledge.

Goldman, R., Pea, R., Barron, B., & Derry, S. (Eds.). (2007). *Video research in the learning sciences.* New York: Routledge.

Gombrich, E. (1961). *Art and illusion: A study in the psychology of pictorial representation.* Princeton: Princeton Univeristy Press.

Greene, S., & Hill, M. (2005). Why research children's experience. In S. Greene & D. Hogan (Eds.), *Researching children's experience: Methods and approaches* (pp. 1–21). London: Sage.

Grimshaw, A. (2014). Delhi at eleven: Reflections on filmmaking as a tool for social exploration and personal expression. *The Asia Pacific Journal of Anthropology, 15*(5), 467–470.

Grimshaw, A., & Hockings, P. (2011). Two recent films from David MacDougall. *Visual Anthropology, 24*(4), 391–399.

Grimshaw, A., & Ravetz, A. (2009). *Observational cinema: Anthropology, film, and the exploration of social life.* Bloomington: Indiana University Press.

Grimshaw, A., & Ravetz, A. (2015). Drawing with a camera? *Ethnographic Film and Transformative Anthropology, 21*(1), 255–275.

Halpern, J. (2001). *From detached concern to empathy: Humanizing medical practice.* Oxford: Oxford University Press.

Harper, D. (2012). *Visual sociology.* London: Routledge.

Harris, A. (2016). *Video as method.* Oxford: Oxford University Press.

Harris, A. (2018). Ethnocinema and video-based research. In P. Leavy (Ed.), *Handbook of arts-based research* (pp. 437–452). New York: The Guilford Press.

Harrow, K. (1999). *African cinema: Post-colonial and feminist readings.* Trenton: Africa World Press.

Hart, R. (1992). *Children's participation: From tokenism to citizenship.* Florence: UNICEF.
Henley, P. (2010). *The adventure of the real: Jean Rouch and the craft of ethnographic cinema.* Chicago: University of Chicago Press.
Hennebelle, G. (1972). *Les cinémas Africains en 1972.* Dakar and Paris: Société Africaine d'edition.
Hickman, R. (2008). The nature of research in art and design. In R. Hickman (Ed.), *Research in art and design education* (pp. 15–24). Bristol: Intellect.
Hickman, R. (2010). *Why we make art and why it is taught.* Bristol: Intellect.
High, C., Singh, N., Petheram, L., & Nemes, G. (2012). Defining participatory video from practice. In E.-J. Milne, C. Mitchell & N. de Lange (Eds.), *The handbook of participatory video* (pp. 38–45). Lanham, MD: AltaMira Press.
Hill, M. (2005). Ethical considerations in researching children's experiences. In S. Greene & D. Hogan (Eds.), *Researching children's experience: Methods and approaches* (pp. 61–86). London: Sage.
Hoey, B. (2014). *A simple introduction to the practice of ethnography and guide to ethnographic fieldnotes.* Marshall: Marshall University Digital Scholar.
Hollan, D., & Throop, J. (Eds.). (2011). *The anthropology of empathy: Experiencing the lives of others in pacific societies.* Oxford: Berghahn Press.
Iacoboni, M. (2008). *Mirroring people: The new science of how we connect with others.* New York: Straus and Giroux.
Ingold, T. (2007). *Lines: A brief history.* Oxford: Routledge.
Ingold, T. (2011). *Being alive: Essays on movement, knowledge and description.* London: Routledge.
Ingold, T. (2013). *Making: Anthropology, archaeology, art and architecture.* London: Routledge.
Iphofen, R. (2013). *Research ethics in ethnography/anthropology.* European Commission, DG Research and Innovation. Retrieved July 13, 2017 from http://ec.europa.eu/research/participants/data/ref/h2020/other/hi/ethics-guide-ethnog-anthrop_en.pdf.
Irwin, R. (2004). A/r/tography: A metonymic métissage. In R. Irwin & A. de Cosson (Eds.), *A/r/tography: Rendering self through arts-based living inquiry* (pp. 27–40). Vancouver, BC: Pacific Educational Press.
Irwin, R. (2008). A/r/tography. In L. Given (Ed.), *The SAGE encyclopedia of qualitative research methods* (pp. 26–28). Los Angeles: Sage.
Irwin, R. (2014). *Radicant teacher education.* Paper delivered at the 2nd Conference on Arts Based Research and Artistic Research, University of

Granada, Spain, 29 January 2014. Retrieved August 20, 2017 from http://art2investigacion.weebly.com/uploads/2/1/1/7/21177240/irwin_rita_y_alumnos_.pdf.

Izod, J., & Kilborn, R. (1998). The documentary. In J. Hill (Ed.), *Oxford guide to film studies* (pp. 426–433). Oxford: Oxford University Press.

Jewitt, C. (2012). *An introduction to using video for research* (NCRM Working Paper). London: NCRM.

Joas, H. (1996). *The creativity of action.* Chicago: University of Chicago Press.

Kellett, M. (2010). Small shoes, big steps! Empowering children as active researchers. *American Journal of Community Psychology, 46*(1), 195–203.

Kogler, H., & Stueber, K. (2000). Introduction: Empathy, simulation, and interpretation in the philosophy of the social sciences. In K. R. Stueber & H. H. Kogaler (Eds.), *Empathy and agency: The problem of understanding in the human sciences* (pp. 1–61). Boulder: Westview Press.

Kuhn, A., & Westwell, G. (Eds.). (2012). *Oxford dictionary of film studies.* Oxford: Oxford University Press.

Leavy, P. (Ed.). (2018). *Handbook of arts-based research.* New York: The Guilford Press.

Lundy, L. (2007). 'Voice' is not enough: Conceptualising Article 12 of the United Nations convention on the rights of the child. *British Educational Research Journal, 33*(6), 927–942.

MacDougall, D. (Director). (1974). *To live with herds* [Motion picture]. USA: University of California, Los Angeles.

MacDougall, D. (1998). *Transcultural cinema.* Princeton, NJ: Princeton University Press.

MacDougall, D. (1999). Social aesthetics and The Doon School. *Visual Anthropology Review, 15,* 3–20.

MacDougall, D. (2006). *The corporeal image: Film, ethnography, and the senses.* Princeton, NJ: Princeton University Press.

MacDougall, D. (Director). (2007). *SchoolScapes* [Motion Picture]. Australia: Centre for Cross-Cultural Research, Australian National University.

MacDougall, D. (Director). (2008). *Gandhi's Children.* [Motion Picture]. Australia: Centre for Cross-Cultural Research, Australian National University.

MacDougall, D. (2011). Anthropological filmmaking: An empirical art. In E. Margolis & L. Pauwels (Eds.), *The SAGE handbook visual research methods* (pp. 99–114). London: Sage.

MacDougall, D. (Producer). (2013). *Delhi at Eleven* [Motion Picture]. Australia: Childhood and Modernity Project, Fieldwork Films and Research School for Humanities & the Arts, Australian National University.

MacDougall, D. (Producer). (2014a). *Eleven in Delwara* [Motion Picture]. Australia: Childhood and Modernity Project, Fieldwork Films and Research School for Humanities & the Arts, Australian National University.

MacDougall, D. (Producer). (2014b). *Eleven in Kolkata* [Motion Picture]. Australia: Childhood and Modernity Project, Fieldwork Films and Research School for Humanities & the Arts, Australian National University.

MacDougall, D. (2018). Observational cinema. In H. Callan (Ed.), *The International encyclopedia of anthropology*. New York: Wiley-Blackwell Publishing, Inc.

MacLure, M. (2013). Researching without representation? Language and materiality in post-qualitative methodology. *International Journal of Qualitative Studies in Education, 26*(6), 658–667.

Margulies, A. (1989). *The empathic imagination*. New York: W. W. Norton.

Marion, J., & Crowder, W. (2013). *Visual research*. New York: Bloomsbury.

Marriner, K. (2018). *The child's eye: 12 films from India by child researchers*. Melbourne: Australian Teachers of Media (ATOM).

Marsh, J. (2012). Children as knowledge brokers of playground games and rhymes in the new media age. *Childhood, 19*(4), 508–522.

Marsh, J., & Richards, C. (2013). Children as researchers. In R. Willett, C. Richards, J. Marsh, A. Burn, & J. Bishop (Eds.), *Children, media and playground cultures* (pp. 51–67). Basingstoke: Palgrave Macmillan.

Maysles, A., Maysles, D., & Zwerin, C. (Directors). (1969). *Salesman*. [Motion Picture]. USA: Maysles Films.

McCormack, D. (2017). The circumstances of post-phenomenological life worlds. *Transactions of the Institute of British Geographers, 42*(1), 2–13.

McNiff, N. (2018). Philosophical and practical foundations of artistic inquiry: Creating paradigms, methods, and presentations based in art. In P. Leavy (Ed.), *Handbook of arts-based research* (pp. 22–32). New York: The Guilford Press.

Mead, M., & Bateson, G. (1977). On the use of the camera. *Anthropology, 4*(2), 78–80. Retrieved from https://repository.upenn.edu/svc/vol4/iss2/3.

Meager, N. (2017). Children make observational films exploring a participatory visual method for art education. *International Journal of Education Through Art, 13*(1), 7–22.

Miller, P. (2013). *Cultural histories of the material world.* Ann Arbor: University of Michigan Press. Retrieved November 21, 2016 from Project MUSE database https://muse.jhu.edu/book/25312.

Milne, E., Mitchell, C., & Lange, N. De (Eds.). (2012). *The handbook of participatory video.* Lanham, MD: AltaMira Press.

Nichols, B. (1991). *Representing reality* (pp. 125–133). Bloomington and Indianapolis: Indiana University Press.

North, D. (2001). Magic and illusion in early cinema. *Studies in French Cinema, 1*(2), 70–79.

Pahl, K., & Pool, S. (2011). Living your life because it's the only life you've got. *Qualitative Research Journal, 11*(2), 17–37.

Pariser, D. (2013). Who needs arts-based research? In F. Hernández-Hernández & R. Fendler (Eds.), *1st conference on arts-based and artistic research: Critical reflections on the intersection of art and research* (pp. 62–69). Barcelona, Spain: University of Barcelona.

Perricone, C. (2006). The influence of darwinism on John Dewey's philosophy of art. *Journal of Speculative Philosophy, 20,* 20–41.

Petheram, L. (2014). Insights into Indian children, their spaces and lives through four films. *The Asia Pacific Journal of Anthropology, 15*(5), 478–479.

Philibert, N. (Director). (2002). *Être et Avoir* [Motion Picture]. France: Maïa Films, Arte France Cinéma, Les Films d'Ici, Centre National de Documentation Pédagogique.

Philibert, N. (2003, June 11–18). Massive hit. In G. Andrew, *Time Out,* p. 2.

Philibert, N. (2017). *A camera gives you incredible power over others.* Retrieved November 10, 2017 from http://nicolasphilibert.fr.

Pink, S. (2001). *Doing visual ethnography: Images, media, and representation in research.* London: Sage.

Pink, S. (2007). *Doing visual ethnography.* London: Sage.

Pink, S. (2013). *Doing visual ethnography.* (3rd ed. expanded and revised). London: Sage.

Potts, R. (2015). A conversation with David MacDougall: Reflections on the childhood and modernity workshop films. In *Visual Anthropology Review, 31,* 190–200.

Putman, H. (2011). Reflections on pragmatism. In J. Shook & P. Kurtz (Eds.), *Dewey's enduring impact: Essays on America's philosopher* (p. 52). Amherst: Prometheus Books.

Quiggin, A. H. (1942). *Haddon, the head hunter: A short sketch of the life of A. C. Haddon.* Cambridge: The University Press.

Ragazzi, R. (2014). Challenging our view of temporality. *The Asia Pacific Journal of Anthropology, 15*(5), 457–461.
Rajchmann, J. (2001). Introduction. In G. Deleuze (Ed.), *Pure immance* (pp. 7–23). New York: Zone Books.
Reisz, K., & Millar, G. (1968). *The technique of film editing*. New York: Focal Press.
Rolling, J. H. (2017). Arts-based research in education. In P. Leavy (Ed.), *Handbook of arts-based research* (pp. 492–510). New York: Guilford Press.
Rorty, R. (1980). *Philosophy and the mirror of nature*. Princeton: Princeton University Press.
Rorty, R. (1982). *The consequences of pragmatism*. Minneapolis: University of Minnesota Press.
Rose, G. (2012). *Visual methodologies: An introduction to researching with visual materials*. London: Sage.
Rotten Tonatoes. (2017). *Critic Reviews Être et Avoir*. Retrieved December 19, 2017 from https://www.rottentomatoes.com/m/to_be_and_to_have/.
Rouch, J. (1974). The camera and man. In P. Hockings (Ed.), *Principles of visual anthropology* (pp. 79–98). Berlin: Mouton de Gruyter.
Ruby, J. (2008). Towards an anthropological cinema. In *European Association of Social Anthropologists E-Seminar Series*. Retrieved December 29, 2017 from http://www.media-anthropology.net/index.php/e-seminars.
Saldaña, J. (2005). *Ethnodrama: An anthology of reality theatre*. Walnut Creek, CA: AltaMira Press.
Sandall, R. (1972). Observation and identity. *Sight and sound, 41*(4), 192–196.
Schuck, S., & Kearney, M. (2006). Using digital video as a research tool: Ethical issues for researchers. *Journal of Educational Multimedia and Hypermedia, 15*(4), 447–463.
Semetsky, I. (2003). Deleuze's new image of thought, or Dewey revisited. *Educational Philosophy and Theory, 35,* 17–29.
Sennett, R. (2008). *The craftsman*. New Haven: Yale University Press.
Shier, T. (2001). Pathways to participation: Openings opportunities and obligations. *Children and Society, 15*(2), 102–117.
Siegesmund, R. (2012). Dewey through a/r/tography. *Visual Arts Research Journal, 38*(2), 99–109.
Sleeper, R. (1986). *The necessity of pragmatism*. New Haven: Yale University Press.
Sobchack, V. (1992). *The address of the eye: A phenomenology of film experience*. Princeton, NJ: Princeton University Press.
Sontag, S. (1977). *On photography*. London: Penguin.

Springgay, S., Irwin, R. L., Leggo, C., & Gouzouasis, P. (Eds.). (2008). *Being with a/r/tography*. Rotterdam, The Netherlands: Sense.

Stille, S. (2011). Framing representations: Documentary filmmaking as participatory approach to research inquiry. *Journal of Curriculum and Pedagogy, 8*(2), 101–108.

Strawson, G. (2011). Cognitive phenomenology: Real life. In T. Beayne & Montague (Eds.), *Cognative phenomenology* (pp. 285–325). Oxford: Oxford University Press.

Stueber, K. R. (2006). *Rediscovering empathy: Agency, folk psychology, and the human sciences*. Cambridge: MIT Press.

Taussig, M. (2009). *What color is the sacred?* Chicago: University of Chicago Press.

Taussig, M. (2011). *I swear I saw this: Drawings in fieldwork notebooks, namely my own*. Chicago: University of Chicago Press.

Taylor, L. (1998). Introduction. In D. MacDougall (Ed.), *Transcultural cinema* (pp. 3–24). Princeton, NJ: Princeton University Press.

Thrift, N. (2007). *Non-representational theory: Space, politics, affect*. London: Routledge.

Turunen, U., & Ruuhijärvi, I. (1987a). *Kun se tapahtuu* [Television Documentary]. Finland: YLE TV1.

Turunen, U., & Ruuhijärvi, I. (1987b). *Koko ajan jossakin* [Television Documentary]. Finland: YLE TV1.

Turunen, U., & Ruuhijärvi, I. (1989). *Tien yli* [Television Documentary]. Finland: YLE TV1.

Turunen, U., & Ruuhijärvi, I. (1990). *Aina eikä milloinkaan* [Television Documentary]. Finland: YLE TV1.

Turunen, U., & Ruuhijärvi, I. (1992). *Elämä* [Television Documentary]. Finland: YLE TV1.

Ukadike, N., & Gabriel, T. (2002). *Questioning African cinema: Conversations with filmmakers*. Minneapolis: University of Minnesota Press.

Vaughan, D. (1999). *For documentary*. Berkeley: University of California Press.

Westbrook, R. (1991). *John Dewey and American democracy*. Ithaca and London: Cornell University Press.

Wolcott, H. (2008). *Ethnography: a way of seeing*. Lanham, MD: AltaMira Press.

Wood, M., & Brown, S. (2012). Film-based creative arts enquiry: Qualitative researchers as auteurs. *Qualitative Research Journal, 12*(1), 130–147.

Young, C. (1975). Observational cinema. In P. Hockings (Ed.), *Principles of visual anthropology* (pp. 99–114). The Hague: Mouton Publishers.